One Clear Morn

Life owes me nothing:
One clear morn
Is boon enough
for being born;
And be it ninety years
or ten,
No need for me
to question when.
While life is mine,
I'll find it good
And greet each hour
with gratitude.
— *anon.*

Terence Collinson

Allyson Publishing

First published 2017

Allyson Publishing
t.collinson787@btinternet.com

Copyright © Terence Collinson, 2017

The right of Terence Collinson to be identified as the Author of this work has been asserted in accordance with the Copyrights, Designs and Patents Act 1988.

All rights reserved. No part of this book may be reprinted or reproduced or utilised in any form or by any electronic, mechanical or other means, now known or hereafter invented, including photocopying and recording, or in any information storage or retrieval system, without the permission in writing from the Publishers.

Typesetting and origination by Allyson Publishing.
Printed and bound in England.

To Julie

*You discovered those couple of chapters begun
and abandoned many decades ago and
you persuaded me to continue to tell my story.
Thank you for the encouragement you gave me
and for all your hard work in producing this book.*

CONTENTS

Preface		vii
Map: Yiewsley and West Drayton		ix
ONE CLEAR MORN		1
Chapter 1	Meeting Aunt Pat	3
Chapter 2	The Walkers Move to Yiewsley	12
Chapter 3	Lost Love	24
Chapter 4	Infant School	31
Chapter 5	After Bobby	36
Chapter 6	Sole Guardian	47
Chapter 7	Uncle Bill	54
Chapter 8	Fred and Doris	61
Chapter 9	Small Portions	67
Chapter 10	The Air-Raid Shelter	76
Chapter 11	Dusty	87
Chapter 12	Junior School	94
Chapter 13	The Winkle Round	102
Chapter 14	The Rabbit Show	111
Chapter 15	My First Business	114
Chapter 16	A Brief Hobby	122
Chapter 17	The Fish Shop	126

Chapter 18	Just Bill	133
Chapter 19	Charlie Ricketts	143
Chapter 20	Arthur	150
Chapter 21	Senior School	159
Chapter 22	Leaving School	165
Chapter 23	The Packing Shed	173
Chapter 24	The Horses	178
Chapter 25	The Strawberry Van	188
Chapter 26	The Oat Harvest	194
Chapter 27	The Mangold Field	200
Chapter 28	Winter	204
Chapter 29	The Decision	211
Chapter 30	The Interviews	216
Chapter 31	The Hanwell Factory	226
Chapter 32	The Trio	234
Chapter 33	The Auditions	241
Chapter 34	Soho	248
Chapter 35	Leaving Home	256
Appendix: Nan's Gems of Wisdom		266

PREFACE

Many years ago, I heard it said that 'everyone has at least one book in them'. The speaker seemed to be convinced that no matter how humble or uneventful a life might seem at first glance, each one of us has within him a story worth the telling. When I added such a thought to my own belief that life itself is a romantic journey that we all travel, over the rocky roads of our difficult times and across the sunlit highways of joyful days, it was inevitable that one day I would want to put some of my own experiences down on paper.

Terence Collinson

YIEWSLEY (to the north of the Grand Union Canal)

WEST DRAYTON (to the south of the Grand Union Canal)

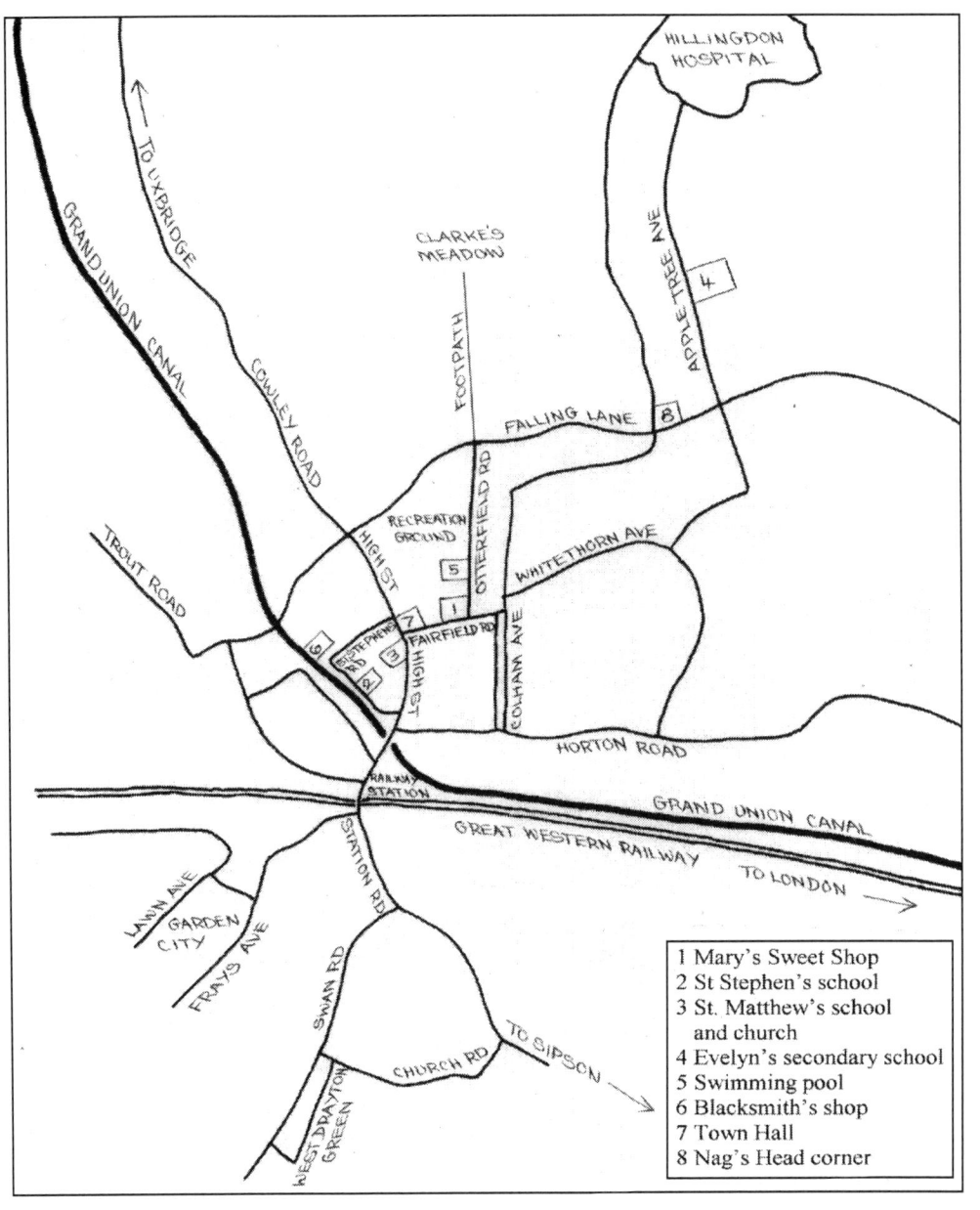

ONE CLEAR MORN

Chapter 1

MEETING AUNT PAT

'She's not in,' I heard someone call. I lowered the knocker silently and turned to see where the voice had come from. A grey-haired man was working in the front garden of the adjoining property. The late afternoon sun was still warm and the man mopped his brow as he took a few steps nearer to the low chain-linked fence that separated his garden from that of the aunt I had come to see. 'She shouldn't be long,' the man added, as he returned his handkerchief to his trouser pocket. He went on in a neighbourly way, 'She plays for the old folks this afternoon, and she's always back by teatime.'

'Oh,' I said, 'Thank you.' Feeling the need to say something more, I explained that I was earlier than had been planned and was happy to wait. We exchanged a few polite words; I admiring his neat garden and he telling me he was pleased to be able to get on with some much needed tidying-up now that the weather was better. I retraced my steps down the narrow concrete path and through the low unpainted wooden gate, which I closed respectfully behind me, still firmly gripped in the gaze of the protective neighbour. I walked a short distance and crossed the small road that served the cul-de-sac to where I had parked my car in the cool of some leafy shade. There I could sit comfortably, with a view as far as the corner around which I expected my aunt would appear.

As I waited, I had time to check through documents that had been completed during the course of my work that day. I had made several successful business calls, on a journey that began on the western edge of Surrey and had taken me across the full width of the county. I was pleased with my day's work and its achievements, and allowed myself a few self-congratulatory moments as I put each of my files in order and stowed them away for attention in the office next morning.

With my duties complete, I could take time to consider a second mission upon which I had embarked that day. A quest to delve into my family history had brought me to where I sat at that moment, a few miles into Kent, the county of my maternal forebears. I had only the scantest knowledge of my mother's family, and the very existence of the aunt I was hoping to meet was unknown to me until just a few weeks ago.

As I sank into my thoughts, I recalled the manner in which I had first learned of my, yet unmet, aunt. On a day I had visited my mother she had casually spoken of her sister, her words taking me by surprise and causing me to wonder if it was perhaps a long-dead sibling that she was referring to. But it was not. As she continued in an uncustomary unguarded way, she revealed little by little that she did, in fact, have a sister who was alive and well.

The very existence of an aunt was pleasing to hear, but it came with a sad reminder of the tenuous relationship between my mother and me. My mother spoke at all times of a 'sister' but never of an 'aunt', oblivious that I might find pleasure and even comfort to have knowledge of a close relative. In confirmation of the slender link that existed between us, my mother went on to let it be known that she and her sister had been in contact for more than ten years, and never at any time in that decade did she consider that I could or should be told.

I was awakened from my reverie when an elderly lady came round the corner walking with difficulty. She was weighed down on one side by a fully loaded music case, the old fashioned kind made of leather with a metal bar over its presently straining handle. As with other people who had appeared, I searched my thoughts to connect myself to her. This time the music case took my attention. Did my interest in music come from the unknown side of my family? If this was the aunt I had come to find, I felt we had something in common already. However, most likely she was no relation and would keep on walking. But no. As she came level with her garden gate, she turned and went in.

By the time she reached her front door and was searching in her handbag, I was at her gate holding my hand in the air in a motionless wave to catch her attention, and calling, 'Excuse me.' She left her bunch of keys hanging in the door and turned towards me.

Meeting Aunt Pat

'Are you Mrs Hoy? Mrs Patricia Hoy?' I asked.

'Yes,' she replied. 'You must be Violet's son. I've been looking forward to meeting you, I hope I'm not late. Come in,' she said, and, after one more glance of curiosity, she turned and started to struggle with her keys again. Her hands were frail and dark with veins. I asked if I could help but, determined and independent, she would not let me.

'Come in, come in,' she said eagerly, and in a moment or two we were inside her small semi-detached house. She was obviously not well off; her furniture and decorations were aged and a little drab but all was neat and clean and her life appeared orderly and respectable. She put her music case down on the piano stool and said she would make some tea. She was becoming quite excited, almost agitated, by the arrival of a relative she had not met before and she moved too quickly for her own safety, it seemed. She hurried to take off her hat and coat, not wishing to waste a moment before making me welcome. Some music was already on the piano and I asked if I could look at it, hoping that if I sat still it might be calming for her. She handed me the album of tunes popular in the twenties and thirties and went out to the kitchen, while I sat thumbing through the book and resisted continuing our conversation through the open doorway so as not to hurry her.

The aunt I had barely met returned with a tin tray loaded with a large brown teapot, almost hidden by a hand-knitted woollen cosy, and cups and saucers in fading colours from different sets; no doubt remainders from many years use and breakages. She bid me sit close, across a low table upon which she placed the tray. She poured the tea and offered the biscuits; the tea was black and the biscuits had been in the tin too long but all was given in generosity and kindness. After a few sips of her tea, my aunt sat back in her chair and looked calmer. Her face brightened and became younger; her skin glowed more pink and her old eyes lit with warmth and loving interest. We were both keen to talk but neither knew quite where to begin. I made approving comments on the book of music that I had looked through while she had made the tea; I said I liked her choice and that I used to play some of the tunes many years ago when I played in a jazz band. She told me that she played the piano for the old people and that was where she had been today. I felt admiration for this elderly lady whose life was so well ordered she could give pleasure to others probably no older than herself. We chatted on about music until we had finished our first cup of tea.

I said, half to be polite, that I would like to hear her play. I was surprised when, straight away, she moved from her chair to the piano. She thumbed through the pages of music that had already served as our leveller and stopped at a Scott Joplin rag. I froze a little as I stood looking over her shoulder; I didn't want her to be embarrassed and this highly syncopated music hardly seemed a good demonstration piece, but by this time I could say nothing and she crashed into it with great style. She had obviously been a good pianist in her day; she played so musically and rhythmically, only her aged fingers letting her down from time to time. At the end of the performance, the player turned round on her stool and our eyes met amid beaming smiles of satisfaction and pleasure of an undoubtedly shared interest. Any reserve that existed between the two people who had just met under quite unusual circumstances was banished at that moment.

'Don't let that tea get cold,' said my aunt with a new confidence, as we sat across the tea tray from one another once again. She poured more tea and, as she put down the pot, said, 'I know, I'll show you some photos.' She went into another room and I could hear drawers being opened and closed. I sipped my tea. In a few minutes she returned with a cardboard box, which would have been pretty once but the flowered pattern was now faded and browned. She put the box on her knees keeping full control of it and its contents, which she was keen to reveal but not until the story she had to tell would be fully appreciated and the members of our family in the photographs understood as to their place in the familial landscape. My aunt leaned forward a little over the box. 'You know how your mother and I met after all these years, don't you?' she asked.

'Just a little. I only found out that I had an aunt a few weeks ago,' I said, feeling that I needed to apologize.

'Well,' said my aunt, 'your mother has known for *ten years* that she has a sister,' giving me a look that showed astonishment that I had

Meeting Aunt Pat

not been told. Then she said, 'Our local paper reported that a Mr Poulton had been knocked down by a car and killed. I wrote to the paper and asked them to pass on a letter, I had enclosed, to the family. I asked if they were the Poultons who had taken my sister away. I got a nice answer from them saying that Mr Poulton's sister had adopted a child many years ago. They gave me your mum's address. I wrote to her to say I thought she was my sister – it must have been a shock. She wrote back and we spoke on the phone a couple of times.' My aunt withdrew a little, sitting back and looking dejected. Then she went on, 'It was good at first, Vi used to come down in her nice car with her husband and their little dog. I was so happy to have found a sister, and I thought she was too.' 'I don't know what happened but after a few times they didn't come anymore. I never knew why,' my aunt said forlornly. 'I used to ring but she could never stop to talk. I only ring now to wish her a happy birthday, and happy Christmas. But she doesn't come anymore.'

I felt sorry for my aunt. To have found her sister and lost her again so soon was clearly a sadness. The weight of not knowing why pressed heavily and the feeling that she had been rejected added to the load. To speak of it caused her a moment of personal reflection; she went on to tell me that her husband had died some years before and that she often felt lonely in her advancing years. She betrayed a tinge of bitterness when she considered some of life's unfairnesses that had befallen her but did not dwell on regrets that touched her life alone, keen as she was to share a story that concerned us both.

During the hour we had talked and shared tea and music, my aunt had decided that I would want to hear her story, would understand and be sympathetic. Every line in her old face looked, at that moment, as if it held a pain that she wanted to let go. She began to talk. For reasons known only to the teller, the story began on a night in 1915 when German bombs were being dropped on London from Zeppelin airships. Not expecting such a dramatic event to feature so prominently in the opening statement to the history of my family, I confess to missing the next part of the story and any significance it had. My attention was restored when my aunt took the first photograph from her faded box.

'This is my mother,' she said sternly. 'Your grandmother,' she added, watching my reaction carefully.

I fixed my gaze on an image that I had never seen, of a grandmother I had not known. After a moment or two, I looked up at my aunt. Some of the pinkness had left her cheeks. Her mouth hardened for just a moment but, as quickly as it came, the severe look dissolved into a sadness in her eyes. She said bitterly, 'There were only two things she was interested in – men and booze!' My aunt blushed to hear herself say out loud words that I imagined she had only thought before. Establishing her own place in the story, she said, 'I was born in Bromley Workhouse. My mother Nell, or 'Eleanor' as she insisted on being called,' my aunt added with a touch of mockery, 'got herself pregnant with me when she was twenty.' My aunt took a sip of her tea, now cold but it did not matter. 'I was given to an aunt and uncle who had lost their own baby. I somehow knew they weren't my mother and father but nobody told me. No one told me, either, that Eleanor was my mother – I called my own mother 'Auntie' for years.' That last memory was so painful as to require a silent moment, after which my aunt went on, 'All I can remember of my childhood is working in fields all day, and some days being given only a raw onion for my dinner.' Her eyes fixed upon me, assuring herself that I had understood the gravity of what she had just said. She took a breath and completed her own story by saying that she had never known who her father was.

There was another moment of silence as my aunt moved the cups on the tray as if to tidy them, and then she continued with her mother's story: 'When she was twenty-four she married the local butcher. They had a son. The boy, my half-brother, although I didn't know until many years later, told me that he did not ever remember being at home, he only remembered a 'boarding school' as he called it. Then they had a daughter, two years later, and she was put straight into an orphanage and was brought up there.'

My aunt sat back a moment as she searched through the box of photographs. Then she went on, 'The butcher volunteered in 1915. He

Meeting Aunt Pat

was persuaded by people who came round canvassing for men to go – the Derby Scheme it was called. He knew that even married men would be called-up soon, and he was afraid of getting the white feather they gave to cowards, so he went. Funny he should be afraid of feathers, and 'im a butcher plucking all them chickens!' My aunt's attempt to show she still had a sense of humour was endearing. She continued to speak of the stepfather who had never owned her, 'He was in France for a long time. When he came home, he found that his wife had produced another child, a girl. He knew the baby couldn't be his, so he divorced her.' The storyteller began to look fatigued but insisted on continuing, 'Eleanor was back to her old tricks; she gave the baby away and went to work in the laundry. She earned enough to pay for her freedom and pleasures once again. The little girl, the fourth child, had more than one home in her first few years and she was with a childminder when she was found by the rag-and-bone man and his wife.'

My wearying aunt had arrived at a point where her knowledge of her youngest half-sister was ending and mine was beginning, so that I was able to take over from her. I had heard the story many times, told with enthusiasm by Mrs Walker, the wife of the rag-and-bone man. She would tell how she and her husband, Bob, were going round the streets on their horse and cart collecting anything that could be cleaned-up and re-sold, or sold for scrap. On one particular day they came to the house of the childminder, where they saw a little girl in the garden in a dreadful condition; dirty and uncared for. When they were told there was nothing for them to collect, Mrs Walker joked that they could take the child away as she seemed to be unwanted. The minder said that the child's mother would be pleased if they did. I could not assure my aunt that there was any evidence of a legal adoption or what arrangement, if any, had been made with the child's parents, but the story I had been told so boldly was that they simply took the child away and gave her a good home.

My aunt's eyes met mine directly and held my gaze as we shared the telling of the facts that closed our story: the child, Violet Eleanor, was not only my aunt's youngest sibling, she would later become my mother. In a moment of emotion, Aunt Pat gently squeezed my arm, as if clutching the representative of her twice-lost sister. Feeling that the tension needed to be released, I added with a smile, 'And the rag-and-bone man and his wife became my grandparents, Nan and Bobby.' My aunt smiled too.

The telling of so much and the walk through the dark valley of memories had weighed upon my aunt. I could sympathize, as learning so much unknown family history in such a short time had tired me too. It was obvious that our meeting must come to an end and, as if to endorse all she had told me, my aunt searched the photographs once again, taking out the half-dozen that she wanted me to have. They were all faded and worn by the years. The hole in one, she told me, was caused by a bullet in the First World War - a near miss for the soldier whose breast pocket it had been carried in. I thought the story was fanciful, but the hole looked like a bullet hole and I marvelled with her. My aunt held each picture and took one last lingering look before passing it to me with a faint smile. I asked if I could lightly pencil some of the details she had given me on the back of the photos and she agreed, slowly repeating facts and dates to ensure my notes were accurate.

Finally, we took our leave of one another. My aunt's aged hands were warm as they gripped mine in a last goodbye. Her eyes sparkled as she said how pleased she was that we had spent this time together and how happy she was to have told of her life and of the lives that touched us both. I thanked her and was feeling more than I could find words to say, relying instead on a gentle embrace, which she accepted and returned in a mutual pleasure of understanding – the impression of the frail shoulders, around which I had carefully placed my arm, would never be forgotten.

Soon I was on my way home, heading towards the last of the evening light in the western sky. As I reflected upon my day, I smiled to myself to think that I had left home that morning knowing almost nothing of my ancestors and that in such a short time the empty stage had been filled with characters, as colourful as any noble family could boast. While I could sympathize with the sadness felt by my aunt and understand a little more of my mother's reluctance to speak of her past, I could at that moment only rejoice to know that where for me there had been emptiness, now there was life, and perhaps a wayward grandmother was better than none.

With all that I had learned that day, I began to reassess my own life and its beginnings and to look with fresh eyes at all of those around me. On that homeward journey, I determined to write my story down. My aunt's knowledge had ended when the Walkers moved away with her young sister, I would begin from there.

Eleanor (middle row, far right), with girlfriends

Eleanor, with 'boyfriends'!

*Eleanor,
having a good time*

(Who has been removed from this photo!)

Aunt Pat as a young woman   *Pat's auntie (photo with bullet hole)*

Chapter 2

THE WALKERS MOVE TO YIEWSLEY

Bob and Carrie Walker and their 'adopted' daughter, Violet, moved from Bromley in Kent to Yiewsley in Middlesex. It was Mrs Walker's desire to move their home, and the new area was chosen for a reason special to her; shortly before, her younger brother had moved to Yiewsley and it was her wish to be near him. The attachment between sister and brother was understandably strong; she was the oldest of sixteen children, and the brother she had followed was the youngest. Carrie was old enough to have been his mother and would certainly have had a lot to do with his upbringing, as a helper or, in times of trouble, even a substitute for their own mother, as happened in large families.

Life, Carrie would say, had been hard for them, and she would tell of ways in which she had earned money to help support her younger siblings. She recalled how, at a very young age, she would go to a wholesaler to buy a piece of 'hearthstone' for one penny, break it into four pieces and knock on doors until she had sold all four at a halfpenny each. Her product was always in demand, as it was common practice then to announce a clean neat home with a front doorstep whitened with hearthstone. With such an excellent profit from her sales she would help feed her younger brothers and sisters, and at the same time learn a lesson in business that would hold her in good stead for the rest of her life.

In the Walkers' daily struggle to earn a living, it was well known that Carrie was the business brains and boss. Bob Walker was a loyal husband and hard working when he was well, but frequently he was ill and confined to his bed. At such times Carrie would run the home on the smallest amount of money, eking out their savings while living off the garden, the chickens and rabbits they kept for meat, and hidden stores of preserved food.

When Mr Walker was well again and ready to go back into

business, his wife would miraculously bring out a small bundle of one-pound and ten-shilling notes to get them started again. Just before producing the money she would have gone upstairs to hunt round her hiding places to find cash that she had tucked away, under the lino or in the back of her wardrobe or other secret places known only to her. The notes would be thrown onto the dark-green chenille table cloth that covered the large kitchen table dominating the centre of the room, and served as planning area for their business, as well as being the family dining table. The notes would be smoothed, laid straight and counted carefully. 'Wod about a load a strawbris?' Carrie would say, 'They should be cheap now.' Perhaps it would be some other perishable commodity, depending on the season, that could be bought cheap when too many had been sent to market for the demand and remained on sale at the end of trading. Mr Walker would sink a little, as his sick bed still tugged at his coat-tails, but he would see the determination in his wife's face and think of the duty he owed to this strong and supportive woman. Another glance at the money on the table convinced him of what he must do. 'Right-o,' he'd say, 'I'll go up to Brentford in the morning.'

Brentford was the fruit and vegetable market for west London, and a long journey when the means of transport was provided by Steamer, their old horse. An early start would be needed down at the stable, preparing for the day's work. Whatever could be found in the market at the right price would be brought home in the middle of the day. If Carrie thought he had done well, they would spend a peaceful dinnertime together before hawking their load around the streets. If she thought he had paid too much or that what he had bought was past its best, there would be an uneasy meal as she bickered and sniped at him, afraid that they would not sell-out that afternoon. The dinner table echoed with pessimism: 'If it doesn't sell today there'll be no chance tomorrow, it'll be rotten in the morning,' she would say menacingly, as she revealed her worst imaginings. Every day brought a new worry, a new gamble, which if lost could result in disaster. There was constant anxiety that a wrong decision, bad luck or ill health would 'bring in the bailiffs' to put them out on the street, and that from there the only place they could go was 'the workhouse'. Carrie voiced her fears repeatedly, and filled all around her with dread.

To add to their burden, they had taken on a child: Violet Eleanor. At first she was pampered and spoiled but soon was expected to take a full part in the hand-to-mouth existence, working long hours alongside her adoptive parents. Many years later she would speak of her childhood, always insisting that she had had a 'hard life', echoing the words she had heard used many times. She was convinced that she was wanted as much for her usefulness as any other reason and would say so, bitterly, for the whole of her life.

By the time Violet was eighteen she was looking for ways to have a life of her own, thoughts of her own, ideas that were not put into her head by her strong-minded adoptive mother. In those days, marriage was one of the few ways a young women could escape an oppressive family home. Violet's husband-to-be worked in the local 'corn shop'. He was in business with his brother-in-law selling all kinds of animal feed; their shop was on Yiewsley High Street and not far from Otterfield Road. The courtship was brief and they were soon married. The haste would have given little time for planning and, perhaps because of that, life did not turn out as Violet hoped; she did not escape the clutches of her domineering guardian but simply added a husband to the household, in which he himself would quickly come under the thumb of his mother-in-law. There was talk of a home of their own but the cost was too great on the meagre income provided by half the profits from a business that was already failing. By the time I was born, two years later, my birth certificate showed my father's occupation as a 'van driver', so the business had gone by then. For my mother, aged twenty, the situation was going in quite the opposite direction to that she had planned and to the freedom she had sought. The pressures of daily life upon my parents' marriage, whilst they lived under the same roof as the overbearing mother/mother-in-law, must have been intolerable. My mother decided to find another way out.

One was found. Fear of the coming war made it easy for young women to enter the services. The Auxiliary Territorial Service, which was formed in September 1938, recruited women to carry out a wide range of jobs; not only secretaries, telephone operators, observers and drivers, but dispatch riders, military police, motor mechanics, even tank mechanics and explosive-shell recoverers. The glamorous posters caught my mother's imagination and she arrived home one day to announce that she had 'joined up'. She was going to be an ambulance driver in the ATS. Soon she was off to basic training.

From that time on, the woman who had given me the gift of life was only ever a visitor in the house in which I grew up. When I was old enough I was encouraged to visit her, it was 'my duty' I was told. I would ride my bike the two or three miles to her house, in Hayes. I would call her 'Mum', but have no understanding of the love and closeness that title should convey or demand. She never touched me in tenderness or spoke to me in a gentle motherly way; I was simply a visitor in her house, as she was in mine.

With my mother's departure, my parents' brief marriage was over. My father was held fully responsible by his mother-in-law, so to continue living at Otterfield Road would have been unbearable. Understandably, he moved out. He went back to live with his mother, his sister and her husband (who had been his partner in the corn shop). He was mocked for going back to his mother and condemned for deserting his child, but maligned for going to court to attempt to gain custody of his son. In time these contradictory criticisms would be seen for what they were and a balanced view of the poor man's actions would be restored.

It was more than twenty years since Bob and Carrie Walker had taken on the upbringing of a child, when they 'adopted' my mother. Now they had fought in the court to keep me in the home in which I had been born, so they were about to begin childrearing again. I am not sure of my exact age at the time their responsibilities commenced but it need only be indicated by the telling of my memories of some years later when, to my great embarrassment, it would be the conversation piece over cups of tea with friends and neighbours that I had to be taken around on their horse and cart in 'long clothes'.

(Apparently, at that time, even boys were put into long dresses for the first months of their lives.) Such was my mortification upon hearing the story that I never enquired further into the matter.

As I imagine the first awareness of any infant is programmed by nature to do, my own awakening consciousness accepted the situation in which I found myself. Two parents brought more stability than many newborn are lucky enough to have. The fact that mine were old could have been nature's way for all I knew and troubled me not at all. Whether designed to avoid confusing the child or to flatter her vanity and dislike of being old, Mrs Walker would on no account be called 'Grandmother' or any diminutive of that title. It would have been most likely that she saw herself as the young nanny she had encountered when 'in service', working as a servant in a big house. I was therefore instructed to call her 'Nanny', mercifully permitting an abbreviated 'Nan'. Mrs Walker became 'Nan', and for me will remain that evermore. The title 'Grandfather' would no doubt also have impinged upon Mrs Walker's vanity so that, regardless of his own wishes, Mr Walker became 'Bobby', and was never anything else. I also accepted, without concern, that the titles of 'Mother' and 'Father' belonged to more distant relatives. The arrangement of our family structure raised no questions in me until different family formations were noticed once I began to move amongst my contemporaries, by which time I was old enough to begin the process of unravelling just a few of the complexities of life.

My acceptance of the situation in which I found myself did not, of course, bring complete peace of mind. Like other children, I had to learn of the problems that adults endure and cause them to act in ways not always understandable. The interrupted breakfast, which took place from time to time, was an example. We would be sitting around our kitchen table, each with a large dish of porridge (usually quite runny, the way 'Nan' liked it). Nan would sound as if she was arguing with Bobby, getting louder and louder until she stood up in a rage, picking up her plate and saying, 'Come on, we're not having our breakfast with *him*.' She would leave the room, balancing her plate in shaking hands, demanding that I follow. I hated leaving the table, being rude to Bobby and seeming as if I was angry with him too. He looked hurt and I felt sorry for him but I had to follow Nan, I was frightened not to. We would have to be careful not to spill our porridge as we climbed our steep staircase. It was difficult balancing our plates on our laps as we sat on Nan's bed to eat our porridge, and the room was cold too. I am not sure that I had a firm grasp of the meaning of irony at that age but it did seem strange that we, the supposed aggrieved, had to have our breakfast in such uncomfortable conditions while the alleged villain ate his on the table by the fire in the nice warm kitchen.

By the time I was remembering more pleasant day to day affairs, Steamer, the horse, was just a talked-about joy of the past. He was not forgotten and frequently spoken of in glowing and affectionate terms. Faces would light up as it was told how he went 'like a train'; Nan would clench her fists and repeatedly punch them out in front of her one at a time to show how the old horse threw out his hooves when he was in full flight. Bobby, by that time, had acquired a motor van for his business. The vehicle must have been an old one, as it was decided that it needed a smarten-up for 'business' sake. The cost of respraying was out of the question so it was decided to hand-paint it. Furthermore, the paint was going to have to be whatever was left over from previous jobs. Most cars on the road at that time were black, and any variation seemed to employ only the most subdued of dark colours. Fortunately, there was plenty of bottle-green and black left from when our scullery had last been painted, so the van would not end up unnecessarily garish or out of place. Bottle-green was used for the main body, while mudguards, front grill, hubcaps and handles were finished in black. The result was considered a success; smart, sharp even, but without excess. The grand appearance has been lost in my memory but the strong smell of domestic gloss paint that followed our van around for the rest of its days made a unique and never-to-be-forgotten impression.

When I was still unused to the routine of attending infant school, and probably on a morning of a disrupted breakfast or something similar, I would feel nervous and consider Bobby's placid company preferable to coping with anymore bewildering adult behaviour that I might encounter that day at school. By the time I left our house to go to school, Bobby's van would have been brought from its garage at the bottom of Uncle Fred's yard, a few doors up the road, and parked outside, ready to go to market. Disregarding any trouble I might be in, I would hide in the back and keep quite still until Bobby came out and drove off. I would remain silent until we were well on the road before I appeared from my hiding place. I often wondered if Bobby knew all along that I was in there; he never seemed surprised or showed crossness but instead invited me over to sit next to him, giving me a smile as I settled in. When he did comment, he would say casually in a knowing way, 'I wondered what Judy was ferreting about with back there.'

Judy was the little black dog that both Nan and Bobby spoke of as if it was a member of the family. They each believed that Judy was *their* dog as, to the slightest command, she would follow either one of them wherever they bid. As to whose dog she was caused the animal no confusion, except on the rarest occasions when master and mistress had business in different directions and a command was omitted; Judy would want to follow them both and could not decide, running back and forth between them and giving out little yelps of distress.

On our journey to market, I asked Bobby why there were big number thirties by the side of the road. 'It means we must not go more than thirty,' he said without further explanation. I pondered for some time. I knew about rationing, and that he used red-dyed petrol for his business and was not allowed to use it for pleasure trips. I came to the conclusion that I had just learnt of another restriction that warned us not to go on a journey of more than thirty miles from our home. After a little more contemplation, I piped-up, 'How do they know when we have gone thirty miles – they must know where we live?' Bobby looked puzzled at my question and the conclusion I had come to. We were clearly at cross purposes; he speaking of speed, and me of distance. I entered another period of private thought as I tried to find the answer to my disquiet. Those thirties could not be just for us. Where were the signs that told other people that they were thirty miles from their homes? There could not possibly be that many signs I concluded, and gave up, confused. After the occasional look over my shoulder to see if the Government was watching us, I forgot all about it. Bobby had already gone quiet having decided to concentrate on the old van's worn steering, which was misbehaving on the heavily cambered road and needed his full attention to control.

We pulled into the market. Great iron gates were open wide and secured back to high stone walls. We found a space to park, on a sloping cobbled area. Bobby was in no hurry while prices were holding still. He took my hand and led me to the steamy market cafe. Salesmen, buyers, porters and the like, all on neutral territory, business left outside for a few moments while the basic needs of sustenance were attended to. Someone said out loud of the proprietor, 'Old Bill doesn't think it's a good cuppa tea unless the spoon stands up in it!' The tea came in pint mugs. Bobby put lots of milk in mine, from a large enamel jug, to make it cooler. He stirred it with a spoon that lay on the counter secured by a length of chain. I was pleased to have a drink, but disappointed that with so much milk in it I could not get a teaspoon to stand up. While we sipped our tea I watched 'old Bill' put a whole packet of tea into a giant metal teapot and squirt in steam and the tiniest amount of water from a tap. Shoosh! Shoosh! could be heard as more steam was added after each customer was served. 'Why does he make tea so strong?' I asked Bobby.

''E's been making tea like that since before your 'ed was as big as a shirt button,' Bobby said, just loud enough for another man at our table to hear. They both laughed.

There was a silence while I thought about that. Then I pulled Bobby's sleeve to ensure I had his undivided attention and 'informed' him, with great certainty that 'My head could never have been that small.'

A wide grin that must have enjoyed my innocence, broke into a loving smile as Bobby looked down at me but said nothing. We shared a sausage sandwich and left feeling refreshed and stronger.

We walked around looking at the produce. The market buildings were open-fronted, with shutters that rolled up high and were noisy as they were pulled up or down with chains. In front, empty bushel boxes were used to make large areas of temporary platforms, and many varieties of vegetables and fruit were displayed on them. Prospective buyers were sampling the fruit; it seemed that they could pick and eat a grape and walk away, but the only time I saw anyone bite into a peach he almost immediately placed an order. Peas seemed to be eaten freely; men stood around the displays breaking open pods, emptying the peas into their hand and throwing them into their mouths as they jerked back their heads. The empty pod was dropped on the ground as they walked away.

Perhaps the apparent lack of respect for peas was due to the fact that there were clearly more sacks on offer than were ever going to be purchased. That was Bobby's signal to move. 'Let's see who's ready to start knocking 'em out,' he said. He held on to my hand, so I would not get lost and he could concentrate on business. He asked the price at a couple of stalls, but they must have had a way of disposing of unsold stock and their prices were still high. Then one man, who had had a good morning and was keen to get home, quoted a price Bobby was willing to pay, and a deal was done.

As many peas as the van could carry had been purchased. Bobby pulled out his roll of one-pound and ten-shilling notes and paid the man. With the help of market porters, the peas were loaded. Our drive home was much quieter than our outward journey; the full load of peas absorbed and suppressed many of the rattles, shakes and bumps that had been amplified by the emptiness of the ageing vehicle. I was kept amused by Judy's antics on the homeward journey. She had found a hole in a corner of one of the pea sacks and was pulling out pods one at a time. By biting not too hard, she could crack open the shell and scoop out the peas, two or three at a time, with her nose. She would then sit back and eat them slowly before scooping out more and eating them.

On such a day, when Bobby was pleased with his morning's work and in good spirits, he would sit me on the edge of his seat, holding me between his knees, and allow me steer the van all the way down Otterfield Road. I remember the feeling still; the mixture of thrill and fear as he slackened his strong grip on the steering wheel and control of the vehicle passed to me, probably for only moments at a time but enough to show me I could do it and embolden me in future years. We would arrive home in a jolly mood; I was excited from the thrill of 'driving' our van, and Bobby was sure his purchases would please Nan and earn us a good profit. Nan had made her usual effort to have a dinner waiting on the table to reward her valiant husband. After casting her eye over the contents of the van, she concluded that the peas were fresh and that the price was right. 'We'll get our money back on these all right,' she said, in an understated way. Dinnertime was peaceful and optimism ruled.

It did not matter that I had not gone to school; now that I was old enough I was becoming useful on the round, and that afternoon, with so many peas to sell, my young legs would be especially valuable. Nan had already guessed my whereabouts of the morning and had planned for an extra helper, seeking out a third 'scoop' from an old set of scales and putting it aside in readiness. After dinner, Bobby drove us onto one of his regular estates. For half a minute he called out his wares, in a loud sing-song voice. We then each took a scoop, into which two pounds of peas had been generously weighed, and knocked on doors, offering 'lovely fresh peas'.

When people came out to the van to see what we had, Nan and Bobby remained to serve them while I ran like a whippet up garden paths with scoops of peas. After each sale, I returned to the van to hand over the money and quickly have my scoop refilled. With each house I called upon I would be moving up the road ahead of the van. When the customers around the van had been served, Bobby would move our mobile marketplace a few yards beyond the houses I had reached and the performance would be repeated.

Throughout the afternoon, housewives would be pleased to see a fresh vegetable that would help them brighten the evening meal and they would buy from us eagerly. As the afternoon turned to evening and preparation of the meal began, there would be no time to shell peas so we would begin to make fewer sales. We would continue to knock on doors, until no sales could be made and it was declared time to give up for the day.

The day had gone well; two-thirds of the peas had been sold, covering the purchase price and a little over for expenses. There was no need to worry about the remaining stock, it would still be fresh and good tomorrow. The unopened sacks were pulled to the back of the van and covered with a few of the empty hessian sacks that had earlier contained peas, and were now viewed as trophies of success. They were guarded for the return of deposit that would be claimed later. The remaining empty sacks were put in a heap behind the passenger seat for me to sit on as we drove home.

'We'll 'ave a good day tomorrow,' said Bobby. 'Those bags are all profit,' he said, nodding at the unsold peas. 'We've done the hard work, now's our chance to get a little bit ahead.' Nan was content and pleased to hear her husband sounding like his old self. Considering that there was nothing she need add to his good cheer, she sat quietly enjoying the comfort of the van as the engine warmed around her feet. After fresh air and exercise, she was lulled to a state of sleepiness.

Cosseted in the comfort of my hessian nest, my review of the day could be nothing but favourable. On that homeward journey my guardian-parents were relaxed and showing qualities that were so often obscured by a veil of anxiety. For the moment, they were at ease on a day that had brought them the modest success – which was all that they asked. With the wisdom of the years, I would cherish them for the good people they were; the decent self-sufficient lives they lived, wanting no more than their fair share in return for their labours. I would estimate that my education had not suffered from missing time in school; in its place, I had experienced the workings of the real world and learned lessons direct from life in all its raw simplicity. But I was a child and at that moment valued them for the security of Nan's strict care and the serenity I felt in Bobby's gentle nature. I was especially enjoying their company as our old van purred along lulling two of its passengers into sleepiness while keeping the third wide awake with the need to wrestle with its worn steering. Bobby took full advantage of his enforced alertness, continuing to voice cheerful thoughts, which, although not directly responded to by his peaceful passengers, added to the atmosphere of contentment that accompanied aromas of moist pea pods, domestic gloss paint and the oily smell of the warm engine. On such a day, how could I be anything but pleased with my life? I was happy and I wanted everything, just as it was at that moment, to go on forever.

Bob and Carrie Walker

Violet, c.1921 shortly after being adopted by Mr & Mrs Walker

Bob walker with his adopted daughter, Violet

Violet, aged 18

Fred, Nan's youngest brother, with Violet (in our back garden)

My father

My parents' wedding day, 1935

*My mother,
in her ATS uniform,
c.1940*

*Me and Nan
c.1940*

Chapter 3

LOST LOVE

Entry to our house, from the road at the front, was gained via a narrow alleyway that ran between our house and our neighbour Mr Knowles's similarly built semi-detached two-up two-down property. The two dwellings were so much alike that on the only occasion I was ever invited into the rather reclusive Mr Knowles's abode, the reverse floor-plan of the otherwise identical rooms was quite disconcerting. Our front doors opened directly opposite one another, and the alley between was so narrow as to convince an agile young lad that he could, if he ever needed to, leap from one threshold to the other without touching the gravelled pathway between.

To reach our respective backyards, the portal arrangements were set at an angle in order to obtain sufficient width of access, a feature of this arrangement caused the slender thoroughfare to end in a pointed formation. Mr Knowles entered his back yard via a close-boarded garden gate that a tall man on tiptoe could peer over. The correct fittings of hinges and latch gave an attractive rustic appearance.

Our gate, by contrast, although set at a similar angle, disturbed the intended symmetry and general good appearance by having an inappropriate design and finish. Our gate had once been a substantial interior door in some large Victorian building, perhaps a school or government office. Traces only of a rich royal-blue paint remained to give a hint of its glorious past, or a lack of present maintenance depending on the beholder's view. Neither were the fittings rustic or even suitable for the outdoor position; large brass knobs inside and out were the means of control and a long steel bolt on the inside was the method of securing the heavy defence when closed. The whole structure towered to a full six and a half feet, adding to its incongruity but giving complete privacy once in place.

The responsibility of keeper of the gate usually fell to Nan. She was aware of the times of her husband's expected homecomings and would listen for a sound almost inaudible to anyone else: the gentle thump, thump, thump made with the side of his clenched fist, which signalled his arrival and wish to be admitted. The bolt would be thrown back to permit entry and then quickly returned to its place of security.

On occasions the request for admission would be almost too weak even for the ears of the vigilant wife and would need to be supported by a call of 'Carrie'. On such a day Bobby was most likely to have been overtaken by one of his bouts of ill health. He would be helped into the house and guided to a chair where he would sit gasping for breath, his face looking more sallow and lined than usual. Nan would rush to him with white medicine, which she administered until his pain subsided. It might have been only the day before that during some disagreement she took the opportunity to remind him of his foolish younger days when, as a heavy drinker, he had damaged his 'constitution' and would 'suffer the consequences for evermore'. On those occasions it seemed to be Nan's mission never to let her husband forget his failings, but when his need was great she tended him with the skill of a trained nurse, disguised only by the tenderness of the loving wife that she could not conceal.

One day, when Nan was piling clothes to be washed into one corner of the scullery, Bobby could be heard out in the alley. Having arrived home at a time unexpected by Nan, he was for the moment beaten by the heavy wooden gate. He was calling 'Carrie, Carrie', almost sobbing and begging his wife to come to his aid. Nan rushed to him and helped him into the scullery. He leaned heavily on the bottle-green gloss-painted brick wall and sunk slowly down onto the pile of clothes waiting to be washed, where he sat until he could be got into bed. There he remained until an ambulance came to take him into hospital. I heard frightening stories of Bobby being 'opened up' and of the stomach cancer being too much so that 'they had to close him up again'. I did not fully understand the meaning of what I heard but I could tell the seriousness of the situation from the tone of the voices. A day or two later, they said he did not have long to live.

One Clear Morn

Such events reunite even the most divided of families, if just for a little while. The only time I ever saw my mother and father together was as they walked in the grounds of Hillingdon Hospital. It was merely on the edge of a car park bordered by a rough hawthorn hedge, still without leaves or adornment in the winds of early March, but to me it was a romantic setting that no Hollywood film could improve upon. For a moment or two, I allowed my sadness for Bobby to transfer to the scene in front of me and to the part that I might have played in it. My parents looked so right together. They were young, like other boys' parents. They were smart, in their best clothes for visiting hospital. I wanted to run to them and hug them both. For an instant, I was aware that my life was different from other boys' lives and I longed for it to be the same. But as quickly as it came, the ache that had griped my heart so briefly, left me, as I saw that my mother and father were not like other boys' parents. My mother was upset and my father wanted to console her, but respectfully kept his distance from the women who now belonged to another man and child. I held back too, and my thoughts returned to Bobby in his last hours, and I knew that losing him would hurt the more. We left that day after being told that Bobby would not last the night, and it was so.

In the days ahead, Nan spoke to other adults more quietly than usual when she knew I was near. She ushered friends and neighbours into our cold front room that we rarely used. I was not invited to go in, and I knew that I should not ask why. When we left the house, I would look back and see that our curtains remained drawn. People who knew Nan, for some distance up and down our road, also had their curtains drawn. The quiet time lasted for several days. There were measured knocks on our front door, visits to the front room and respectful comments in sympathetic low voices.

One day Nan was up earlier than of late. She dressed herself in her smartest, dark clothes. She tried to have some breakfast and, after, sit still with the usual last cup of tea while giving me instructions for the day. Mr Knowles, next door, would be home and said that he would look after me but I was only to trouble him in an emergency. Soon, a knock came on the door and several men, dressed smartly in dark clothes, went into the cold front room and carried out what I knew by then was Bobby in his coffin.

After Bobby's funeral, Nan returned slowly to a limited daily routine. No activity considered 'unnecessary for the time being' was undertaken. She seemed to need to spend time out of doors, and tending a flower border next to the path that ran the short way to our garden shed became almost a place of commemoration. I had never seen her pray but she now spent time on her knees while she loosened winter-compacted soil around the roots of plants that she knew were waiting for warmer days. 'They don't look much now but they'll be lovely soon,' she said, sounding as if she was not sure whether she cared or not.

Nan was not an educated gardener; she knew no Latin names, and cared not for rhizomes, corms or tubers – to her, roots were roots. Her border contained common herbaceous flowers that could be found in any cottager's garden. Most would thrive without expert attention and some were even invasive varieties, for which the most important implement was her small spade with the broken handle. With it, plants that had outgrown their allotted space could be divided, bringing them under control and providing a gift for a friend or neighbour. As she hacked into a clump, she would say 'Mrs So-and-so will love a bit of this'.

Although untutored in the language of plantsmanship, Nan had learned common names over her years of experience. The ones she knew she said to herself, as if the sound created a picture in her mind of the flower in all its glory: London pride, goldenrod, phlox, gypsophila, pink or iris she would repeat as she worked. 'That's a peony' she would say proudly, considering it to be the aristocrat of the border. As in other years, her noble plant was too advanced for its own safety and would require a covering of ashes to protect it from a late frost.

A large clump of lily-of-the-valley, still unattractive to anyone who had not experienced it in summer, seemed to have some special meaning for Nan. She knelt over it and with bare fingers picked off a winter's debris, making way for the heavily-scented creamy-white flowers that would follow soon. Nan was not one to cry easily but one late afternoon she remained with her head bowed low for a long time as she worked unhurriedly on the still-sleeping miniature lilies. She found signs of new growth, of new life and of the potential beauty of another season to come, and it seemed to comfort and encourage her. She stood to take one more look, saying, 'That'll be lovely soon,' and went indoors.

If Nan could not be found in the garden she would be with Mrs Howe, who lived two doors away. Nan and Bobby had known Mrs Howe for many years; she had owned a greengrocer shop and they had many business dealings with her. An old friend could be a comfort and Nan found herself spending many afternoons having tea and long conversations next-door-but-one. Mrs Howe had an additional means of stimulating Nan back into life; she was a knowledgeable lady and a good conversationalist but she saw life from her own particular point of view, which she could put forward rather directly, and on some occasions with the tactlessness to which she was prone. On such a day, Nan would return home showing signs of irritation. Exasperation with Mrs Howe would turn to anger with life and its unfairnesses, and then to rage at the untimely death of her husband. But Nan had had many setbacks in her life to deal with, so the frustrations of her afternoon would settle, finally, into a visibly grim mood of determination not to be beaten.

One day, a government letter fell on the mat. Nan hesitated, then picked it up and opened it cautiously. Inside was her Widow's Pension Book, which she examined for a few moments before throwing it down on the kitchen table. Fury and fear welled up inside her. The mix of emotions and the reminder of her sad new status made her body rigid and her face fierce. 'How can yer live on ten-bob a week?' she said, in a voice indignant and pathetic at the same time. 'Our rent is thirteen and six. This won't even pay that.' After a short pause, 'Well, that's it! We've 'ad it now! The bailiffs'll be round to put us out on the street and we'll end up in the workhouse.' I had no idea who bailiffs were or what the workhouse was but 'They', the unknown, would always be waiting to ensnare us, and the unknown has an insidious way of being more frightening than the known.

Bobby's death had dashed Nan down and she was struggling to survive her time of mourning, so there were many frightening days when she voiced her worries loudly and it seemed, at times, that she might sink into total despair. Fortunately, there was in her a resilience that kept her going through a long period of thought, after which she came to the conclusion that she had to go on because there was no other way. She had let time pass, she had let old friendships comfort her and she had managed to do the things necessary to maintain daily life – perhaps it was the mundane tasks of day to day affairs that gave her time to think and come to her decision.

In normal times Nan could be quite forgetful, especially concerning a matter such as cooking, which she found less attention holding than a walk down our long garden and perhaps a chat with a neighbour across the fence. Potatoes put on the stove to boil were often forgotten. Perhaps understandably, the lapse took place more frequently after Bobby's death, as it did on the day of the arrival of the pension book. The old aluminium saucepan, which must have had nine lives, had been soaked overnight as usual, and next morning created plenty of thinking time for the forgetful cook as she scraped and removed an inch of black 'volcanic rock' from its inside.

After half an hour's intensive restoration work the saucepan was improved, and it seemed that Nan's outlook on her new life was too. She came in from the scullery and commanded me to sit with her at the kitchen table, where all planning took place. 'Right,' said Nan, 'Never say yer mother 'ad a jibber.' I had not, at that age, unravelled the full meaning of that particular saying, but I knew it was good news and meant that Nan's defiance was returning to take on the wrongs that assailed her. 'We'll 'ave to come up with some of the old tricks,' she went on, 'We'll 'ave to find some lodgers. We've done it before, we can do it again.' Concerned with my part in this new strategy, I noticed that it was 'we' who were going to have to 'do it', so I listened intently and with a concentration I had not achieved before. Fortunately, there was no silly speech to the effect that I, still two months away from my sixth birthday, was now the 'man of the house', that was not Nan's style at all. Nevertheless, without ceremony, my life changed. I was spoken to like an adult from that day on and was not spared any detail of the facts that would influence our lives. Some that affected me directly, gained my attention more than others. 'If we don't work, we won't be able to afford to eat' sounded serious to a growing lad with a good appetite. I decided then and there that wherever my labours were required they would be given unstintingly to ward off that dreadful day. I condensed Nan's statement into a slogan that I would remember, 'No work – No eat', and it remained in my mind always, coaxing me into many and varied occupations, some probably far beyond my years. Nan saw to it that I never went to bed without a supper, of course, but my industriousness was not wasted; I learned so many things that cannot be taught, convincing me that it was then that my education at the 'University of Life' began.

Chapter 4

INFANT SCHOOL

The smell of wet leaves instantly gives me the ability to summon up a picture of St Stephen's Infant School, the first school I attended. In front of the building was a playground, around which grew large horse chestnut, beech and London plane trees, all appearing as if they had grown out of the tarmacadam surface. I have no recollection of the summers I spent at St Stephen's, in my memory the school stands in perpetual winter. The days are cold. The days are wet. The fallen leaves on the ground are cold and wet. I stand about shivering, or I shuffle through the mush of leaves trying to avoid older boys who, in groups of half a dozen, go around the playground linked, with arms across the shoulders of the boy next to them. They surround new arrivals, chanting menacingly, 'JOIN OUR GANG OR BE BEATEN UP.' When I am surrounded and challenged, I meekly put my arm across the shoulder of the end boy and join the group. I feel foolish and have not enough aggression to chant. I feel no comradeship with these truculent boys and I leave the group at the next corner, I hope unnoticed. I long for playtime to be over and to be marched back into the warmth and safety of the building.

Once inside and lessons are about to begin, I feel more secure and my confidence rises slowly. I am pleased that adults are now in charge as they will be wise, sensible, fair and kind, and all the things that children have not yet learned. I forget my fears of the playground and open my mind to learn.

As the days go by, I begin to wonder if my expectation of adults has been set too high. My first awakening came in the class of Mrs Lee, a teacher close to retirement age with a large 'bun' of grey hair on top of her head, who would walk up and down between the rows of pupils while addressing the whole class loudly. She would pick on a child who she thought needed 'extra attention' and stand over him (it was usually a boy) shouting her lesson still. As she continued to teach in her own peripatetic fashion, she would be, at the same time, sharpening her pencil, usually a new full-length bright-yellow one. Once she felt the point of the pencil was suitable for her purpose, she would apply it to the boy's scalp who she had settled upon that day, twisting the pencil left and right at a pressure she considered appropriate.

Any questions she had for the class would now be directed at the boy, at an unchanged level of decibels. If no coherent answer came, pressure on the pencil would be increased. Success in giving a satisfactory answer seemed to be kept tantalizingly out of reach of the chosen boy's known abilities, so that Mrs Lee only ever ceased when her victim appeared as if he might break into tears or into a rage, which would draw attention to her method of teaching.

The only revenge the boy with the damaged scalp and injured pride could exact was to engage a few loyal friends who he would organize to ambush Mrs Lee as she was leaving school on her way home that day. The boys would gather behind a hedge, ensuring that they were in earshot but well hidden, and proceed to chant:

> OLD MOTHER LEE
> CAUGHT A FLEE
> PUT IT IN A TEAPOT
> AND MADE A CUP OF TEA

Mrs Lee would fly into a rage; waving her umbrella like a hussar brandishing his sabre, while shouting, 'I know who you are, I'll see you in school tomorrow.' There would be a scuffling behind the hedge and the boys would be gone.

Mrs Lee had demonstrated the fallibility of adults – even teachers. She had introduced the simple fact that violence only begets more violence but, probably like mankind itself, her pupils were too young to learn that lesson.

I left Mrs Lee's class more alert, but as I had only observed her actions and not been her victim, I still had a hopeful respect for my elders and betters. My next experience, however, was mine alone, and would fill me with the pain of injustice and cause me to reassess again my opinion of those older and supposedly wiser. One day, I found myself in the distressing situation of being late for school. The teacher who dealt with my 'misdemeanour' was a young smartly-dressed woman who, because of her youth and attractive appearance, I thought would be kind and sympathetic and not at all like Mrs Lee. I was sure that she would understand my problem. I had been brought up to believe that if I told the truth nothing bad would happen to me, so in innocence I began my story. It quickly became apparent that I was not going to be listened to. Nevertheless, I continued to explain, as well as she would let me, that our alarm clock failed to wake us and it was not until children could be heard going to school that the problem was noticed. 'Our alarm clock was wrong,' I pleaded, talking myself right into her trap. Had I said 'broken', as it turned out to be, I would not have made such an easy target for her, but with my limited vocabulary, I had grabbed at the first word that conveyed the simple fact.

'Ah! Wrong was it?' said the smart young teacher. 'If it was wrong, was it fast or slow?'

I could feel her closing in. I panicked. She did not give me a 'don't know' option. Was it 'fast' or was it 'slow'? She wanted an answer.

'Fast,' I said in nervous haste.

'Ah!' she said again. 'If it was fast you would have arrived at school too early. You are lying. Go and stand outside the headmistress's office.' My own fear of breaking rules had already loaded pressure upon me and now I had told the truth and not been believed. I said to myself, 'It's not fair,' and could hear Nan's voice saying, 'Who said life's fair?'

My recollection of other classrooms is vague. I have no memory of anything I learned; no nursery rhymes or poems or songs, no 'two plus two equals', or even the rules of a simple game organized by teachers. Most vivid in my memory is a great assembly hall, in which we spent much of our time waiting in long queues for some form of health care. An example was the visiting nurse, known by the children as 'Nitty Nora', who would examine our scalps for lice. After a long wait in the queue, each child would arrive in front of the nurse and in the few seconds allotted would have his or her hair pulled to the left and to the right, each time revealing the scalp for examination. If nothing was found, the child would receive a tap on the back of the head ending in a short push, firm enough to ensure that he or she needed to take a smart step forward to regain balance and, more importantly to a nurse with limited time, to propel the child forward and out of her way.

If signs of lice were found, the infested child would be separated out and sent home, with instructions for the mother to go through the laborious routine of delousing. Half an hour at a time would be needed, combing through wet hair with a fine-toothed comb to find the 'nits', as the eggs and immature lice are known. The process would have to continue for several weeks to ensure the problem was cleared. Even after combing, many nits still need to be picked off individually, (leaving our language with the useful and descriptive term 'nitpicking').

We were cared for internally too, and that required more time queuing in the great hall. Earlier in the century, it had been decided by governmental decree that the diet of the 'British urban working classes' was deficient in vitamins and minerals and that the situation could be tackled through the schools. To correct the matter, children were administered large spoonfuls of cod liver oil during the course of their day at school. Oil alone had proved so unpalatable that, fortunately, by the time I and my contemporaries were being dosed, malt had been added to make a sweet treacly substance; it was golden-brown and looked like soft toffee. A nurse controlled a very large brown jar of cod liver oil and malt, into which she would dip a spoon, turning it a few times to hold the runny substance in place. As each child reached the front of the queue, the spoon would be thrust into his or her mouth. The mixture looked appetizing and there was a moment of sweetness, but that was followed by a fishy oily taste that no amount of sweetness could disguise. Each child dealt with the unwelcome sensation in their own way. The 'fainters', 'kickers' and 'screamers' were removed from future such line-ups, their parents being informed of the need for the additional supplement at home. Most others, to their credit, were stoic, accepting their dosing and its aftermath, and contenting themselves to pull faces at one another in comradely sympathy.

A poster on the wall, attempting to make our dosing with vitamins and minerals attractive to us, proclaimed that cod liver oil and malt had been given by Kanga to Roo and Tigger in *The House at Pooh Corner*. I, and many of the 'urban working classes' I am sure, had not encountered the stories of Winnie-the-Pooh, causing the well-meaning advertising to be wasted upon us.

I left infant school well vitamized and a little more aware of the dangers of personal infestations by *Pediculus humanus capitis*. I was a little wiser, if, perhaps, not entirely in the way the authorities had intended; the naivety that gave me such high expectations of the adult world had been moderated to a more sensible level, which, I am certain, stood me in better stead to deal with much that I encountered in the years that followed.

Chapter 5

AFTER BOBBY

As spring began to show signs of its intended arrival, at that time of year when a fresh vitality enters all living things, Nan followed nature's way, rising up in spirit and taking a fresh outlook on the new life that had been thrust upon her. She had been helped by the many heart-warming tributes from friends, neighbours and business acquaintances, who did not spare to add to their condolences praise for the man who had been her husband. There were kind words for Nan herself, telling of the esteem in which she was held for her loyalty to her husband and stoicism through his periods of ill health. Sincerity of the sentiment was confirmed by the invitations she received in her time of need; friends locally opened their homes to her, and letters from further afield asked her to visit and stay a while if she could. Afternoon cups of tea with Mrs Howe continued, probably more amicably as Nan's outlook on all things improved. Mrs Rawlins, across the road, asked Nan over to tea more frequently than before. Mrs Taylor, who had recently had her small back bedroom converted into a bathroom, must have considered that a warm soak would be therapeutic to Nan's recovery and invited her to take advantage of her new facility. At intervals, Nan could be seen going to Mrs Taylor's with a bundle of clean clothes wrapped in a towel under her arm. The new bath was described as 'lovely' by a pink and glowing Nan upon her return from a session.

As Nan's confidence grew, she thought seriously about the invitations she had received, wondering if she could perhaps take a little time to herself before committing to the restricting presence of lodgers. She had been used to surviving for periods without income and it occurred to her that, with a large portion of our rent paid by her widows' pension, she could perhaps manage to do so now. Marshalling her resources was the first thing to be done and, as happened when the need arose, she went upstairs to search her hiding places where small amounts of money would be found. A few notes laid flat under the lino would not give their presence away and as less obvious places were often chosen, Nan, like the squirrel, would forget them and temporarily lose part of her hoard. However, on this occasion, with adventure in mind and with a newfound vigour, she made sure that no treasure trove was missed. Diligence required the movement of furniture, with the associated bumps and bangs that could be heard downstairs for a full half-hour.

It must have been decided that we were in funds, as I was told that we were going to be doing some visiting. Scotland was one possibility. Another was the countryside of Kent. Letters of acceptance were written on small pieces of off-white lined writing paper in Nan's self-taught handwriting, which followed the copperplate style of her day but with her own excess of loops and flourishes. From the possible dates and lengths of stay, it was clear I was not going to see much of school that summer. In answer to any comments to that effect, the response was that I would learn more where we were going. I was happy to agree.

While we waited for answers to Nan's letters, we went on a day visit to one of her old friends who lived in London. There was no direct route to the part we wanted to get to so we zigzagged across the metropolis, hopping from one bus to another. It was a journey that began my lifelong dislike of urban areas and the landscapes created by humankind. We dragged along drab streets between sooty buildings, through shopping High Streets blighted by ugly iron railway viaducts, an overload of street furniture, and poles carrying overhead cables catering for every need of the Londoners as they went about their daily lives below. Only where a building had been completely destroyed by a wartime bomb could any respite from the work of man be found, where nature had rushed in to clothe the scar with grasses and wildflowers.

When we arrived at our destination, I was told that we were going to see Nan's friend who was called Ada and, although she was no relative of mine, just to be polite, I was to call her 'Auntie Ada'. I suffered immediate discomfort at the thought of calling someone I had not met 'Auntie Ada'. I had never heard the name Ada before. I thought it must be an old person's name and I immediately tainted it with all that I had seen and disliked on the journey of the morning. I would be polite, of course, but perhaps getting away with simply calling the lady 'Auntie', if I had to call her anything.

Nan was greeted boisterously. I was welcomed but with a sideway glance that suggested that my presence was a mystery. We followed 'Auntie Ada' upstairs to her second-floor flat. The two old friends were soon drinking tea and chatting excitedly while I looked out of the window onto a narrow roadway that ran between the aged building that we were in and a row of brick-built arches, which appeared to support a viaduct. The viaduct might have carried a road or railway or even a canal but, whatever its nature, it was hidden by brickwork that formed a skyline as far as I could see to the left and to the right. The arches created semicircular caverns below, which were enclosed by varying designs of boarded walls, windows and doors. They had the appearance of a row of workshops in which many different trades were carried-on. In front of each was a clutter of paraphernalia relating to the kind of work being done; large crates of incoming or outgoing goods in front of some, and cars being repaired or being resprayed in front of others.

Soon, the nature of what the arches supported became clear. Cups and saucers between the two old friends began to make a small tinkling sound. 'Aunt Ada', knowing what was about to befall and not wishing to miss a word of Nan's news and gossip, held a finger in the air, suspending the conversation while the cups progressed to a violent rattle. Into my vision, far to the left, came a train of low red carriages, four or five of them, each with London Transport written on the side. As the carriages passed across the skyline, the fabric of the apartment shook and vibrated as if a minor earthquake was being experienced. Their passing took no more than half a minute but for that short duration there was no point in continuing the conversation as even a shout across the tea table would not be heard. Once the train had gone and a London-kind of normality returned, Nan's friend seemed not to have been perturbed by the experience. 'It's all right,' she said, 'the next one isn't for half an hour,' adding that it was the underground train that went to a place I failed to hear, bemused perhaps by a train that seemed to fly across the sky being called 'underground'.

Our homeward journey was no less drear than our morning sortie. Others like us, keen to get home, added to the difficulty of finding buses and slowed our progress once we were aboard. I was glad that at the end of that day, when our struggles had finished, we were twelve miles outside the city.

In a day or two, a letter arrived from Mr Walter McLaughlin of Glasgow imploring his 'English mother' to come to visit him and his wife. The wholehearted welcome told of great affection built up during Mr McLaughlin's military days when based in the south of England. He had boarded with Nan and had received the kind of attention she could lavish upon a person she had taken close to her heart. She would tell how he appeared at her door one day looking for lodgings, and had reminded her of her younger brother who had also worn khaki but at the age of sixteen had been killed on his first day in France. At the end of Walter's furlough, his departure caused English mother and Scottish son to part with tears in their eyes, Nan would tell with full emotion as she caressed a silver-framed picture of her brother proudly wearing his uniform, as if he and Walter McLaughlin had become one person.

While Nan plotted her Scottish adventure, I plotted mine. I was going to see another country, the vision of which I had built up from pictures on railway posters and porridge oats packets; I would have my first experience, I felt sure, of mountains and lochs and rugged countryside, of men in kilts tossing cabers, and I might even run into bands of marauding highlanders all looking like Rob Roy!

The realization of my fantasy was very different. Reality was a tedious steam train journey that went on forever, broken only by dry sandwiches brought from home. It is true that we passed through magnificent countryside, the like I had never seen, but it was outside the carriage window and I was trapped inside. I could not enjoy what I saw, for no sooner was it shown to me than it was taken away as we thundered onward. When finally I could escape the incarceration of the journey, it was into a city, grimy like London. We made our way to where we were going to stay, in an aged backstreet tenement building in what surely must have been one of the less attractive areas of Glasgow. Mr McLaughlin and his wife were very kind and lavished attention on Nan in an impassioned generosity. My wellbeing was attended to in kindliness, but I saw no mountains or lochs, and the most rugged terrain I encountered was in the concrete corridors and iron-railinged staircases taking us several flights up to our hosts' apartment where we remained enclosed, it seemed, for days.

After a few days back at home, recovering from our excursions and catching up on some necessary jobs, we were off again, this time to see Mrs Geary, another of Nan's old friends. Nan knew Mrs Geary from their days together in service, her name was familiar to me having heard it spoken of with some reverence, for her position of cook, when Nan held a more lowly place in the order of things 'below stairs'. My enthusiasm for visiting was refreshed because this time we were going to the countryside of Nan's reminiscences. She would speak so frequently about her home in Kent, making it sound to be all woods and bucolic beauty. She would say the names of places, savouring the sounds as if they conjured a vision of the mini-paradise of her memory. As she eulogised, seeds were sown in a young mind eager to see for himself.

Our Greenline bus, on its way to Westerham, dropped us at the end of a narrow lane that would take us to our destination. In the warmth of the spring day, we needed to remove our top coats. With coat over one arm and suitcase in hand we set off to walk a mile or so down the lane. Immediately, I was captivated by my surroundings: grassy banks on either side of us were laden with the strong green growth of yet-to-flower meadowsweet and cow parsley; under hedges, safe from the field-hand's scythe, primroses still clustered; and insects hummed loudly, as the heat of the sun reflected a moist-green humidity across

After Bobby

the stony surface of the lane. When we needed to rest and cool ourselves, Nan sat on her suitcase while I collect sheep wool from a barbed wire fence and told myself this *really* was the country. Had Bo-Peep appeared with a shepherd's crook I would not have been shocked, such was my childish fantasy about the countryside.

We walked onward and were about to take another rest when Nan said, 'There's the house.' There was no hesitation, because she knew that it was the only dwelling on the lane before the village was reached two miles or so further along. The house, not generous in proportion or adornment, lay back from the lane almost hidden. It was more ordinary than I expected, having heard it said, with much admiration, that Mr Geary had built it himself, in a way that suggested something grand or unusual. Mrs Geary was expecting us and was soon at the door hugging her old friend. She had lost her own husband a year or so earlier and her greeting was full of understanding and sympathy for Nan. I received the glance of curiosity that I was becoming used to but it did not delay the welcome and soon we were inside drinking glasses of cool cordial.

As the two women talked loudly and laughed frequently, I was left to wander about. The house was set in its own grounds, now untended and overgrown. I found derelict sheds that I could explore in the coming days. I found an old bicycle that I hoped was not quite too big for me and, to my delight, a gypsy caravan that was almost lost in undergrowth and branches of trees that hung down around it. My initial excursion was cut short as I responded to a call from the house. Nan was being shown around and I was invited to join her. The important matter of a 'call of nature' was being attended to first, which only required Mrs Geary to point across the garden to a small, wooden building that could be described as a closed-in sentry box. All that was required would be found there, she said. Next, we were shown where we were going to sleep. My room was tiny with an overlarge pattern on the wallpaper that made the room look even smaller, as if it could have been plucked from the pages of a book of children's stories. The closeness of the overgrown copse outside the little window was a delight that would allow me to lie in bed and imagine that I was sleeping in the woods. This *really* was the country I told myself again.

Nan was being shown the kitchen by the time I tore myself away from my musings in my bedroom. Mrs Geary was proudly demonstrating a pump in the kitchen sink that brought water from the well. 'We used to go out with a bucket,' she said, pushing a wooden handle back and forth that jerked water into her kettle. A paraffin stove heated the kettle for tea and, later, saucepans for cooking. A strange looking arrangement that appeared to be a large tin box balanced on top of a paraffin stove was where she was soon going to place the chicken that sat prepared nearby. The type of oven, which I had never seen, thrilled me for being a piece of real country-style equipment, I thought. Later, I found that it roasted the chicken perfectly well, giving the meat only the slightest hint of paraffin.

The day had been warm but as the evening arrived temperatures had fallen sharply. We can still get a frost in May, the two women agreed. By the time the table was laid for the evening meal, a wood fire had been lit directly on the stone floor of the main living room. The hearth that had no need of a metal basket or iron grate was so natural in its primitive simplicity, and gave the blazing wood a magic that excited my schoolboy imaginings. On either side of the fireplace, inglenooks accommodated settles, which had unpadded wooden backs high enough to keep the draft from a tall occupant; both were antique in style, built of unpolished timber from the workshop of Mr Geary, we were told. When the meal was ready for serving, dusk and the small-windowed room made it necessary to provide additional light, so a pressurized-paraffin lamp that burned like a gas mantle was hoisted high and lit the table. Firelight and lamplight combined illuminated only the end of the room that we occupied.

After dinner, we moved from the table to sit by the fire. The two old friends had taken a settle each, slipping into the deepest corners, and with only the fire between them there was nothing to prevent reminiscing going on until bedtime. The conversation did not require my participation, so I began to peer around the room. Just visible, at the extreme of the lamp and firelight, was a piece of furniture that took my attention. Strips of wood created a curved section at the top of the large polished cabinet. Places where feet might be accommodated aroused my curiosity. Mrs Geary, aware of my exclusion from their talk and wanting to occupy me, said that I could examine the mystery item more closely. The stripped top, I found, was a lid that rolled up to expose a keyboard. 'It's a harmonium,' Mrs Geary called to me, adding, thoughtfully in Nan's direction, that her husband loved to play it. 'It doesn't work very well now, the bellows are broken,' Mrs Geary warned. But, 'Try it,' she said, pointing to the flat carpeted pedals. I pressed one. The other rose up inviting me to press it too. I pressed and the first one rose again, as if tempting me to continue 'pedalling'. I accepted the challenge and maintained a steady rate. With a single finger, I pressed one of the yellowed ivory keys but no sound was produced. Only when I pedalled furiously could I extract a feeble wheeze from somewhere deep within the ailing machine. I closed-down the roll-top cover and returned to the fireside. My thoughts turned to the man who was absent and yet was all around us. I admired the home he had built, with its snug and secure inglenook corner where at that moment I was bathing myself in the warmth of the fire. I stared into the red embers that waxed and waned as draughts harried and disturbed them while I planned the adventures I was going to have tomorrow.

 A little before bedtime, Mrs Geary wanted to mention a matter that was on her mind. She first assured her old friend, again, of how welcome we were and went on to say that she hoped we would be able to stay for a week or two. To show that she had considered the matter seriously, she explained that she understood that my education was important so she had spoken to her friend at Tatsfield Village School who would be happy to let me attend all the time my grandmother was 'recuperating' locally. Nan thanked Mrs Geary and, wanting to extend her contentment of the evening, said that we would like to stay. The excitement of going to bed in my fairytale bedroom was slightly marred by the fear of being plunged into a school where pupils and teachers were unknown to me. I wrestled with my worries for a while and came to the conclusion that, with Nan's openly admitted dislike of school, she would probably forget about the arrangement.

Next morning, I was awakened by the unmistakable aroma of bacon sizzling in a frying pan. The joyful smell transferred me from my deep slumbers to a state of full alertness in moments. A few seconds of uncertainty came with the less familiar odour of paraffin-cooking that rolled into my room like a thick dusty carpet. The aromatic herbage outside my bedroom window, mixed with the slight mustiness of my room, added to my temporary confusion until the overlarge pattern on the walls reminded me where I was.

As I tucked into crispy bacon enclosed in doorsteps of white bread, Mrs Geary and Nan were again talking but, this morning, about more serious matters that had affected their lives. Mrs Geary was speaking about her husband and the reason they came to live so far away from the village. He had, she said, been gassed at Ypres in 1915 and invalided out of the army in a dreadful condition. He was ill for a long time. He was in despair about the actions of his fellow man who could do such things, and full of anger for a society that had sent young men unsuspectingly to suffer and die in such terrible ways. At first he found it difficult to mix with other people, 'We came here to be away from it all,' Mrs Geary said. Nan listened intently with great understanding, thinking once again, no doubt, of her young brother killed in France.

As the two old friends continued talking, I was given a wave that said I could go outside. There was no need to tell me to be careful on the lane as there was no traffic and there would be none until about eleven o'clock when the postman came on his bicycle. The only motor vehicles that would be seen belonged to the milkman and the baker, and they both had old vans that could be heard long before they arrived.

As I emerged from the porch that protected the kitchen door, the bright sun struck and I needed to shade my eyes. After a few moments I could see that the overgrown garden came close, almost smothering the house, as if attempting to drive back man's intrusion. In waist-high grasses that glistened in the sun, narrow brick pathways, almost hidden, marked plots that were once under the gardener's control. A vegetable patch now produced only seasonal weeds. Flower borders thrived upon neglect and were made more vibrant by the intrusion of wild flowers that joyfully disturbed the gardener's once co-ordinated colour scheme.

At the back of the garden, a low wooden gate gave access, through an overgrown hedge, to an orchard of forgotten fruit trees. Un-pruned branches burdened the trees, some laden with blossom providing nectar for a thousand honey bees who went about their work noisily. Several hives were placed about but were empty of the miniature workers and falling into disrepair. Next to the orchard was an area of former industry; implement shelters, storage sheds, a stable with hay loft above, a large workshop with rusting hand tools stored on cobwebbed shelves or in dusty drawers, a tool chest filled with smoothing planes, rebate planes of every shape and a full set of carefully-ground chisels and gouges that only a skilled craftsman would appreciate to the full.

Another low gate, with one remaining hinge, could be lifted open to let me through into small fields, once cultivated or grazed but now turning to scrub. Beyond was a meadow down to a small stream where lesser celandine and wood anemone found their chosen habitat of sun or shade. The stream was shallow and clear as it rippled over the flint and chalk of the North Downs. I removed my shoes and socks to paddle in the cold water and, after, dried and warmed my feet in the sun.

In the coming days, as spring turned to summer, I had the kind of freedom I had not known before. While Nan sought consolation in the company of an old friend, and for the moment found respite from matters that she would need eventually to address, her release was my release. I was free to roam in any direction that my fancy took me and, as the days passed, I explored every corner of Mr Geary's land. I rode the bicycle that was not quite too big for me up and down the lane, almost as far as the school, which I viewed from a distance while children were tightly enclosed and at their work – I never did see the inside. I revisited the gypsy caravan and set up home inside, while I imagined a horse between the now crumbling shafts as we clopped along the lanes. In the warmth of the day, I returned to paddle in the stream, and lay on my back in the soft grass of the meadow or in the shade of the orchard while all that I had encountered penetrated my very being.

Every day I saw the hand of the man who had found solace in his toil in the fields and in his workshop; his influence was everywhere and I felt regard for all that I saw. I was drawn to know more about him; I found unfinished projects in his workshop that my own practical nature appreciated and I felt close to him. I examined, again, the dusty cobwebbed tools and imagined the master at his bench, and esteemed the man who could do justice to such fine equipment, could build his own house, and make music too.

Many years later, I understood that it was during that summer that I began to form ideas of what I might want life to hold for me. It is clear that I was not destined to be a studious child who would collect and catalogue specimens of nature, or an artistic boy who could capture the beauty of a single bloom in crayon or paint, or a literary lad who might immortalize the wonders he saw in a poem. In my own way I wanted so much more than all of that; I wanted to be a part of the natural world that I saw around me and to experience it with all my senses. I wanted to remain in the countryside that was every bit as wonderful as the stories I had been told about it. I wanted to find the peace that Mr Geary had found there as he worked with the natural elements of life. I wanted to learn the skills that he had possessed and had enabled him to fashion his world to his own desires. I wanted all those things and made myself a childish promise that one day I would have them, in the certain knowledge that if a wish is truly meant and firmly held it would come true – one day.

By Nan's flower bed

Chapter 6

SOLE GUARDIAN

Nan's self-financed sabbatical completed her recovery, in as far as it ever could be achieved. She had been shown affection by all who knew her, and that friendship, and her love for the husband she would never forget, brought her back to an appearance of her 'old self' and she felt ready to do whatever needed to be done. The responsibility of bringing up another child, had been taken on when her husband was alive, now it fell upon her shoulders alone and she knew that she would need to organize her affairs accordingly. Resources had been run as low as she felt it safe to do, so she decided that it was time for the 'old tricks' she had spoken of. She let it be known that she would welcome lodgers and, the arrangement being common practice at that time, responses came quickly.

Our first lodger was a mysterious man called Mr Auditon. He rented our upstairs front room, which he exited to go to work and entered upon his return so silently that we were never sure whether he was in the house or out. Only two events of his daily routine let it be known that he still lived with us at all. The first was the distant pandemonium created by an old wind-up alarm clock, which had two bells on its top and stood next to his bed on an empty two-pound Blue Bird toffee tin. On the lid of the tin, around the clock, he placed half a dozen old copper pennies that jumped and clattered in sympathy with the vibrating ringing clock. Mr Auditon was a self-confessed heavy sleeper whose work, he said, was so important that he must not be late. If his apparatus of arousal only succeeded in waking the rest of the house, but failed to stir Mr Auditon into consciousness, we were authorised to beat upon his door until we gained a response.

The second opportunity of the day to confirm Mr Auditon's continued presence in the house, and the time we were most likely to see him 'in the flesh', was for a few fleeting moments only, during the course of the evening. A modest creaking on the staircase and a restrained knock on our kitchen door announced that he was about to enter. He would politely pass the time of day, briefly perhaps due to his attire of pyjama trousers and singlet vest when, with towel over his arm and washbag in hand, he would cross the room and enclose himself in our scullery, where he would carry-out his ablutions under the cold tap, which was over the sink in the corner of the room. His return would be equally swift, wishing all present 'Goodnight' as he passed to go upstairs and enclose himself, once again, in his room. Any visiting neighbour of a finer cut, would glance at Nan in anticipation of a comment on the speedy, half naked man who had just passed, but none would be offered and the conversation would gradually pick-up where it left off.

We knew very little about Mr Auditon other than he worked at the Royal Air Force Camp at Uxbridge. All he could tell us about his work was that it was 'hush-hush', secret war work and very important. How he spent his days, we had no idea. Gossipy neighbours were concerned and we received warnings to be careful in case he was a spy. But Nan was sure that he was 'all right' because he worked at the same place as the 'nice Mr Knowles' next door. Mr Knowles's introduction was the only reference Nan wanted, although she did say that in all the years that Mr Knowles had lived next door she had never known what work he did. The reticent and slightly reclusive Mr Knowles would only ever say that his work was 'important and secret'. But he was 'very nice' and could not possibly have a spy for a friend, Nan said, so Mr Auditon had security clearance and any tittle-tattle that came our way was ignored. While Mr Auditon remained with us, we were free to resume normal daily lives. The extra income from the renting of one room, while supplementing Nan's pension, would provide only a meagre living, but it must have been sufficient to keep the bailiffs at bay as Nan seemed content and even cheerful.

Now that Nan was my sole guardian, I spent more time in her company and was beginning to be noticed by her friends and acquaintances. Questions as to my very existence created unguarded conversations that embarrassed me but, at the same time, advanced my education on the general woes of life and the problems of day to day affairs. How and why she had custody of me was a regular enquiry. She would explain that I was the son of her daughter, Violet, who had been let down so badly in marriage. She would say many times, very convincingly, that I was born 'in wedlock'. That particular statement did not bother me too much as I had no idea of the importance attached to it, or to its alternative – 'Wedlock' could have been a quaint little town somewhere for all I knew.

Equally, my health and general condition exercised the conversation. Nan always seemed to be fending off comments on my slight physical build: ''E's tall for 'is age', or ''E's wiry an' 'e's well covered' I would hear her say. In private she sounded more concerned and would say, in confidence to a closer friend, that the doctor had told her that I would be at risk from all the childhood ailments until I was seven. No doubt he would have said the same about many children before 1948 and the arrival of the National Health Service, in the days when the main healers were home remedies, bed rest, the patient's own resilience and letting nature take its course.

Nan, like many people, avoided the expense of a visit to the doctor's surgery by dealing with manageable illnesses and accidents at home. She had at her fingertips a whole range of potions, purges and cure-alls and was quick to apply one of them at the first sign of trouble. I was sent many times to the chemist for one of Nan's all-healing remedies. I was given a small blue hexagonal medicine bottle. It was very greasy, with an even more greasy much-worn cork. With the bottle was a sixpenny piece, from which change was expected. 'It's no good going up the High Street', Nan would say, meaning that the assistant who worked in the modern shop selling patent medicines would not know what was wanted. Fortunately, there were still one or two old-fashioned shops where the man who served was the pharmacist and knew what to supply. There was a tiny shop near the Nag's Head public house on Falling Lane; chemist and one customer overfilled the small space that remained between bottles and jars of all sizes on shelves that covered the walls from floor to ceiling. I would present my bottle, and ask for, 'Some green oils, please.' The chemist would use a stepladder to reach several large bottles, which he would bring down and, with the help of a small funnel, mix just the right amount from each into my bottle. A new cork was supplied. Most times the charge was threepence. Some shops charged sixpence and these Nan carefully noted and avoided next time. The oil was examined when I got home and if it was the right shade of green it was approved and put into the little black medicine cabinet that hung in the scullery, until needed for one of Nan's panacean bread poultices.

    I always seemed to be having to 'sit still' while Nan aimed one of her hot poultices at one part of my body or another. Children seemed to get endless numbers of boils in those days; small ones on the lower leg, larger ones on the thigh, and the worst made sitting down impossible! For these, and many cuts and grazes, a bread poultice and green oils was the cure. A slice of bread was soaked in boiling water and then wrapped in lint and squeezed dry. After green oils had cooled the poultice a little, it was applied to the affected part and bandaged to hold it in place; the hotter the poultice could be borne by the patient was apparently important in its efficacy.

    I gave Nan plenty of opportunity to practise her skills, as any cold that I caught would go on to my chest; the resulting cough would turn to a bark, which I could 'perform' for anyone upon request and gain much sympathy. Colds and coughs were eased with medicines bought from the chemist shop; Galloway's cough mixture was always in the house, and Vicks vapour ointment was rubbed onto the chest when the cold went in that direction. Only if the problem persisted, or was more serious, would a doctor's opinion be sought. On one occasion, I was sent to Hillingdon Hospital for an X-ray. I heard a hushed conversation suggesting that a 'spot' had been found on my lung, apparently indicating a problem with tuberculosis. Nan had a great fear of illness having lost her beloved sister in the flu epidemic that came after the Great War, and made sure not to miss the hospital appointments recommended. The treatment prescribed was probably only preventative and turned out to be not at all distressing. It entailed having all my clothes removed by a soft and sweet smelling nurse, who then directed me to stand in a small area surrounded by moveable screens onto which several sunlamps were directed. I had to wear nothing except dark goggles, and simply enjoy the pleasant feeling of nakedness and electric sunlight. A few sessions, and the problem was never mentioned again. My first experience of hospital was not an unpleasant one.

Bedrooms would normally be unheated all year round and would be icy-cold in winter. It was then that the feather bed became the savour. A giant bag of feathers covered the full length and width of the bed, which when first made would start out about a foot deep and look quite flat and smooth. Sheets and blankets would be tucked in with great care ('hospital corners' being spoken of when being taught to make the bed). Children would change into pyjamas and warm dressing gowns by the kitchen fire, then be allowed to get warm ready to face the run up to bed. 'Jump into bed' would not be an exaggeration in a freezing-cold bedroom. Once in, the occupant would sink into feathers; walls of feather would build up all around throughout the night, so that by morning the sleeper would be lost in a warm hollow of a giant nest. (The days of a 'firm mattress' and worries of anything less than a 'straight back' were many years in the future yet.)

On colder nights, an eiderdown would be placed on top of sheets and blankets. Perhaps in days of yore, or maybe still in the wealthy apartment, down of the female Eider duck would fill this top covering, but from my 'eiderdown' what appeared to be the common filling of chopped chickens' feathers escaped, just a few each night – perhaps not true to its name, but just as warm and attractive in its decorative silky finish.

The only time that bedrooms were heated was if the illness was serious enough. One winter, when a cold went to my chest and my well-known bark developed into something more sinister sounding, Nan 'prescribed' confinement to my little back bedroom, which she was planning to heat in her own inimitable way. I heard her shouting to clear the way as she climbed our narrow staircase with a shovel full of 'hot coals', as she called the already burning lumps of coal from the kitchen fire. She would be blowing smoke away from her face all the while she climbed the stairs, continued across her own bedroom and descended the two wooden steps into mine. The amount she could carry would fill the tiny grate and give an instant fire. Whether or not she had dropped any of her 'hot coals' on the way up did not seem to matter, it was the easiest way to get a fire going. Even then, it would be hours before any warmth would be felt; the black decorative iron surround would be cold and any heat the small fire could produce would be absorbed for ages.

Nan, who was demanding when I was well, was attentive when I was ill. She would come upstairs several times a day and help me out of bed onto wobbly legs to sit on a chair while she remade my bed. When being helped back in, the ungrateful patient would complain that the bed felt damp and was 'smelly'. One morning, my bed was made a little earlier than usual. On this occasion, the sheets were changed and the room was tidied round. The doctor was expected to call, and always the doctor's brief presence caused a little discomfort in the house. Just before Dr Bobbit arrived, Nan would tuck the bottom corner of her apron into her waistband, as if a triangular apron was some form of respectful salute, (or perhaps aprons became invisible if worn in that way)! I could hear the doctor entering our front door and Nan being excessively polite, subservient even, in a way that was normal then but would be considered ridiculous years later. As the doctor climbed the stairs, the creaking of the woodwork was greater than usual, as if even the staircase was apologizing for its narrowness and steepness, its construction too meagre to support a man so grand in importance and stature.

'Hello, young man,' Dr Bobbit said, as my wrist was taken by a dry warm hand and held between finger and thumb as my pulse was checked. The doctor took his stethoscope from his bag, fitted the earpieces and breathed several times on the part he was going to place on my chest, to 'warm it' he said. He listened to several places on my chest and then on my back. He placed his left hand on my back and tapped the back of his own fingers with the fingers of his right hand. He looked stern but said nothing. He thought a moment and then asked Nan to go and get half a glass of water and a bucket. He opened up his brown leather bag and took out a small glass vial containing a dark-red liquid. When Nan came back, he put two drops of the substance into the glass of water. I was just about to receive some pre-penicillin treatment. The medicine would not go about its work internally and quietly as penicillin would have done; this medicine was far more direct and quick acting. The doctor handed me the glass, suggesting its attractiveness as a drink by calling it 'ipecacuanha wine'. I obediently drank it down, and instantly exploded inside. After a few violent moments, every tube in my body seemed to have been cleared. Dr Bobbit pronounced that I should be kept in bed another day or two, and then he left, no doubt collecting his five shillings at the bottom of the stairs.

As the illness receded and the patient began to feel a little better, the days began to be enjoyable. My room, by this time warmed all through, was snug and comfortable, the fire having been kept in during waking hours. The atmosphere and the warmth were pleasant and the patient, now well enough to sit by the fire, was savouring release from his sickbed. The joy of sitting by an open fire – being mesmerized by the red glow and flickering movement, being seduced into stillness by the comfort of the radiated warmth – was learned at times like these, and has remained evermore.

Chapter 7

UNCLE BILL

In my earliest memory Uncle Bill was an enigma. Long before I met him I would hear stories of 'Willy Walker' who was such a 'wonderful' pianist, with 'such a lovely touch' – he had his own dance band and they were 'ever-so-good'. In my infant imaginings someone with a funny name like 'Willy Walker' could only be a cartoon character; I saw him as a clown with baggy trousers and white painted face. But Nan was not speaking of a clown; she was revelling in the happiness of her younger days and times spent with her husband and his family. Willy Walker was her nephew who's music had clearly been an important part of the merry-making and the music-maker of those halcyon days had remained joyfully in her affections.

The first time I would meet Uncle Bill was when Nan had been invited to spend Christmas with him, his sister and her husband at their home in Shepherd's Bush. It was the first Christmas after Bobby had died. It had been a busy year; we had been to Scotland and to Kent, our first lodger had moved in and we were getting used to sharing our home. Nan was still missing Bobby and, occasionally, I would interrupt her in a quiet moment and she would be caught wiping away a tear. A chance to spend Christmas with her husband's relatives was accepted eagerly.

Our journey into London revealed more of the bomb damage that we had seen just a little of near home, and even now we were a long way from the most severely attacked areas. Nan was emotional to see shops that she liked badly damaged. She was proud of her appearance and would travel many miles to frequent a furrier to select a fox-fur stole or visit a tailor to be measured for a new costume – a dark blue, pinstriped tailored jacket and skirt was a favourite. Seeing the shops now with broken windows and rubble strewn around shocked and distressed her.

We asked directions and were sent along oppressive streets of sooty, formidable, terraced houses. Masbro Road was similar and equally sombre. We found number twelve and knocked. I was agitated by the strangeness of the place and of the thought of meeting people I did not know, but my fears were quickly dispelled when we were greeted warmly and welcomed by Uncle Bill's sister Claire and her husband Charles who occupied the ground floor of the house. Uncle Bill lived alone upstairs and came down when he heard us arrive. A few moments of confused kissing, hugging and words of greeting, all mixed in with belated condolences to Nan on the loss of her husband, soon took away any remaining nervousness I had.

Soon we were settled in and everyone began to relax together. With cups of tea in hand, the pleasures to come over the next few days were spoken of. Nan made congratulatory comments on the Christmas fare that was displayed around the room. Difficult-to-find items of seasonal luxury were offered generously with 'please help yourself to anything you want'. Stories were told of how tangerines had been found for sale in Shepherd's Bush Market, or some oranges from this shop or that. Even a bowl of nuts, with nutcrackers laying in readiness, was on the sideboard; 'Brazil nuts!' said Nan with raised eyebrows, 'Haven't seen them for a long time.' Brazil nuts and tangerines were the subject of the conversation until the first cup of tea had been drunk; even the price of the festive article was not out of bounds, with the usual gasps of surprise that adults seemed to make when talking about the 'cost of things today'.

The conversation turned to Christmas dinner. We were to have chicken, it was announced. That was a pleasing thought to me with my good appetite: I began to feel at home. Oven-ready chickens were not available then and the ones that could be purchased from a poulterer's shop, with or without feathers, were expensive and would require many ration points. If a householder did not know someone who kept a few cockerels, he would rely on his own 'farming' abilities. Even in small London gardens, a way was found. Our chicken had not arrived yet. It sounded as if a neighbour was going to bring one that evening. Charles looked at the clock and commented on how early it was getting dark, as if it was particularly important that day. While the rest drew up to the fire, talked, laughed, ate mince pies and drank more tea, Charles again looked out of the window, 'It'll be dark before he gets here,' he said to his wife.

It was quite dark when, finally, the knock came that Charles had been waiting for and he went to welcome the visitor. All in the room exchanged polite season's greetings, while I wondered why there was no chicken to be seen. Charles and his friend sat by the fire and shared a Christmas drink while having what appeared to be an important discussion. Uncle Bill, not being included, settled back in his chair with a cigarette while he chatted with his sister and Nan on congenial matters of family, Christmases past and old times in general.

Quite suddenly the conversation, taking place by the fire, came to an end. Both men got up meaningfully and, with torch in hand, went out into the back garden. I was told I could go with them, but not to get in the way. The garden was in almost complete darkness; the windows of the surrounding houses being blacked-out in compliance with regulations that would have brought reprimand from the patrolling warden, for any chink of light that might aid an enemy aeroplane. By torchlight and brief moments of a hazy moon, I could see a small square garden surrounded by shoulder-high walls of the same soot-stained brick as the houses.

The two men made their way to a small wooden building in the furthest corner of the garden. I was allowed to watch but told again to stand well back. Charles opened a latched door and crouched down to make himself small enough to go through the opening into what I could see by then was a chicken house. His hunched figure could be seen inside as he reached around feeling in the dark for the cockerel, who he hoped would be sleeping and unsuspecting of his immediate future. Charles and his neighbour exchanged loud whispers through the wire mesh between them; reports from Charles and encouragement from the neighbour. Suddenly, pandemonium ensued; Charles had reached and caught hold of the cockerel but had lost his balance in the process. He and the flapping bird had fallen into a row of roosting hens, knocking them like dominos from their perch and launching them into flight around the darkened hen house. The air was filled with wings, feathers and hens. The clucking and flapping threatened to alert the neighbours for several doors up and down the road and expose the deed in hand.

Charles's exit from the hen house was less dignified than he had hoped, but the hens soon found their perch again and quietened down. Apart from his slip and loss of balance, the whole operation had been planned carefully, as was about to be shown in the second half of the evening's work. A solid chopping block had been placed ready and a short billhook, usually used for firewood, laid across the top. This is where the neighbour's help was most needed. The two men held the cockerel firmly on the block. The billhook fell only once, doing its work quickly and completely, and the bird was soon hanging to await plucking and further preparation for the kitchen.

By the time Christmas Day came, and we were all sitting around the dinner table, Charles entertained us by reliving his experiences in the hen house, perhaps exaggerating, just a little, the havoc his fall had caused. Everyone enjoyed his story and laughed heartily, including Uncle Bill who, it dawned on me, had not taken part in that evening's affair even though Charles had needed help and had called upon his neighbour. It would take a year or two before I would understand and appreciate Uncle Bill's gentleness, which had excused him. In the meantime, I was about to be introduced to him just a little more on that Christmas Day in 1943.

Uncle Bill was proud of a new shirt he had bought to wear on that special day, wanting to look his best in the company of the guests. He had particularly chosen a shirt that required cufflinks as it was his wish, also, to show off a gift from his friend, Jeff. He told us how he had spent a pleasant time in Shepherd's Bush Market and how he had seen this stylish shirt and bought it at such a 'good price'. 'This make is so much more expensive in the shops,' he said, pulling aside his tie and feeling the material of the shirt himself, as if his action would confirm the quality to all around the table. Murmurs of agreement of 'Yes, nice', or 'Smart', were returned politely.

As dinner went on, Charles made a casual remark. 'Aren't cufflinks meant to be on the lower side of your wrist, Bill?' We all looked across the table and, sure enough, Uncle Bill's cufflinks were fully visible on the *top* of his wrists. And, as he was a man of short stature with correctly proportioned arms, most of the cuffs protruded beyond the end of his jacket placing the links in an unhindered view in their aerial position.

'That's how they should be,' said Claire, thinking her husband's remark rather impertinent and rushing to her brother's defence.

'I don't think so,' said Charles, laying down his knife and fork having cleared his plate. 'They shouldn't be up there,' he said, with a little more assertiveness now that his wife needed to be convinced as well.

Poor Uncle Bill looked confused; moments ago he was proudly showing off his new shirt, now it was being examined for an oddity by everybody around the table. Charles was most rigorous in his investigation, being positive there was something wrong. Claire was trying to balance her husband's vociferousness by saying she thought the shirt was all right and looked very smart anyway. Charles would not be deterred and moved round the table to Bill, wanting to help him off with his jacket so that the shirt could be examined more thoroughly. Claire protested, but Uncle Bill put up no resistance. It was clear to Charles from his close observation that the shirt did, in fact, have a defect: its sleeves had clearly been put into the body incorrectly, he pointed out. Still Uncle Bill and Claire would not believe Charles, but he went on until the error could be denied no longer. Finally, it was accepted by all that the shirt was imperfect, and several possible mistakes were then spelt out in embarrassing detail. Whatever the problem was, the cufflinks projected upward high on Uncle Bill's wrists and not more discreetly underneath, as they should have been.

Then came the second wave of embarrassment for poor Uncle Bill. His sister, finally being convinced that the shirt contained an error, turned from defence to attack and pointed out, in no uncertain terms, her brother's foolishness in buying such an item from the market: 'You know it's all rejects down there. No wonder it was cheaper than the shop. You'd think you would have learned better by now.'

Charles, afraid that he had been too forceful and perhaps caused his brother-in-law embarrassment, now turned from attack to defence: 'Well, we all make mistakes. You can sometimes get a good buy down there.'

Claire, not sure whether she was cross with her brother or annoyed on his behalf, her ambivalence causing her to smile, added as her final rebuke, 'Not so cheap now is it?' But then relenting, 'The rest of it looks nice.'

'Like the curate's egg,' muttered Uncle Bill, no one quite knowing what he meant.

'Never mind,' said Nan, 'It'll do you a turn,' feeling that a comment of some sort was due from her and deciding to balance matters in support of her nephew – although not really wanting to put much thought into the affair as she poured more cream onto her Christmas pudding.

'It's not *too* bad,' said Uncle Bill, finally deciding to mount his own defence. 'I don't think it will notice too much,' he added, and continued to eat his Christmas pudding with his cufflinks fully visible as they sparkled high on top of his cuffs. The quizzing ceased and laughter gradually took over; Uncle Bill joining in, and being the one to laugh last was the one to laugh loudest and longest, wagging his cufflinks a time or two to keep the jollity going.

After that Christmas in Shepherd's Bush, Uncle Bill began to appear at Otterfield Road. I had not remembered him coming to our house before but now he would arrive, either alone or with his friend Jeff, for a Sunday afternoon visit. Nan would get out our best china and lay a good tea by the fire in our kitchen in the winter or, in the summer, in our best front room, if the days were warm enough. The visitors always entertained us with animated conversation, like travelling troubadours wishing to earn their supper. Nan joined the congenial atmosphere as if she felt echoes of the jolly days spent with her husband and his family. The junior 'Willie walker' had now matured and had taken his father's place as Bill Walker which Nan called him freely, as if he were his father's true representative.

Such visits were infrequent, but continued throughout my early years. My own part, at first, being no more than an observing shy child in the room. Nevertheless I wanted to listen to Uncle Bill; he held a strange fascination for me and a little of the enigma remained. It would not be until I was older that the influence he had on my life would begin to be felt and I shall tell about that in a later chapter . . .

Chapter 8

FRED AND DORIS

After several months of early morning starts brought about by the rattling of bells and pennies on tin, Mr Auditon found digs more suitable to his needs. He had departed on good terms, saying that he had found his room very comfortable but it would be more convenient for him to be nearer his place of work. Nan was not concerned about the loss of income and was, in fact, looking forward to an improvement in her purchasing powers, having already been asked if she could provide full board and lodging to a family of three.

It was quite common for a widow to provide meals as well as accommodation for her lodgers, giving her the opportunity to sell her culinary and domestic skills learned over many years, thereby maximising her income and gaining most benefit from the living quarters she had to offer. Some of Nan's more 'refined' acquaintances tried to assuage the loss of esteem they imagined she might be feeling by referring to her 'paying guests' and avoiding the demeaning term of 'lodger'. Nan seemed to find their consideration more embarrassing than helpful but had learned to take such things in her stride and avoided either title for the rest of the conversation, if it could be done.

In a day or two a lady called Doris Mere came to see Nan to discuss what arrangements might be made to accommodate her, her daughter Vera and a Mr Frederick Watson, who she was planning to live with after recently leaving her husband. Mrs Mere was eager to have as much privacy as our small abode could afford and took a liking to the idea that Nan's big middle room and my small back room comprised a suitable suit of adjoining rooms, offering as much seclusion as she might expect to find at the price they were willing, or able, to pay. Nan, also wanting Mrs Mere's particular arrangement to be kept to themselves and drawing as little comment as possible, came to the conclusion, when considered in the light of the attractive new financial situation she was anticipating, that the rooms in question could be made available.

Over the next few days, furniture was moved about as our house was rearranged to fit the new requirements. All traces of our occupation were removed from the apartment to be leased and the rooms were fitted out as best we could to suit the future need. This would be the first time I was going to have to give up my little back room but it was 'in a good cause' I was assured. Nan and I were going to have to find other sleeping quarters and I wondered if our best front parlour that was rarely used might, at last, be plundered to help us in our time of need; it would be 'in a good cause' echoed in my head. But it was not to be. Nan decided that our top front bedroom could be divided into two private compartments, and with strategic placing of furniture and interior curtains she proved her point. My seclusion was provided by a high wall created by the back of Nan's old mahogany wardrobe, which had been placed in the centre of the room. The front of the magnificent piece was conveniently approached on her side, allowing normal use and the privacy necessary in the circumstances. I had been sorry to leave the only room I had ever known but soon grew to like my cosy corner behind the wardrobe.

It was not many days before our lodgers arrived to take up residence. Vera and I eyed one another cautiously while Mr Watson and Mrs Mere moved a few personal possessions into their rooms, tested the comfort of the bed that was to be theirs and, as they began to unpack, closed the door to claim a little of the privacy they desired. Meanwhile, Vera and I followed one another about as she examined things new to her. She was perhaps eight years of age to my seven, and until that time we had experienced lives very different from one another; we were both children without brother or sister but brought up in quite different family arrangements, conditions, customs and ways. We would have much to learn about the other and about the world outside our own particular early environment. It was natural that we began, tentatively, to ask questions, each answer being absorbed in a few moments of silent contemplation before another enquiry was ventured. Vera was an intelligent child and curious about all that she saw. With so much being unfamiliar, her wish to know more caused an increasing flow of questions, which were soon being thrust at me with a rapier precision: why did we call our living room the 'kitchen' (adding in support that we sat by the fire there, we had our meals there but no cooking was done there) and why did we call the room where the cooking was done the 'scullery'? I had no answers to give, but she began in me an awareness that much I had taken to be normal would perhaps not be considered so by others. I had encountered my first contact with the proverbial saying 'To see ourselves as others see us'. By the time the adults appeared, Vera and I had moved out into the garden, where questions persisted and my eyes continued to be opened to the ways of my life which until that day I had taken for granted.

Now that there were five occupants in our small house, we found ourselves thrown together as one family. We would frequently all be present in our 'kitchen' enjoying the same fireside, and perhaps one of the popular radio programmes of the day. When it came to mealtimes, Mr Watson took what he assumed to be his rightful place at the head of the table. On the first occasion before sitting down, he made suggestions as to where everyone else might sit. Nan charged back and forth from the 'scullery' with plates of already dished up hot dinner until we were all accommodated and ready to settle.

During our meals together, I had time to observe the mannerisms of our lodgers. Mrs Mere appeared to act in a high-class way; holding her knife and fork at a steep angle to her plate, she would spear small amounts of food, transfer them neatly to her mouth and then, behind tightly closed lips, chew sedately. I wondered if she was trying to compensate for Mr Watson who ate with his fork alone, holding it in his clenched fist so far up the implement's handle as to give the impression that it had no handle at all. He scooped food rapidly into his mouth, noisily sucking it in with sounds that were not allowed to be made by children. His method of attack required him to bow his head low over his food, into which he dangled considerable amounts of straight greasy hair that hung in an unhindered perpendicular column from his forehead. Once his scooping had begun it continued until his plate was cleared, at which time he immediately dropped his fork noisily onto his plate and, in his own inimitable way of complimenting the cook, asked, 'What's for afters?'

Once dinner was concluded and a cup of tea was on the way, Mr Watson would sit back and toss a tin containing loose tobacco and cigarette papers onto the table in front of him. He carefully unlidded the tin, took out a meagre pinch of Golden Virginia tobacco and rolled himself a small misshapen cigarette. As he struggled to take his first few puffs, he was ready to commence holding court. He liked to speak of his successes, which he did on many occasions interrupted only by loose dentures that clicked increasingly until he was forced to remove his top plate momentarily to correct the matter. Otherwise he talked freely of his achievements and, without inhibition of modesty, told all around the table of his skills in this subject or that.

It could not be denied that Mr Watson had a lively and an inventive mind. He would study his copy of the *Daily Mirror* newspaper and, after brief attention to the more obvious attractions, he would settle upon news of a subject closer to his heart. On one occasion, he held up his copy of the paper to show us a page containing photographs of models inadequately dressed against the storm apart from transparent plastic mackintoshes. He said that he had invented plastic a long time ago, and had even thought of the value of the material's waterproof qualities and its suitability for a lightweight raincoat that could be folded and kept in a pocket until a shower of rain was unexpectedly encountered. Had he been able to obtain financial backing, he explained, his raincoats would have been on the market long before those of the company advertising in his newspaper.

On another occasion, an article in his newspaper prompted him to reveal what would have been his greatest achievement. He explained that long before it was known that Frank Whittle had invented the jet engine, he, Frederick Watson, had thought of such an engine and had made convincing working drawings. Prospective backers were impressed, but could not be persuaded to put up any money. If only he had had the chance to develop his engine, he would have been rich and famous by now. As the vision in his mind of what might have been faded, his smile fell away as he let out a small sigh of disappointment.

As Mr Watson continued to puff his fast disappearing cigarette, Vera's mother would take out one of her Du Maurier cigarettes, with its modern built-in safety filter, and lay it on the table next to the exclusive box-packet that was the trade mark of the tobacco company. The icons of smoking excellence would remain for all to observe for the few moments it took Mrs Mere to find the gold lighter that Mr Watson had given her as a gift. After lighting her cigarette, she would lean back in her chair and blow her smoke towards the ceiling, elegantly raising the cigarette between her fingers in the same direction almost to arms length. As she enjoyed the first deep inhalation of nicotine, she would invariably say, 'I don't smoke normally,' to which Nan, if out of Doris's earshot, would mutter under her breath, 'You could 'av fooled me.'

While Nan and I had to get used to the close proximity of our 'paying guests', they, too, had adjustments to make. One of the occasions when intimacy was at its maximum was on Friday bath night. Although the landlady saw to it that as much arrangement was made as could be made, participants of the evening routine were expected to take their part. In the late afternoon, a fire would be lit under the brick-built copper, which was situated in the back corner of the scullery. Buckets of cold water filled the cauldron, built into the copper's centre with its rounded bottom exposed to the fire. After the evening meal, a galvanized tin bath, long enough for a child to lay in or an adult to sit in, was brought from the shed and placed on the floor in the middle of the scullery in front of the copper's fire. Hot water from the cauldron was bucketed into the bath and cold water from the tap over the sink in the corner was added until the temperature judged just right. Vera and her mother would appear in pyjamas and dressing gowns ready to take their baths; first Vera and then her mother. After, when dried and dressed for bed, they would sit by the kitchen fire while Mr Watson bucketed more hot water into his bath to bring it up to temperature. He would then refill the copper with cold water and stoke the fire under it for the benefit of those to follow. Apart from a gentle splashing, there would be little to be heard while Mr Watson took his leisure in the warm water in front of the blazing fire. When sounds of metal on metal could be heard, it signalled that the bather was dried and dressed and scooping water from his bath with a galvanized bucket and pouring it into the sink. The last few pints would be emptied by lifting the bath and pouring them directly into the sink, the highest end of the bath touching the scullery ceiling as the bath drained dry.

The second family of bathers (Landlady & Co.) would then mop out the bath and the process would be repeated. I would be the next to be immersed. When my cleansing was complete, I would join Vera by the kitchen fire, pyjamad and gowned, while Nan took her repose, prolonging her soaking as long as she dared. When metal on metal was heard, all hands appeared to help with emptying, clearing away and carrying the long bath back to the shed, where it was hung on its hook until next week.

So it was that our 'paying guests' were installed and our lives had turned, once again, in a new direction. The bailiffs would be kept from the door and Nan could continue to say, as she liked to do so boldly, 'We don't owe anybody anything.' Of course, such freedom comes at a price; the responsibility she had taken on would occupy her every day of the week and she would need all of her skill to manage a home in the particular circumstances. She would need, also, much ingenuity in the days of rationing to procure and prepare sufficient essentials to fulfil her obligations.

Chapter 9

SMALL PORTIONS

I had been born in a country about to enter the Second World War. I was too young to be a soldier or sailor or airman, or a merchant seaman who not only faced the dangers of the sea but also attack by our enemies who sought to starve our island into submission. I was even protected from the feeling of deprivation that adults endured, as I had no knowledge of the 'good times' before the war they spoke of so frequently. My only misfortune was to experience the shortages of food and luxuries that persisted during the war and for some years after. Rationing controls gave rich and poor alike a fair share of what food was available, so I was no worse off than many others. I was able to accept the challenges that I found around me and, in the process, learn skills of self-reliance, which cannot have been anything but a good grounding and preparation for life.

When I was sent to do the food shopping for the five members of our household, I would be given five ration books, a one-pound note (from which change was expected) and one shopping bag, which would be more than adequate to hold my purchases. My first call was at Saunders dry goods shop, where large sacks, with tops rolled back revealing their contents, were set around on a tiled floor. An assistant would use a scoop to put dried peas or beans, rice or tapioca into a paper bag to be weighed. Tapioca and rice were regulars, to make milk puddings. Split peas made pease pudding, which was often found on our dinner plate; children, perhaps confused by the language of wartime, called the dull-yellow leguminous paste 'peace' pudding and had to be encouraged to eat it because it was 'good' for us.

Next on my shopping trip was a visit to either The Home and Colonial or Sainsbury's where, first, I would queue at the grocery counter. When it was my turn to be served, an assistant would stamp my ration books and weigh out allowed amounts of sugar or flour or biscuits or dried fruit, if it was in stock. Next, I would queue at the provisions counter where another assistant would cut cheese and weigh it, adding or taking back a sliver if she had misjudged the exact allowed amount. Then, with wooden spatulas, she would scoop a piece of butter, weigh it and pat it into shape. Lard was treated similarly. Each item would then be wrapped individually in greaseproof paper. Both assistants mentally added my bill as they fetched and weighed, informing me of the total as the goods were pushed across the counter to me.

Regardless of any inconvenience that short rations would cause when I got home, I was happy to have so little to carry as would not hinder my enjoyment of practising my newly-learned skill of roller skating; one partly filled shopping bag would not disturb my balance, so I could indulge my desire to travel everywhere on my skates. It was my fervent wish not to remove them for a moment longer than absolutely necessary. Nan, not quite understanding my enthusiasm, could only comment, 'I wonder you bother to take 'em off when you go to bed!'

Once my prized cargo was handed over, change checked and swoons over 'the price of things today' expressed, Nan was reminded of how much her skills of survival were going to be needed to feed five people for a week on the food in front of her. In a voice first doom laden and then with a sarcasm that was not totally disapproving, she added, 'You're so good at skating, skate up to Mr Ellis and see if 'e's got a bone for me.' Mr Ellis was our local butcher in a small shop on the High Street. He had known Nan and Bobby for many years and would help-out whenever he could. My request for a bone sent him into the back room of his shop. He reappeared with what, to me, looked like the whole leg of a cow, which he sawed into pieces and handed to me wrapped in newspaper.

The bone would be boiled for hours, steaming out our scullery. Nan would occasionally lift the lid and peer into the saucepan, fanning away steam from her face that left her glasses in a dripping grey mist. After a length of time (known only to Nan), the bone would be left to 'stew in its own juice' until it was cool enough to be picked clean of marrow, meat, sinew, gristle and solid matter of any kind, all of which would be returned to the liquid; only the bleached bone would be discarded. The liquid and pieces would be left to cool in a basin, standing overnight in the larder or, in the summer when the larder was not cool enough, outside in a cupboard made of fine wire mesh, which would keep out insects. The cupboard hung on a wooden fence and was surrounded by a jasmine bush, which had grown almost completely around the improvised larder creating a permanent shade from the sun by day. By night, the cool air would help set the liquid into a solid jelly, which would be turned out onto a plate next day; in suspension were the pieces but it was mostly jelly, firm enough to be sliced and served up with whatever vegetable could be found in the garden at that time of year. 'Get that down yer,' Nan would say proudly, as she brought her 'brawn' (as she called it) to the table. 'It'll stick to yer ribs like glue,' which presumably meant that it would be good for us (although the statement remains unexplained). One or two comments were ventured cautiously about the lack of content of Nan's brawn but it was admitted to be 'very tasty', and none was ever left on the plate.

One of Nan's friends knew somebody who worked at a food processing factory that was situated by the side of the railway into London; I would see the great advertising hoardings as I went past on the train. Employees were allowed to buy chicken carcasses after they had been through a machine that stripped the meat from the bones. Several would be delivered to us, wrapped in newspaper, for just a few pence, and, like the beef bone, not counted against our ration. They, too, would be boiled for the same endless time to make soup or stock for stews. To complete the meal, I would be sent to Clinche's, the bakers on Fairfield Road, to wait for a crusty loaf to be taken from their ovens on a long-handled peel. It would cost fourpence-ha'penny, and be hot in my arms. The crust was irresistible and by the time I got home I would have picked a hole in one end of the loaf; the nibbled end would be sliced off and given to me with my bowl of steaming soup to make a delicious supper.

When ration coupons ran out, we tried whale meat, which had the texture of tough beef but tasted fishy and oily, and tins of an ugly fish called snoek, which came from South Africa; neither were popular, and, therefore, not on ration. We sampled both but did not repeat the experience. Some people bought horse meat. We tried it once from a specialist butcher in Praed Street, near Paddington railway station; the shop was full of foreign people talking and laughing and seeming to know exactly what they wanted. We were the only English people and felt very out of place. We did not enjoy eating it and never considered it again.

One of the pre-war luxuries that adults talked about was bananas. They sounded so exotic, and I confess to being quite beguiled by the desire to try one. So, one day, it was a wonderful surprise to see that Mr Lane's greengrocer shop had just received a supply. Large bunches hung on rails, almost at ceiling height, on three sides of his shop. The real thing was so much more wonderful than I had ever imagined, they were so yellow and so bright. I rushed home and tugged at Nan to come quickly before the bananas were all sold out. Without questioning me, she tucked in the corner of her apron and, hand in hand, we went to the shop. Mr Lane laughed, saying he did not think anyone would mistake his *wax* bananas for the real thing, he simply hoped his display would cheer everyone up! On the short homeward journey, Nan was cross with me, muttering under her breath because her pride had been dented by being both laughed at and seen in public in carpet slippers and apron.

An item of rationing that affected children directly was confectionary. A lady of great personality, called Mary, became important in many children's lives, she worked in the sweetshop on the corner of Otterfield Road. She was only an employed assistant, but for miles around the shop was known as 'Mary's'. The owner and his wife both worked alongside Mary, seeming content to take a secondary role. They were kind and obliging to anyone who went to their back door on a Sunday, when, probably in breach of Sunday trading rules, they would hand over some 'desperately needed' item, but somehow their presence was unnoticed during the time of opening hours and it was the plump middle-aged blond lady whose engaging qualities filled the minds of her customers and gave the shop its name.

Children would go into 'Mary's' hopefully and she would pull out a cardboard box from under the counter, gleefully expecting to please her young customers, saying, 'We have some of these today.' The prospective purchaser would be crossing fingers, hoping that one of their favourites would appear. On days when no favourites were available, we would be longing for something sweet and consider anything on offer. Liquorice Wood always seemed to be in the window but would only be purchased in desperation. It came in sticks, about the size of a new pencil in thickness and length. The wood was yellow and fibrous, and when it was chewed it softened and gave a slightly sweet liquorice taste. In better times this raw ingredient would have been processed into a syrup to flavour Pontefract Cakes or Liquorice Allsorts.

Carob Beans were, usually, also to be found in Mary's window; they were like very large runner beans, dried and so dark-red as to appear almost black. Many of we children dismissed them out of hand with the highly articulate assessment of 'Yuk'! Many years later, I feel humbled to find that throughout history mankind seems to have had a love affair with the carob tree. The beans, which are also know as locust beans or St John's bread, are said to be part of the locusts and honey that St John lived on during his time in the wilderness. It is also said that the Prodigal Son ate the locusts he was feeding to the pigs. Many people survived on carob beans in times of drought and famine because of the tree's resilience. Until sugarcane became widely available, carob pods were an important source of sugar. Carob syrup was highly valued and known as 'black gold'; it was used for all sorts of culinary and even medicinal purposes. In Roman times the tree was called 'carat' and twenty-four of the seeds equalled the weight of a pure-gold coin that was in circulation; '24-carat' became the measure of pure gold that we still use today.

Producing the main meal of the day was perhaps easier at that time when many people had gardens and grew their own vegetables, and when it was still common practice to cook simple meals. Our garden was narrow, being only the width of our semi-detached house. It was, however, seventy yards long. Our cultivated area ran like a narrow ribbon of civilization through an untamed jungle; some of our garden and those on either side being uncared for and overgrown. We grew many vegetables and could forage for a variety of fruit from neglected bushes and trees. Preparation of many meals began with harvesting: perhaps a root of potatoes; or a few carrots or parsnips; or some horse radish or mint; or a picking of raspberries or loganberries or redcurrants, which I hated collecting because it took so long to fill a basin; or, from next door's garden, a few Cox's Orange Pippins or Egremont Russets or Worcester Pearmains; or, from Mr Knowles's garden, some of his Morello cherries that were so large and dark-red but tasted so bitter until cooked and sweetened.

When I was old enough, I was expected to be the main workforce in the garden. I learned about digging and double-digging, and trenching, when dung, which I had collected from fields around in one of my home-made carts, had to be dug in. After digging, the soil had to be broken and smoothed down to make a seed bed. As soon as spring began to warm the soil, Nan would hand me a packet of seeds, saying, 'I think we'll have a row of these,' and as the season went on, the garden would be filled. Seedlings had to be watered, which meant cans of water had to be carried down the long garden. Although water was not metered, people must have become so used to wartime restrictions that even *it* was not wasted; on washday, baths full of rinse water would be left in our backyard to be scooped up and used on the most needy vegetables.

Our garden also produced meat. We kept rabbits, which I had no problem in thinking of as both pets and meat for the table. Frequently, another rabbit hutch would be needed to house our increasing stock. As usual, I was delegated to build it. The materials needed would come from the pile of old timber at the bottom of our garden. The wood had been used more than once already, but for the whole of my childhood, foraging in the great heap produced enough good pieces to complete whatever project was in hand. The nails needed would also have to be scavenged from the pile; if I complained that they were rusty and bent, the answer would be to find some that were not too rusty and straighten them. The only expense that would be undertaken was for a roll of tarred felt for the roof of the hutch, to keep the occupants dry and snug.

Keeping our stock in comfort would require trips to Mr England's corn shop ('Old England's' Nan called the shop, so I imagined there must have been an old Mr England who Nan and Bobby had dealings with before my time). We never spent so much that we could have a bale of straw, instead I would be sent to buy a 'truss', which meant I could stuff a sack as tightly as possible for just a few pence.

At Nan's request her brother would call in to kill a rabbit; using only his strong builder's hands, the job was done in seconds. I was always pleased that the rabbit made no sound or showed any sign of distress. Uncle Fred would do no more after this but pass the still-warm carcass to me, knowing that I could do the rest. The rabbit was hung by its back feet on a nail over the sink in our backyard. With a razor-sharp knife, its throat was slit and it was left to bleed clean. The same knife was used to slit the stomach, to remove the intestine and all other unwanted viscera. It was then skinned, making sure no damage was done to the pelt, (or I would have to answer to the lady who would cure it and make mittens from it). Once the meat was cut into joints it would be handed to Nan to be made into rabbit pie or stew. The meat was white, like chicken, and tasted good. Nan said it was because of the pure food our rabbit had eaten and the care it had received during its lifetime. She declared that she would never eat a rabbit if she did not know where it had come from.

One day, I was informed that half a dozen point-of-lay pullets would be arriving. My instruction was to prepare the chicken house; clean it out and repair it. Once the young hens arrived they were made 'comfortable'. 'Give 'em a few days to settle down, give 'em some good grub, an' we'll 'ave some eggs,' Nan predicted confidently. I was sent once again to 'Old England's', this time to buy mixed corn and some bran, which would be mashed into boiled potatoes and fed hot to the chickens. The potatoes were the very small ones called 'chats', sold off cheaply by the corner greengrocer, or by Nan's friend Beatie who had several stalls in Yiewsley High Street and sometimes gave Nan some free, for 'old times' sake'. All of our potato peelings and any leftover vegetables went into the feed. The hens seemed to love hot food; they fought to get to it first, not waiting for it to cool, which caused them to strut around with heads reaching high as if gasping for cooling air. It certainly seemed to bring them on to lay, and kept them laying well too – or perhaps it was because they knew that if they did not, they would end up in the pot!

On one occasion, some special care was needed. Chickens, like many birds, are prone to have a problem with mites and the malady had affected the scales of our hens' legs, which had recently been bright yellow-orange and smooth but were now rough and dull, as the scales were infected and lifted. Treatment in those days was usually administered by the knowledgeable owner; a veterinary surgeon could never have been afforded by the average householder and would only have been consulted by attending the free clinic supported by the RSPCA, which was more suited to deal with a dog or cat.

On this occasion the knowledgeable owner was Nan. She placed an old saucepan, which had several inches of paraffin in it, firmly down near the chicken run. One by one she caught up the hens, subduing their flapping and clucking as she moved them to be held gently under her left arm. Once secured, the hen seemed to either enjoy the experience or simply give up the fight. The bird's feet were lowered into the paraffin and Nan bathed its legs by lifting handfuls of paraffin with a cupped hand. When released, the hen immediately continued scratching and pecking for food, seeming to take no notice of the noxious foot bath it had just undergone. In a day or two, after several applications, the mites seemed to have been defeated and the hens were returned to their previous, excellent condition; the scaly nature of their legs and feet giving just a hint of the animals' prehistoric dinosaur past, in its correct livery of yellowy-orange.

Soon, as predicted, there was a 'cheerful' cluck-clucking and I was sent out to see if an egg had been laid. The hen house was built in such a way that a row of nest boxes protruded from one end of the main house. A single weatherproof lid could be lifted to expose four compartments half-filled with straw. A brief look along the row showed a warm brown egg in a hollow of straw, which had recently cosseted one of the hens. I carefully lifted out the egg and closed the lid, making sure that it was safely latched to keep out any intruders. I took the egg in to Nan, who said without ceremony, 'Put it in the isinglass,' reminding me that it was not a game. She seemed a bit less pleased than I had expected; she had just received the electricity bill that was demanding more than she had anticipated, and to her, at that moment, the egg was just another gamble that had paid off.

For a little while, I held the egg in the palm of my hand. I ran my fingers lightly around its perfect shape and fixed my gaze on its golden smoothness. It was still warm, reminding me that it had not been produced by a machine but by a living creature. I wanted to share my excitement with Nan, but she was occupied with a new concern. In later life, I read that we should enjoy our successes as well as our plans, and here was just such a time when that advice was instinctively felt. If my enjoyment could not be shared it would be experienced alone, in a way I had learned to do. For another minute or two, I marvelled at nature's wondrousness and felt thrilled to be a part of it, and even to have had some small influence in its outcome.

As the number of eggs in the bucket of preserver increased over the coming days and weeks, I began to wonder when we were going to eat them. It turned out that they were considered rather special, almost as if they had curative properties. At the first sign of an illness, the patient would be encouraged to drink down a glass of milk with an egg beaten into it; from an early age, I had no qualms about this particular practice. If the invalid was confined to bed or prescribed light meals, an egg custard could be expected to arrive at the first mealtime. On healthier days an appetite still needed to be satisfied, but a suggestion that eggs might be just the thing brought out another of Nan's sayings: 'Gotta live tomorrow, you know.' This rough and ready wisdom hid two truths of which I was unaware: first, that isinglass would keep an egg 'fresh' until the winter, and second, that we would be glad to have real hens' eggs when other foods were less available and at the time of year when the need was greatest. If only enjoyed medicinally, they would not be wasted. I was sure that Nan was right, and went off down the garden.

Chapter 10

THE AIR-RAID SHELTER

The story of our air-raid shelter had begun in 1939 when one morning there was a great noise out in the street; the shouts of workmen, the sound of lorry engines and the clattering and clanking of iron being unloaded onto concrete pavements could be heard from indoors. 'What's that great hullaballoo?' said Nan with indignant curiosity. She grabbed my hand and, leaving Bobby at the breakfast table, we went to see what was going on. Many of our neighbours were already standing outside in the street and many more were coming out of their houses as the lorries moved up Otterfield Road discharging their loads noisily outside each house. The watchers were chatting to one another loudly over the hubbub. At first glance it could have been a joyful occasion, the chatter was animated, even excited, but the conversation was of war and the dangers heralded by the arrival of these materials.

The local council were delivering the components with which each householder could build a structure of defence: an Anderson air-raid shelter. The council workers were carefully counting the number of curved and straight corrugated galvanized steel panels that were being supplied to each family: 'Six curved. Straights for the back. Straights for the front. That's the lot.' And so they went on up the road, finally adding to each pile a small sack of nuts and bolts and a cheaply produced spanner, to aid the householder in bolting the panels together.

One signature was all that was needed to say that the materials had been received. In previous weeks, officials had been round to collect the necessary information and complete forms that amounted to a simple means test, which made provision for households with an income of less than £250 per annum to have a shelter free of charge. Larger earners would have to pay seven pounds.

A time was planned for my father and his brother-in-law to come round to build our shelter; by way of inducement, my father would have been unnecessarily reminded that it was for his son's protection. Bobby was too ill to be of much help but was there to give what support he could. Uncle Fred appeared, to give advice but no more than that, as was his usual way. A site for the shelter was decided upon: it was to be half-buried in our vegetable garden, in a pit six feet six inches long and four feet six inches wide. The corrugated steel panels were carried in from the road, where the council men had left them, and placed in readiness behind our shed near to the chosen place.

The determined diggers, with no more than garden forks and spades, dug down to the recommended four feet depth. Care was taken squaring the hole and levelling the bottom, which would serve as the floor of a part-time dwelling so would need to be flat and firm. The side panels were put in place and each held with a single bolt, loosely fitted. Flat end pieces were lined up and held similarly. Only when all panels were temporarily assembled could the nuts be tightened and the construction made rigid. Once the shelter was considered to be as strong as it could be, the soil that had been removed was shovelled onto our little tin home-from-home, filling gaps around the edge and banking up on its top; this was recommended in the government leaflet, as it would help absorb the shock of any nearby bomb blast. The householder, the leaflet also said, could continue gardening and grow vegetables around and on top of the shelter. Some people chose to grow flowers, and many local gardening clubs – in wonderful defiance of the grim situation – organised 'Best Kept Shelter' competitions.

In the following days, our shelter was completed inside. We put lino on the floor but, despite having flattened the soil underneath, stones pushed upward and punctured where our feet touched; the addition of old mats helped hide the damage and keep the soil at bay. Wartime mass-produced bunk-beds were fitted. Nan tried to make the inside comfortable for an emergency but we found that it could not be left in a state of readiness for night-time occupation as any bedding or materials of an absorbent nature became damp and soon smelled musty. The outside did, however, naturalize and become part of our garden scene; it matured and seemed to belong. It took part in our games: it was a hiding place for 'hide-and-seek', and a dark dungeon in 'Robin Hood'. The adults mainly ignored it, except to declare that they would never spend a cold damp night in it and if a bomb was going to kill them they would prefer to be tucked up in their own nice warm beds indoors when it did.

For some time, it seemed that our shelter was going to be just another unnecessary precaution. We were in a period that became known as the 'phoney war': for months after the declaration of war, the expected swarms of German bombers failed to appear. Nan read aloud to Bobby and me, from her newspaper each morning, articles about the war: thirty-eight million gas masks had been issued; a million school children had been evacuated out of cities; one and a half million people had been recruited into civil defence; street lights and motorcar lights had been banned, (the first casualties of war were pedestrians who, unable to see in the unlit streets, broke their ankles, and motorists who were involved in accidents caused by blackout restrictions). But still nothing more than threatening propaganda leaflets had been dropped by German aeroplanes.

It was in September 1940 that the need of a place of safety was taken more seriously, when the bombing of London began in what the newspapers were calling 'the Blitz'. Nightly we heard air-raid warning sirens, a menacing wailing sound that rose and fell in pitch and sent shivers down our spines. The heavy drone of aircraft filled the sky overhead, and the dull thump of bombs in the distance could be heard at intervals. We were twelve miles from the city but could see the sky above London glowing red. Anti-aircraft guns were so loud that I was convinced they were in the street outside our house and tried to run out to see them. Notwithstanding her self-professed lack of education, Nan continued to devour the newspapers in her lust for knowledge of the second world war in her lifetime. She would fill with emotion as she read of casualties, near or far; their loss was her loss. As she read to herself she would exclaim, then read aloud the article that had shocked her: 'On the seventh of September, the first night of the Blitz, almost two thousand Londoners were killed or wounded. The docks of the East End were targeted. Fires burned non-stop and guided German bombers to their destination on successive nights.' Nan empathised, feeling herself to be a Londoner; both she and Bobby had many connections with the East End in the days before my knowing, and she proudly claimed to have been 'born within the sound of Bow bells'.

We were spared the worst of the war. Bombs that fell near to us were the result of miscalculation or bad weather, causing the target to be overshot. The load of high-explosives would then be jettisoned before turning back, in hope of a safer homeward flight. 'Bombs were dropped at random' was a phrase used on the radio to account for such damage outside target areas. There were many nights when the war seemed to be coming our way. Had it not been for my sake, Nan would have remained sunk deep in her feather bed, but when the ravings of man's foolishness became too loud for sleep she would come to my little back bedroom with bundles of warm clothes and outdoor shoes. We would make our way by torchlight down the garden on the ever cooling evenings. She would carry a roll of bedding and make us as comfortable as she could. Only during the most severe of raids did the shelter seem preferable, as no amount of clothes and covers could keep out the cold that radiated from the steel walls, or the damp from the soil all around us. Only a child could fall back into sleep, until woken by a wheezing chest that could absorb no more moisture. Nan would go to the house and make a hot drink, which we would enjoy while she reported that Bobby had the best idea, ''E's fast asleep and snoring 'is 'ed off in 'is nice warm bed,' she would say, affecting pique but betraying the pleasure that she felt knowing that her sick husband was in the best place.

Daily we were shocked by radio news bulletins, newspaper reports or cinema newsreels, but human nature protects us from fully understanding until we see for ourselves. On one of the nights we spent in our shelter, bombs had fallen closer than we realized and it was not until I went on an errand that I was able to see for myself and understand a little more. I had been sent with some rabbit skins to Nan's friend who lived at the top of Otterfield Road on Falling Lane. For a small payment, she would cure the skins and make fur mittens from them; the mittens made fine presents for distant relatives and

The Air-Raid Shelter

friends at Christmas or for birthdays, but from close family members groans could be heard under the breath of 'Oh, no. Not *more* mittens'! The house of the skin-curing lady and a public house stood on the edge of a cornfield with no other properties nearby. When I arrived, both buildings had been badly damaged; bricks and broken materials were strewn around. People were saying that the pub had been full of customers when it received a direct hit at the back; many had been injured but, luckily, none were killed. Nan's friend had since gone to live with her daughter, as her house was damaged beyond repair. When I got home, Nan wanted to know what was the matter and why did I still have the skins. 'She's not there,' I told her.

'Never mind. She'll be back later, you can take them then,' Nan said.

'No. She's not there. The house has been bombed and so has the pub,' I explained. 'The lady has gone to live somewhere else.'

'Oh! The poor woman,' said Nan, 'I thought that raid was close but didn't know it was that close.'

What I told Nan was clearly a shock to her, and she thought it might be a good idea if we slept in the shelter from now on. For the next few days we went to the shelter as soon as the sirens sounded, but as winter came on and nights became colder I found myself being woken fewer times. By the spring, raids seemed to have stopped and nights were quieter. Reports were then of bombing raids on our historic cities, where cathedrals, churches and grand houses were to be found; indomitable wartime humour joked that Hitler must have found a tourist guide book! For the time being our shelter was less important and a place of play once again.

After Bobby died, Nan had reached out to relatives and close friends, accepting invitations to visit and inviting them to us in return. We had spent a few days with Nan's brother and his wife, and now their son Jimmy and his wife Lily were coming to stay with us. With them would be their son Michael and his cousin David. By that time, our lodgers were well established, so our little house was going to be overflowing.

One Clear Morn

On the day our visitors were to arrive, we went to West Drayton railway station to meet them. Vera and I had been playing so she came along with us. Near the station was the De Burgh Hotel, which it was thought would be a congenial place to greet our guests. We went into the sunny garden where 'Uncle Jimmy', as we were to call him, spread a broadsheet newspaper on one of the tables (not too near the adults) revealing several pounds of Kentish cherries, which had been parcelled within. 'From the "Garden of England",' he announced, with a smile that was friendly and full of pride for the county that was his home. The great heap of cherries covered photographs and reports of war that we children easily managed to ignore in favour of the sweet red fruit.

While we ate cherries, the adults became reacquainted. There were hugs and kisses for Aunt Carrie, and thanks for the opportunity to escape the war for a little while and perhaps achieve a few nights uninterrupted sleep. With a drink in her hand and cheeks beginning to flush, Nan listened to the experiences of her nephew and his family. They told her of the many nights they had to leave their beds to go to a place of shelter, worrying that when they came out in the morning they would find their home and business destroyed like so many of the damaged buildings around them. They all laughed and agreed how well the newspaper headline-grabbing name of 'Bomb Alley' suited the swathe of Kent under the flight path of German bombers on their way to London, from where our guests had travelled that day not only for respite but, in wartime spirit, a brief holiday and a jolly good time.

With our house filled with the younger members of Nan's family, her own youthful sparkle returned and with it a determination to make her guests welcome. Her resourcefulness saw her reaching into backs of cupboards and bringing out hidden treats for the table that would give them pleasure and prove her a good hostess – a matter in which she took great pride. Aware of the reception that awaited him and wishing to respond, Jimmy, who owned a greengrocery and fruiterers business, had brought a generous amount of fruit; some, Vera and I had never seen and had to touch it to prove it was not wax, like so much we saw as decoration displayed in fruit bowls on people's sideboards. As a special treat for Nan, her nephew had brought her fish and prawns from his father's fish shop. 'Just arrived from Billingsgate as I got there, so it's all lovely 'n' fresh,' he said.

High Tea was important when there was leisure time to be enjoyed, and a family visit would create a special reason to have the best and turn the affair into a grand occasion. Today, all of our best china would be needed to lay enough places for guests, lodgers and ourselves. Every upright chair in the house, and the piano stool too, was placed around the table, leaving little room for people. The children were given the task of laying the table while adults worked in the scullery cutting bread, making sandwiches and loading dishes. Gradually, the prepared food was brought to the table, everything being displayed from the beginning: a homemade Victoria sponge on a raised cake-stand towered over shellfish, slices of spam and a dish of tinned salmon. Cups were filled from the large decorative teapot, which was immediately refilled in readiness. We each squeezed into a chair; Vera, being the smallest, was given the high piano stool. A last minute hunt for large safety pins in the sideboard drawer of bric-a-brac was necessary, as they were the best implement for removing a winkle from its shell. They could be used, too, to unblock salt and pepper pots, as plenty of each, as well as Sarson's vinegar, would be required to make the cockles, whelks and winkles palatable to anyone not quite a connoisseur.

Such a convivial gathering creates pleasant conversation and there was much that day, everyone around the table contributing. Happy matters caused laughter, and personal reminiscences brought moments of thoughtfulness. Of course, the war that surrounded us was not forgotten, the difficulties of obtaining food being particularly relevant as we sat around the well loaded table. Nan was asked how she had made 'such lovely' cream for the sponge cake. She apologized that it was only 'National Margarine' and some icing sugar she had managed to get. Less popular were the pineapple chunks. A tin had been purchased from a street trader on Uxbridge High Street. We children judged them to be hard and decided we could not eat them. The adults hastily examined them and agreed. Mr Watson said in his usual manner (that told you he must be right), 'They're not pineapple.' Soon everyone around the table was dissecting the chunks; cutting into them and declaring that they were not the texture of pineapple but solid and more likely to be flavoured swede. It was agreed that Mr Watson must be right.

'And the jam is homemade, isn't it?' asked Uncle Jimmy. Nan confirmed that it was, and went on to explain that it had kept well for two years. She always received compliments for her jam, but I was less impressed because we could never eat it until it had grown an inch of mould on the top. By that time, the new batch that tasted so good had been stored behind last year's to await a similar fate – such was her diligence in looking after tomorrow and the ever expected day of need. However, Nan had proved that she also knew how to live for today as we shared that truly High Tea.

By the time sleeping arrangements were discussed, it was clear that the adults already had a plan. With promise of adventure, and the safety factor brought in for good measure, we children were bribed. Our shelter, once again, had an important place in life, if only as a spare bedroom. David and Michael needed guidance in preparing for bed as they had not encountered our type of shelter half way down a long garden. We had to explain that we could not change into pyjamas in the shelter; it was too small, too dark, and our day clothes would be in the way and become damp by the morning. A combination of pyjamas, overcoats and outdoor shoes was recommended. The overcoats turned out to be necessary as an extra bed cover, as we were surprised how cold even a starlit summer night could be.

We were escorted to our beds by Uncle Jimmy, Aunt Lily and Vera's mother. They watched us settle down and told us that the back door of the house would be left open in case of an emergency; they emphasised that we were not to leave the shelter unless it really was an emergency. We were left with a torch, and told not to waste the batteries.

Once the adults had returned to the house, we lay in our bunks not yet ready for sleep. First, we talked about things that children talk about, and then we began to say silly things that made us giggle. All

The Air-Raid Shelter

the time, Vera held on tightly to the torch and shone it on each of us, at intervals, to assure herself that she was not alone. Her nervousness showed and, perhaps to cover our own fears, we teased her. When she spoke of what might happen in the night, we took over her story and made it more frightening. Our cruelty made us giggle louder, until Vera said in an impassioned whisper, 'Be quiet the German's will hear us.' Her plea sounded so sincere but so funny that we all, including Vera, went into hysterical laughter, which was so loud that we thought it possible that some demon of the night might hear and be drawn in our direction so we all shushed each other to be quiet.

One by one, we drifted into sleep. First David, and then Michael fell silent. Vera shone her torch around once more before she, too, became quiet. I lay awake a little longer worrying what form an 'emergency' might take, and being reminded of the smell of earth and of dampening bedclothes. The atmosphere thickened as our breathing filled the air with moisture; the moist air struck the cold steel walls and ran down in little rivers of liquid breath. Soon, I joined the others in sleep, but less peaceful than they appeared. Uncomfortable dreams brought German soldiers through the makeshift covering of our shelter's entrance; bayonets ripped through the carpets and sacking that had been fashioned to keep out the night. My anxious slumbers were brief, broken by the sound of sirens; once again, the doom-laden sound warned that German aircraft had been sighted on route to London. Vera woke and switched on the torch she had clung to so firmly and shone it around to assure herself once again. Suddenly, she let out a shriek of terror, and shouted, 'SCORPION!' She leapt out of her bunk and pushed her way out into the moonlight. As we three boys sleepily crawled out after her, she was jumping up and down, her screams adding to the noise of sirens, aircraft, guns and distant bombs. Without coat or shoes she ran off up the garden to raise the alarm.

David, Michael and I stood shivering. Without the torch, which had gone with Vera, we were afraid to return to our beds inside the dark shelter. In a few minutes Vera returned with her mother and stepfather, followed, at intervals, by the other adults. The entire household stood around the shelter entrance watching as Mr Watson crawled around the floor, cursing as his knees hit protruding stones. In-between unintelligible mutterings in the direction of his step-daughter, he asserted impatiently that it could not possibly be a scorpion: 'You only get 'em in hot countries, and if it was one, you'd be dead. They're poisonous. One bite, and you're dead.'

But Vera was convinced that it was a scorpion. Still jumping up and down, as if to emphasise her words, she screeched, 'It *is* a scorpion, I know it is. I know they can kill yer. I know what they look like, I seen 'em in a book. I *know* it's a scorpion. I *know* it is.' Mr Watson was not in a good humour, having been dragged from his warm bed, and was becoming less patient as his fruitless search went on. Adding to his annoyance was his step-daughter's irritating assurance that she was right, but, rather than show his displeasure with her, he decided to save his breath and not offer any more reassurances – instead, he would let her continue to frighten herself with her own vivid imagination and her precocious certainty that she was right.

Still the only available light came from the one torch that we children had been given. As it was pushed under a bunk in pursuit of the scorpion, the shelter went dark bringing more screams from Vera (her distress at not seeing seeming to be greater than her fear of seeing). When an extra torch was brought from the house and shone into the shelter, Mr Watson could be seen more clearly, still on his hands and knees and about to make one more circuit of the floor. As he turned his back to us, Vera saw her 'scorpion'; it was riding on the centre of her step-father's back just below his collar, and moving towards his neck. The torchlight caught it, dramatizing its appearance against the dark interior of the shelter. We three boys joined Vera in her jumping and screaming. As the giant insect was about to climb onto Mr Watson's neck, the visiting aunt and Vera's mother added to the excitement with only slightly more dignified exclamations of horror and warning. The intrepid Mr Watson was helped out into the moonlight, finally convinced that a scorpion was about to bite the back of his neck and showing signs of anxiety himself by this time. The great pincers were now clearly visible to everyone, except Mr Watson.

'It's a *stag beetle*,' said Uncle Jimmy. 'They're not dangerous –

The Air-Raid Shelter

it's all right Fred, you're not going to die!' he added, brushing at the creature with the back of his fingers.

'Don't hurt it,' shouted Vera, totally reversing her role in the events of the evening now that her 'scorpion' was declared harmless.

The stag beetle fell onto a clump of chamomile that had self-seeded in the sandy soil on the top of our shelter. The great brown beetle sat for a moment looking at us all, as if unsure whether he had enjoyed his sport with us or was annoyed to have had his night's rest disturbed. Either way, he was going to move on, and he launched himself into the air, and, sounding like a clockwork toy, flew off into the night.

As we all stood in the garden, the comedy of the situation dawned on the adults and they began, one by one, to laugh, until everyone was laughing; we were all, adults and children alike, out of the house, out of the shelter and standing in the bright moonlight while the bombs seemed to be coming nearer and the guns seemed to be getting louder. Witticisms from the adults helped keep the laughter going: we're more frightened of a stag beetle than Hitler's bombs, was the general direction of the mirth. The dull crump of explosions came even nearer. 'They seem to be following us,' said Aunt Lily, 'We came to get away from bombs. We didn't know you had it as bad as this.' Just then, the sky lit up with a flash of light followed immediately by another of equal brightness. Someone went on to exclaim surprise but was silenced by two deafening explosions in quick succession.

'Blimey, that was near,' Uncle Jimmy said, 'We had better get inside.' We children were persuaded back into the shelter with assurance that the stag beetle would be miles away by now, and that if there were going to be any more bombs we would be in the safest place. We were tucked up once again, and the adults went back to their nice, warm beds indoors.

Chapter 11

DUSTY

Dusty, my dog, may never have been mine had it not been for the practical arrangements necessary to aid Nan in earning our keep. Having vacated our rooms to accommodate lodgers, we found ourselves sleeping in a divided upstairs room. Our makeshift dormitory, being at the front of the house, allowed all noises from the street to be heard, whether wanted or unwanted, especially in the still of a warm summer night when windows were left open for the comfort of the occupants. Allowing for Mrs Mac, who would be heard on frequent occasions returning home sometime after closing time, there were usually no sounds to be heard.

One particular night, from my corner behind the wardrobe, I could hear the sound of rustling as Nan was putting on her dressing gown and searching for her slippers. 'What's the matter?' I whispered, loudly enough to be heard around the wardrobe but not so loud as to disturb the lodgers in the room on the other side of the staircase.

'There's a funny noise,' said Nan. 'I'll see to it. You go back to sleep.' Being a young lad who liked his sleep, I had no difficulty in following her instructions.

I was woken again when Nan was putting a tiny puppy into bed with me. I managed to wake a little more this time, but it was through sleepy ears that I listened to the story of how she had heard a whimpering coming from the street. Her curiosity had taken her downstairs and outside where she was surprised to find the puppy in the dusty gutter, seemingly not far from giving up the struggle for life. She told how she had brought him in and given him some warm bread and milk. He had lapped at the milk weakly and must have taken enough to send him off to sleep. He was now wrapped in a piece of old blanket and looking more dead than alive as his slumbers claimed him. 'He'll be all right there,' said Nan, leaving the puppy on my bed and returning to her corner of the room. 'Let's get some sleep. Goodnight.'

Dusty

In the morning, I was delighted to find that my dreams were not dreams but true; there was a puppy and he was real. The only food we had to offer him was bread and milk, which turned out to be ideal as he still had not enough strength to take anything more. Nan found some old blankets and made a bed in the most draft-free corner of our kitchen, next to the fire place. Full of breakfast, the compact little bundle of unkempt fur stretched out on the blankets while I continued stroking him. It seemed he could only be bothered to open one eye to peer at me before falling back into sleep.

I managed to give some attention to schoolwork that day but was pleased when it was time to go home, to see what was happening with the puppy. When I got home, Uncle Fred's advice had been called upon and he was there looking at the puppy with Nan.

Uncle Fred was an ambitious man who liked the good things of life and, by his own hard work, could afford to have them. I admired his good taste and knew that when I grew up I would try to have some of the nice things he had. Strangely, as if wishing to deny anything pleasurable to anyone else, the only advice he ever gave to his oldest sister or to me throughout my growing up years was not to bother: 'Why do you want the trouble?' or 'You can't really afford it, I shouldn't if I were you.'

Nan was getting this kind of lecture as I arrived home, and not a good thing was being said about the puppy. Giving weight to the condemnation, an imperfection in the poor little animal had been found; some damage caused at his birth. 'Probably the reason it has been abandoned by its owner,' Uncle Fred said enthusiastically. 'It was probably thrown out of a car in the middle of the night,' he went on with some relish, adding that if veterinary work was required we could not afford it and even if we could find the owners they would not want the mongrel back. So, the best advice he could give was to take it to the free RSPCA clinic and have it 'put down'.

After Uncle Fred had gone, I asked Nan what was the matter with the puppy, who was at this time enjoying my attention; wagging his tiny tail and licking my hand. Nan rolled him over and showed me a lump on his stomach. She called it a 'hernia' and, interpreting for me, said it was where his 'tummy-button' should be. 'Does it hurt him?' I asked. She did not know, so it was decided to take him to the free RSPCA clinic, not to have him 'put down' but to ask the visiting vet what we should do about the problem. We were delighted to hear the long explanation, although many words were not understood they unmistakably conveyed the fact that the swelling should be left as it was. It was not hurting the puppy and nature would take care of it, healing it inside. The only reason an operation would be needed would be for appearance sake, but even appearances would be taken care of naturally; the lump would reduce in size a little and what looked large on this tiny puppy would hardly be noticeable on the full-grown dog.

We returned home satisfied; we were happy to accept at least some of what Uncle Fred had said, that no one would want to claim the puppy, and especially happy to accept all that the vet had told us. Nan decided it was safe to keep the little dog. All we needed now was to know what we were going to call him. As he had been found in the dusty gutter of our street, it was not difficult to settle on the name of Dusty, a name that fitted him so well and always reminded us of the night of his arrival.

As the days went by, Dusty grew stronger. He explored the kitchen and even the scullery, not being put off by falling down the single step that separated the two rooms. He seemed to have fur rather than hair and it became so long and thick as to give him the appearance of a toy teddy bear. He fell down many steps without damage, rolling like a ball inside his thick fur. Commenters suggested he was a husky in the making. As he became bolder, he would follow me into the garden, going a little further each time before running back to the safety of his bed in the draught-free fireplace corner.

When it came time to keep him safe by the control of a lead, it was found that his thick fur made a collar ineffective, as it could not be tightened enough to hold him and he could slip out anytime he wished. Nan thought a puppy harness would be safer and more comfortable for Dusty. We found one in Mr England's shop when we next went to buy puppy biscuits. The harness was far too big, and looked comical on the tiny puppy, but some more holes were made in the leather straps with our two-prong meat fork (the usual tool for such a job) and Dusty was safe and secure. 'He'll soon grow into it,' said Nan, and it was left at that.

Dusty grew strong. He attached himself to me, saving his energy through my school time and only bursting into life when he knew I was due home. He was always ready for an outing, and when I was off on some errand, pulling my box-cart trolley, Dusty would run with me. When he was small, he would tire quickly, and was then happy to sit on the trolley and be pulled along. At the top of a hill, I would ride on the cart with Dusty between my knees, hugging him gently while we whizzed along a downhill run.

The puppy harness was let out a notch at times as Dusty grew until, finally, it was at full stretch and, despite its puppy name, still fitted when he was fully grown. By that time, he was too strong for me to hold with one hand and pull my trolley with the other. One day, without planning it, I sat on the trolley still holding Dusty's lead. I could not hold him back and we went off up Otterfield Road at great speed; he had been called a husky and now he was proving that he was one. The thrill of riding a highly-powered vehicle was quite overwhelming and my heart began to thump. I was afraid that someone might step from their garden gate into our path, so I shouted, 'Whoa, Dusty,' and dragged my feet on the ground to convince him that I meant 'whoa', and we stopped; I was glad I could bring my 'husky' under control. I hoped I was not being cruel to him but, far from seeming abused, Dusty was delighted with his own performance; wagging his tail and licking my face, while panting at the same time.

Chores would be much more pleasure from now on. Trips to Clarke's Meadow to collect rabbit food were a regular need in the summer months, and to have company would make it fun. Dusty would get excited at the very mention of the meadow and would jump all over me as I tried to roll up the giant hessian sack that the food was going to be collected in. He did not seem to bother too much when I went to school in the morning, resting his muzzle on the edge of his basket as he looked up at me and smacking his tail down on the floor a couple of times. After school it was different, he would follow me around and not let me out of the back gate without him.

Once out onto the pavement, I would sit on my trolley clutching the sack. Dusty would rush off in the direction he seemed to know we were going, pulling the trolley and me with ease, making the well-oiled wheels hum and whir as they bump-bumped over the paving slabs of Otterfield Road all the way up to Falling Lane, the highest point of our journey. Dusty, remembering his puppy days, would jump onto the trolley in a most demanding way and sit in front of me. I would grip him between my knees, my feet resting on the front steering-bar. We would glide along on the smooth tarmacadam path, down a gentle slope all the way to Clarke's Meadow. Dusty, who obviously had no intention of relinquishing his position until it was absolutely necessary, sat firmly in place panting in the cooling breeze, occasionally turning his head just long enough to wipe a wet tongue across my cheek, as if to say 'Ain't it fun'?

As we came to the end of the path, the grass of Clarke's Meadow would quickly stop the trolley. Dusty would leap off, he knew he was allowed to go free while I was busy. He would take a drink from the shallow stream and then run about in all directions. After each sortie, he would return and bark once, as if asking if there were any new instructions.

Meanwhile, I would drag the sack over the grass as I sought out the rabbits' favourite food. As I grasped juicy young milk thistles, I could imagine our rabbits seeking them out first and nibbling joyfully at twice the usual speed, as the tasty treat was devoured. Tender young dandelion leaves, and flowers too, were equal favourites, and perhaps to add variety and help speed my work, some clover and sweet new grasses were gathered too. At particular times, docks took over areas of the meadow and if rabbits would eat them a sack could be filled in no time. But rabbits did not like them and they were just a nuisance to be avoided; if one leaf was accidentally included, it would be found in the bottom of the hutch after all the other leaves had gone.

Once the sack was stuffed tight, it would be laid on the trolley; with one end wedged in the box seat to hold it in place, it would take up the full length of the trolley. Dusty would be whistled up and we would make for home. I would now be pulling the trolley, with Dusty running free until we came to the main road and crossed into Otterfield Road. After so much running about, Dusty would be very well behaved and happy to walk by my side, accepting the control of the lead. Back at home, a generous handful of the succulent leaves would be delivered to each hutch, they would be pounced upon and the sound of mass nibbling could be heard as the occupants settled down for their evening meal. Dusty would sloppily empty a basin of cold water and leap into his basket, still panting and dripping water from his tongue.

I was pleased to find that I was just in time to hear *Dick Barton Special Agent* on the radio, which would start at a quarter to seven. For a quarter of an hour each day I would be held in suspense by the daring deeds of Dick Barton and his two assistants, Jock and Snowy. The music at the beginning was exciting and the tension grew as the story built up to some new cliffhanger situation as the programme ended, leaving you unable to wait until tomorrow to find out how they got out of it. The latest dilemma would be talked about at school next day.

As for Dusty, he seemed to have no interest in Dick Barton and was by that time resting his head on the side of his basket with his nose pointing in my direction. If he wanted to keep an eye on me, he need only flick one open. However, he seemed to have no wish to do that for the moment, preferring to doze while snoring gently, in-between tiny yelps or growls that suggested he was enjoying sweet dreams.

Chapter 12

JUNIOR SCHOOL

It was, by now, more than clear that Nan had little regard for formal education. She liked to tell that she, herself, had never been to school, adding, with a chuckle, that she had 'only met the scholars coming home' (a statement that I have never fully understood). Frequently throughout my schooldays, to my great embarrassment, I would see Nan appear at the school gate and come striding across the playground, in full sight of my classmates, to take me off for any one of a variety of reasons, trivial or important, it seemed not to matter. The interruption to my studies might be anything between half a day or even several weeks when accompanying her on one of her jaunts.

The second establishment I attended for my formal education was St Matthew's Church of England Junior School. The Victorian building was back to back with St Stephen's, my old infant school and adjacent to St Matthew's Church. Entrances to both church and school opened onto Yiewsley High Street. From school to home was only a few minutes run for a junior scholar and could be travelled without incident, providing the Belisha crossing on the High Street was used correctly and the stiff end of the duty policeman's motorcycle gauntlets were avoided for any failure to follow the rules recited to us on one of his recent lectures at our school.

Our classroom at St Matthew's was a high-ceilinged room with plain flaking walls. Black woodwork was dominant; ceiling beams, wainscoting, doors and window frames were all blackened by numerous coats of dark varnish applied over many years of maintenance. Desks, also varnish-darkened, were constructed in pairs with a bench seat attached to accommodate two children side by side. Desktops were divided in two; each side could be lifted to reveal individual compartments, with ink stains fading in chronological order of spillage. The undersides of the solid-wood lids were carved with the initials of bored schoolboys who were lucky enough to own a penknife. On the assumption that all children were right-handed (or perhaps would be persuaded to be so), a white china inkwell, the size of an eggcup, was set into an appropriate-sized hole on the right front corner of each desk; it was the duty of the child chosen to be ink monitor to ensure that all wells were filled for the day's work.

At the front of the room, in the corner opposite the entrance door, was a large black cast-iron fireplace and around it a heavy-built matching iron fireguard. In the winter, a fire blazed, consuming oversized scuttles of coal that were brought in by the caretaker at intervals. Crates of milk bottles, containing one third of a pint each, would be placed in the hearth to warm. During the coldest part of the winter, the bottles would be near frozen but the heat from the fire was so effective that a proportion of them would boil over, ejecting their tops and frothing hot milk down the sides of the glass and onto the hearth.

At morning break time, the crate of milk would be pulled away from the fire and the milk monitor would take charge of handing out a bottle to each child. A straw monitor would clutch a box of paper straws, handing one to each pupil, and perhaps two to his friends. Drinking would begin quietly but become noisy as the bottom of the bottle was reached, when air and milk were sucked up together. Lively chatter would commence and build in volume as bottles were emptied, until the teacher clapped his hands and shouted to announce the next lesson.

Our class teacher dealt with several subjects, so that much of our time was spent in that room. Lessons were frequently without text books; the master, like a great orator or a fairground barker, projecting his voice to be heard by between thirty and forty children, orally instructing us or quizzing us on mathematics, history, English or geography while we wrote our answers in notebooks, which would be marked later. Teaching by rote was an accepted method too. I have always been grateful that we were pressed to learn our 'times tables' by heart; the ability to know that 'seven sevens are forty-nine' without having to think about it was evermore an anchor in the reality of daily affairs.

Junior School

Art was taught by another teacher, in a special room where the appropriate materials were kept. I cannot remember any future artists in our class. Little girls mostly drew square houses with four windows and a front door, and perhaps a row of flowers and a matchstick man and woman. Little boys only ever seemed to draw machinery of war; aeroplanes and tanks firing bullets of dotted lines across the page, and German aeroplanes, with badly formed swastikas, shooting at English parachutists, which is what we were told happened.

The lesson I had learned at infant school was going to have an effect upon me all the days of my schooling; now less trusting, I needed a strategy to get me through. Without adult guidance, my simple childish logic told me that the only way to cope, was to be unnoticed. My observations showed me that the teachers' 'pets', probably the brightest children, sat in the front row of the class; I was aware that I was not one of the most academic and would not have enjoyed the spotlight so frequently shone on that position. The back row was inhabited by the noisy, the troublemakers and, no doubt, the least scholarly: I certainly did not want to be associated with them and receive the kind of attention they attracted.

As I watched the teacher performing his art, it became clear that to gain a response from the class as a whole he first directed his questions to the front row, where already minds were engaged and hands were raised. At unexpected intervals, questions were aimed like a bullwhip, at one of the 'unwashed' in the back row, whose eyes were still full of sleep and threatening to pull him back into last night's neglected slumbers. It was easy to see that I should establish myself in the moderate even ground of the central plateau. If neither the lush pastures of the front row nor the rocky terrain at the far reaches of our enclosed universe were for me, perhaps I could lose myself in the hinterland, where I would be surrounded by likeminded pupils; average, not too ambitious and simply wanting to get through their day with the least pains. I could listen, I could learn, and I could survive.

In the following months, I achieved my aim to be unnoticed. It had the advantages I wanted, and some features I had not bargained for; unnoticed meant un-remembered so, while I was never punished, I was never commended. I never let it be known that I knew that seven sevens are forty-nine, or offered a line of poetry, or put myself forward for the Nativity play to be considered for a leading role or even a member of the chorus of angels. I did not learn to express myself in any way, so that in time my own voice became an embarrassment to me. My work was marked in ignorance of the individual who had produced it so, for safety, a 'C' average was the usual result. I never became head boy or monitor of milk or ink or straws. I achieved my wish for anonymity, and paid the price in obscurity.

My desire for a peaceful existence included my journey to and from school, so that I always crossed the High Street correctly and avoided the wrath of the duty policeman. But, of course, not every contingency can be planned for. On one of my homeward runs, I was attacked by a bully from a higher year. He liked to hide near the school until a younger boy came along, then appear and kick the junior. Why the assailant needed to hurt, and why kicking was his method of attack, I never understood. One day, my turn came for the hostile treatment; unfortunately, I had squatted down to tie my shoe lace, making an easy target of the bottom of my spine, when the flying shoe came my way. I hobbled homeward crying, which triggered Nan's nursing skills; Goddard's Horse Oils was applied generously and I was made comfortable, and rewarded with one of the medicinal eggs from the isinglass bucket, presented in a delicious egg custard, the cure for many ills. After a while sitting, my bruised coccyx made it too painful to stand up straight. My hunched body caused alarm. The warmth of my bed was considered to be the best cure and I was helped up the stairs, like a bent over old man. A day or two of school was lost.

When I was ready to be sent out into the world again, I went with instruction on self-defence. I was a little hesitant to think that it was all up to me, but to be self-reliant was the only way Nan knew. Articulate parents might have made demands on the school, but I would be shown 'the old one-two'. Nan held her fists high in front of her face. The left was rotating in a small horizontal circle. She then said forcefully, 'You say to that boy, "See this?",' she nodded to her moving left fist, 'that's number one. When he looks at it, 'it 'im with the other one, that's number two. Give 'im the old one-two an' 'e won't trouble you again.'

Regardless of my pugilistic instruction, I went to school warily, and still a little tender in the rear. Several days passed before the bully appeared on my journey home. On that day, I was walking along and able to face him and measure up the situation; I was as tall as him but he was a solid stocky lad, I was sure that my leanly covered frame would be no match for his if it came to exchanging blows. He moved closer and I automatically put up my fists, as I had been drilled to do. My own action shocked me. 'Why did I do that?', I asked myself. I have just given him the signal to begin. I was sure I was about to get a beating.

In my fearful state I could hear Nan's voice: 'Never say yer mother had a jibber,' in the usual persuasive tone, and then more firmly, 'You've started it, and yer don't start something you can't finish,' and for good measure the voice added some gruesome assurance and further encouragement, 'The bigger they come, the 'arder they fall.'

My desire to run away was great but my dread of the shame that would be heaped upon me if I went home crying again was greater, so I stood firm. I began to move my left fist around as I had been shown, 'That's number one,' I said to myself. As the bully's eyes fixed upon my circling left fist, I pulled back my right. This was the point at which I was supposed to strike, but timidity, lack of belligerence or simply good common sense said wait. To my surprise, the boy looked full of fear – turned and ran away. I watched him go, not quite as rigid in shock as I might have been if he had just delivered a solid punch, but fixed in surprise for a moment before relief was felt. I was pleased not to have taken a beating and equally happy that I had not needed to become the aggressor, so I could live by another of Nan's maxims (of which it must be clear to see she had one for every situation in the average life), I could 'Live and let live'; I liked the sound of that one, it suited my own personality and the conclusions I had come to in my brief span so far. I continued my journey home, feeling pleased with myself and enjoying the lesson I had just learned about dealing with bullies.

Towards the end of my time in junior school, Nan decided I should be 'put into long trousers'. It was usual for junior schoolboys to wear short trousers, and the change from short to long was a rite of passage that usually took place at the beginning of senior school. At that time, denim jeans were not worn and the leg apparel of the male, child or adult, was almost without exception of a grey-flannel nature; boys and men were grey-legged as if by an officially prescribed order of uniformity. Before the event of the washing machine and machine-washable clothing, trousers, whether short or long, would be worn for great lengths of time before expensive dry-cleaning was undertaken. Once short grey-flannel trousers had been installed upon a junior schoolboy, they would remain in place throughout his day; a physical training lesson may require removal of jacket or jumper, perhaps tie and even shirt, but grey-flannel short trousers would endure, suspended by braces, and sometimes an elasticated belt with the popular snake-hook buckle, too.

A boy with new trousers could easily be identified. To gain the longest period of wear on a rapidly growing child, thrift on his mother's part guided her to a garment several sizes too large, so that when 'fitting' them on her son she would need to assure him more than once that he would 'soon grow into them'. Braces would be shortened, narrowing the space between trouser-waistband and chin, and the elasticated belt would be fully employed reducing the voluminous girth of the grey-flannel and bringing it closer to the waist of the incumbent.

Contrasting with a recently fitted-out pupil was a comrade overdue for new attire; he would have grown into and long since out of his breeches. One boy, known throughout the school for increasing in height by fifty percent in one academic year, had acquired the name of 'Turk' and longed for the time when his new trousers could be afforded. In the meantime, his braces had been extended to their maximum length and material which once touched his knees was now ten or a dozen inches above, revealing a large area of chapped thighs as well as the usual grazed knees common to schoolboys.

Possibly it was the sight of winter-scarred legs that convinced Nan I should have long trousers early instead of waiting for the accepted time; she had tended to my damaged knees many times, applying Germoline ointment and bandage, or perhaps it was her desire for my advancement into adult life to come sooner, with all the advantages that might bring. Whatever were her innermost thoughts, I was taken to Foster's Outfitters on Yiewsley High Street and measured for my first pair of long grey-flannel trousers. It took a while to become accustomed to the weight and touch of the additional material; I felt restricted in movement and less available for playground games. Had I the makings of head boy or even monitor of milk or ink or straws, I could have carried out my duties with such convincing authority; strutting through my day enjoying the admiration of my fellow pupils, while my appearance convinced one and all of my mature efficiency.

But I was seeking to be invisible and my early refitting rendered me conspicuous, so unwanted attention had to be endured until some of my friends convinced their parents that it was their time for transformation.

My old black bike

*Me, 'Turk' and Arthur
(centre, back row)*

Chapter 13

THE WINKLE ROUND

I was told one day that my father was going to take up Bobby's winkle round. We would be trading on the good name built up over the many years that Bobby had gone out on Sundays selling well-prepared home-cooked winkles and a small range of other shellfish.

The plan had been hatched by the 'senior members of our little consortium' and, by the time I was informed, only advantages for all parties could be envisaged. My father had a van and he was free on Sundays. He wanted to earn some extra money and he knew that a respected reputation would give him the best chance to make a success of the venture. It would also give him the chance to spend time with his son, he said.

For our part, Nan could not bear to lose the valuable business connection, and, as we could not drive and had no vehicle, even an alliance with a dysfunctional son-in-law would be acceptable to achieve her wish. Any profits from our work were to be shared. I was never told in what proportion, but our share would go to Nan to be used for our keep.

My father's contribution would be essential but we, too, would play our part, as he was free only on Sunday to go on the round and there was much preparation to be completed on Saturday. The plan was only possible now that I was old enough to help. I had been to Billingsgate Market with Nan and now I was going to be trusted to go alone. Also, I had been on the round with Bobby and I could show my father the houses and streets where we were best known.

The first job on Saturday was to go to market, and that required an early start. Before leaving the house, I was instructed firmly not to lose the money I had been given to make the purchases, to ensure that I spent wisely, not to pay too much and only buy the best and the freshest. I would set off on foot to West Drayton Station, buy a day-return ticket to Paddington and go onto the platform.

The Winkle Round

If there were a few minutes to wait for the train, I had time to find the machine that stamped letters into an aluminium strip. It was a great drab cast-iron box on short legs with a heavy pointer that could be moved around a large dial to select the required letter. When a lever on the side was pulled hard, the letter would be punched into the strip. The last pull of the lever would cut off the strip. I would usually write my name and nail the strip to my latest soapbox trolley when I got home.

When the train pulled into the station it would be necessary to wade through steam and smoke to find a carriage door. Once in the third-class compartment, it was warm, steamy and smelled sooty. Our journey to Paddington was about twelve miles and we would make several stops. While we sat waiting for the guard to wave his green flag to signal to the driver to proceed, a 'fast train' travelling in the opposite direction would thunder past vibrating the whole station, tracks, platform, waiting room and our carriage too. More steam and smoke obscured all that could be seen a few moments earlier. The speed of the express train would tell of the long journey it was making, perhaps all the way to the end of the line at Penzance in Cornwall, covering a large part of Brunel's Great Western Railway (or God's Wonderful Railway, as people said GWR stood for).

As our train gathered speed out of the station, my attention would be taken by posters in the carriage, they were framed and protected under glass, which made them look like valuable paintings. I was captivated by the title 'Cornish Riviera', which sounded so exotic, and beguiled by the pictures of the faraway places. I imagined that the passengers making the long journey to such a wonderful place must all be smartly dressed and such important people.

Soon we were stopping at Hayes and Harlington, Southall, Hanwell, Ealing Broadway, Westbourne Park and then on to Paddington. As I walked along the platform, amongst the crowd of people who had just alighted from the train, I observed the great buffers that marked the very end of the line. In my schoolboy mind, I wondered why the driver had so carefully slowed and stopped the train quite some way back. Why had he not glided in and let the buffers stop us? They seemed designed for the purpose, so strong and able, but appeared never to be used.

Then, I handed in the first half of my return ticket and quickly crossed the station to go down the stairs to the Inner Circle line of the Underground. On the noisy journey, I watched carefully for the Monument station, where I must get off. I walked down Pudding Lane, past Christopher Wren's column (the monument itself, near the place where the Fire of London had started in 1666) and then onward across Lower Thames Street into the market. From the entrance, my eyes were greeted by an unnerving number of white-coated men spread across the vast floor of the indoor market; wholesalers surrounded by stalls loaded with all kinds of fish and seafood, porters in coats of tough white sailcloth, some heavily soiled, some less so, many wearing specially-designed flat-top leather hats for carrying boxes of fish or anything that needed moving to a purchaser's vehicle.

I wove my way between the daunting multitude of men and fish to find the whelks, cockles, shrimps and prawns that I had been instructed to buy. Prawns were expensive and were only purchased on a holiday weekend or when a good day was anticipated. I examined the goods of several stalls and when I saw freshness at the right price, I was ready to buy. I would approach a salesman who, like most of his fellows, was a burly Londoner, large and gruff – perhaps gruff because he had been working since four o'clock that morning.

I ask, 'Can I have a gallon of cockles, please?'

The stallholder looks down at me and says, 'What?'

I control my shyness and repeat my question louder. He reaches up to a roll of cream-coloured stockinet, woven into a tube. He ties a knot in the bottom and then cuts off about a yard. He opens the top and shoots in cockles from a one-gallon measure. The top is tied and the 'parcel' is dropped casually in front of me. All his produce looks good, so I have a gallon of shrimps and a gallon of whelks from the same stall. They are netted in the same way as the cockles. I decide to have his prawns too, and they come in a gallon tin, in which they remain for the journey home.

As usual, I have been told to buy an eel for dinner. Eels have been sold at Billingsgate for hundreds of years, probably even before a charter for a market was granted in 1327, although, at that moment I was more interested in the eel than the history. With prawn tin under my arm and nets gripped in my fingers, I stop on my way back across the market at any stall that has the finless fish on display. They are kept live in deep trays of water, in which they swim freely. I seek the liveliest and ask for an eel please, my chosen one is taken from the tray and parcelled alive in stockinet.

Each week, with arms loaded, I returned to the Monument station and boarded the underground train. On most journeys, no one was aware of the nature of my purchases. Only on rare occasions did any fellow passenger notice a movement in the net on the floor between my feet, which drew their attention to the wriggling eel and cause them to move quietly away. At Paddington, on the mainline train, I could go into the guard's van, with the bicycles and parcels, to avoid the hot steamy carriage and close proximity with any nervous passenger.

Arriving home, the nets and tin are put in a cool place outside. The eel is put into a bowl of water and swims around briskly, seeming no worse for its earlier experiences. As soon as Nan approves the purchases, the eel is taken from the bowl, chopped into pieces about an inch long and dropped into boiling water. It is delicious with parsley sauce and mashed potato.

Dinner time was brief, as there was much to be done and the nights were drawing in at that time of year. Four bushels of live winkles, in four sacks, were waiting in the alley outside our back gate, where they had been left by the Carter-Patterson van bringing them from the railway station. They had been sent to us direct from Scotland by train. Nan boasts that they are 'Scotch winkles', not 'Scots' or 'Scottish' but 'Scotch', which was not meant to offend but as her sincere tribute to their superior quality. I would drag the sacks into our backyard, one at a time because they are heavy. The winkles must be washed, cooked and salted down. All the implements needed had been carried by Nan from the shed and put in readiness in the back yard. Baths were in place for washing, electric copper for cooking, and hose pipe, fitted to scullery tap, coming out through the sash window, which is open wide for the purpose.

Two buckets of winkles were put into an oval galvanised tin bath. The hose ran into the bath while the contents were stirred with a broom handle, kept for the purpose. The bath was allowed to overflow taking grit, sand, seaweed and unwanted flotsam over the side. When the winkles were considered clean, they were scooped into a metal basket. By that time, the copper was boiling furiously, and standing in an inch of water with hose pipe and electric cable laying by its side - health and safety rules, if there were any, seeming not to apply. The basket of cleaned winkles was then plunged into the boiling water. The copper groaned as it struggled to get back up to temperature. The winkles were left to cook.

Salt was needed, so I would run up to Mary's Sweet Shop on the corner. Six blocks of cooking salt were purchased, and probably a bar of Nestlé's chocolate if they had one. By the time I got home, a 'bungalow' bath had been placed on the upper side of the yard. The hose was already putting in the required amount of water. The salt was placed in the water and broken up. As the winkles were cooked, they were drained and tipped into the salted water where they would remain until next morning.

More winkles were put into the washing bath and the process carried out as before. Washing, cooking and salting down would go on until well after dark; each batch preparing three gallons of winkles and there are thirty-two gallons to be dealt with in all.

Early on Sunday morning, my father would arrive, the winkles would be drained, put into the oval baths and loaded into his van. The cockles, whelks and shrimps were displayed in enamel washing-up bowls. The prawns would remain in their tin. My father would then drive to Cowley, where our round began. Our first call was at a big house on the main road. I ran to the front door. They usually had a pint of winkles, so I would take a full pint measure in readiness. In hope of encouraging them to spend more, I would take a half-pint measure of shrimps as well. Sometimes the business-booster worked, they had the winkles, and seeing the shrimps, they had those too. Of course, the plan could fail, if they decided to have a change and ask for a pint of shrimps only, I would run back to the van and make a second journey up the garden path.

Further along, we pulled on to an estate. People came out of their houses to buy from the van. When they were all served, we would both knock on doors and make more sales. We moved on around the streets of several estates throughout the morning.

We aimed to get to the Pear Tree public house by two o'clock, when men were leaving to go home to their Sunday dinner. Jolly people crowded around the back of the van and we sold more of the expensive prawns. Some men bought whelks to eat and pass around like sweets as they stood talking to their friends. Most took a pint of winkles home for the family's tea.

When everyone had gone, we drove off. As we moved away from the Pear Tree, I would think about the times I had helped Bobby on this round. When he had served most of the pub customers, he would leave me to deal with the stragglers while he went in, just before closing time, for a 'quick pint'. After a few minutes, the bar door would open and he would call me over to give me a glass of lemonade. I was pleased to have a drink, but the lemonade was not to my liking. Because it came from a pub, I was convinced that it was only for grown-ups. It tasted different to the R. White's lemonade or cream soda or orange-coloured Tizer that came from Mary's Sweet Shop. Pub lemonade took my breath away, and the bubbles were like needles in my mouth. I would push the bar door open a few inches until Bobby saw me. When I had told him my problem, he would drop a half-crown piece into the glass, and bubbles would rush to the surface leaving the lemonade placid and drinkable. Only when I had drunk down to the coin did I see what a filthy ill-used half-crown had been dropped in, and wished I had not complained in the first place.

My father would drive on to more housing estates and we would continue serving at the van and knocking on doors. On winter afternoons, our energy would start to fail and the cold begin to get into our bones. Something to eat would have been warming but nothing we had on the van was inviting. As the day began to fade, my father would start to worry about the amount of stock we had left to sell. He would waste valuable time counting the takings in hope of some reassurance. I understood his anxiety; I had seen Bobby dealing with the same problem. In innocence, but perhaps sounding impertinent, I repeated what I had heard Bobby say to himself, 'It won't get any more by counting it.' My father seems not to have heard anyway. He knew that what we had left must be sold if we were to profit from two days hard work. We moved on.

The next street was well lit, a good number of people come to the van and we made sales where we knocked. Another street and then another went well. Soon it is too late. No one came to the van and, through the doors we knocked on, we saw families already sitting around the table. The savoury food, including shellfish, is enjoyed at the beginning of a Sunday tea and nobody wants winkles after they have tasted bread and jam, and cakes. We have a few pints of winkles left, almost no cockles, whelks or shrimps and, thank goodness, the expensive prawns have all gone. We decide to call it a day and make for home.

In the dark, we put baths and bowls into the backyard to be dealt with tomorrow. So many of our working hours are spent in our backyard, scullery door and window wide open to aid our work, causing our home to be without warmth or comfort. Tonight will be different. Nan knows that the arrivals will be frozen through. She will make sure the homecoming is a warm one. We are pleased to get inside the house and close the scullery door. The Suffolk latch finally clicks shut, and bolts, top and bottom, are thrown as we have no intention of venturing out again. The kitchen is warm and bright, a big fire in the hearth was timed to be at its best at this moment. Nan's promise to have 'a fire up the chimney' waiting for us is fully realized, and is welcome. The fact that hot coals will fall out and further damage the carpet, which already has the appearance of black leather where burns have covered much of its area, only the outer edge showing any signs of the woollen pile and pretty pattern it once had, is, tonight, considered a small price to pay.

While a hot cup of tea was enjoyed, the leather money bag was emptied onto the dark-green chenille cloth on the table in the middle of the room. The scene reminds me again of Bobby. When I was very small, he would shoot out his money in just the same way and encourage me to count it. Half-crowns would be stacked, then two-shilling pieces, followed by other coins going down in value. My education from the beginning was a practical one; I was taught to count money and have respect for it at the same time.

During the season my father took over Bobby's round, our arrival home at the end of the day, was a time we could have enjoyed together. When the takings were counted, there was always ample recompense for the work of two long days. There would be a silent sigh of relief as the worries of the afternoon subsided. We could sit back, soaking up the warmth, while Nan happily bustled in the scullery, dishing up piping-hot dinners, which was her way of rewarding her heroes of the moment. For just a little while, I saw the man who was my father. Tension fell away from his brow as we listened to one of the popular radio shows of the day. He began to laugh freely, as we became engaged by the voices coming across the airways. Brief connections between us were made as we glanced at one another while we shared the audio pictures of one absurd situation or another, created by a well-known comedian and his team.

As the radio programme came to an end, we settled back, now warmed and restored. My father would turn his attention to me. 'Well, how are you getting on then?' he would ask.

'Fine, thank you,' I would say.

'Oh, that's good,' my father would say in the kindest voice he could employ.

There would be a silence, neither of us knowing what more to say. There was tension. I knew my father wanted to love his son. Long ago, he brought me impressive toys, but his advances had been beaten back by his disapproving mother-in-law. He was kept at a distance, while daily I was reminded of his supposed sins and weaknesses.

On such an evening, after we had shared a working day and together had achieved success, recuperated and laughed, a gentle exchange of words could have helped us across the invisible barrier between us. But we had, in common, an inability to easy conversation, which was exacerbated by the presence of the third person in the room. Throughout the whole of my childhood, I would sacrifice any closeness with my father for my own well-being, as to engage Nan's disapproval would bring about days of discomfort. For my father's part, he had tried and had failed. As his mild nature dictated, he had acquiesced to the wish of the unyielding senior member of our broken family.

After a few more minutes of uneasy silence, my father would say he must go. Nan would move closer to the fire, making herself comfortable to listen to a play that was about to start on the wireless. My father would pull on his coat and I would go with him to the front door. He thoughtfully insists that I stay in the warmth of the house. He gently grips my upper arm – our first embrace of the day. He smiles down at me, with a look that must have imprisoned a thousand words, but none come, until he says, 'Look after yourself then.' Giving my arm a final tender squeeze before releasing it, he says, 'Goodbye then.' He disappears into the darkness, and I hear him drive away.

Chapter 14

THE RABBIT SHOW

The rabbits we kept, being of no particular breed – apart from 'Heinz 57 varieties' as Uncle Fred's humour would have it – were almost always born wearing the grey livery of their wild cousins. Minute flecks of grey, black, brown and white suggested a very mixed family history, and to anything less than the closest examination, left them with the appearance of the dominant grey. Only on one occasion, in my experience, did this plan of nature vary, when one of our new broods contained a little animal unlike any other of his siblings, appearing in a coat thicker and softer and in the richest uninterrupted colour of smokey-blue.

As the delightful cuckoo in the nest grew, there was much discussion as to how, from such a long line of grey ancestors, a single rabbit could appear and be so different. From our knowledgeable and wordy acquaintances, we heard about 'spontaneous genetic mutation' and we nodded in full agreement! Our more everyday friends spoke of 'throwbacks' or 'sports' and such words we could understand and settled for the possibility that we were witnessing a 'throwback' to some noble forebear. 'No doubt accidental' as more of Uncle Fred's sardonic wit suggested.

I decided to ask the opinion of my school friend Michael who knew lots about rabbits. He kept pure-bred Old English, Lop-eared and little black and white Polish, which he had entered in shows and won prizes, his best rabbits had won cups too. He knew about 'throwbacks' but, as far as he understood, it was something that 'just happened', usually in quite the wrong way he bemoaned when one of his prize-winners produced young that looked like a wild rabbit.

Michael thought my smokey-blue was quite beautiful and said I should put him in a show. I was surprised that an animal without pedigree would be accepted but I let Michael help me fill up an entrance application. When the form was completed, it was obvious that my entrant had nothing to offer in grand parentage, and that fact could be seen clearly from the number of blank spaces that remained on the form. I expected a rejection but instead, in a few days, I received a registration certificate and details of the arrangements for the day of the show.

In the hall, on the day, owners stood behind a long row of trestle tables. On the table in front of them they held their potential prize winners, keeping them still and fussing with their appearance. Under the tables had been placed all of the transporting cages, all in individual styles ranging from simple-functional to very fancy. I felt momentarily embarrassed as I carefully toed under the table my cardboard box that had served as my transporter.

There was no order as to where each contestant stood along the row. Later, I could see that the confident experienced owners, feeling that they were showing a good example of their breed, favoured a position nearer the top of the table, while the modest and the less confident would allow themselves to be jostled to the lower end. No one would actually place their rabbit at the very top of the table; the space there was held in some reverence and reserved for the show-winner. In my newcomer's ignorance, one space was much like any other and, as the places were filling up quickly, I took the opportunity to put my rabbit on the table in the only space that seemed to be available. I commenced to act as if I knew what to do, smoothing my entrant's coat and removing unwanted straw and other foreign matter from his feet. As I glanced down the row of faces from my 'prized' position, I received every manner of look, from as far as I could see along the tables, ranging from contemptuous glares to deferential respectful smiles. I smiled uncertainly back. It was not until the judging began and I could see how a rabbit with merit would be moved up the table towards me that I realized I had at least begun the day in the winning position.

The judges continued picking up, examining and moving rabbits up or down the table according to the considered order of fineness. I managed to nudge along a little, to escape from the winner's spot. Soon Michael's Polish rabbit was moved up to take the place I had just vacated. He knew his entry was an extremely good example of its breed, but being a modest person had chosen to begin his day somewhere about the middle of the entrants. Another rabbit was moved up ahead of mine, and then another. I began to feel more relaxed, to be out of the uncomfortable position I had put myself in.

The judges continued examining and moving rabbits. I then began to feel a second wave of discomfort from the sudden awareness that I might be moved downward continually, and end up at the extreme end of the table from where I had started the day. After all, my rabbit had been bred for meat; it was no prized or sacred beast improved over generations for its symmetry, its ideal length of back or the shape of its head and now considered by man to be perfected beyond improvement.

My rabbit was picked up and examined once or twice more and replaced without movement up or down the table. By the end of the judging that's where he remained, in fourth position. I looked down the table at a dozen or so pure-bred animals and thought something must be wrong and the error would be noticed and corrected; perhaps I was about to be thrown out as an imposter. In fact, I and my mongrel rabbit remained in fourth place and I was given a certificate stating so. Michael won first place with his Polish. His certificate commented on his rabbit's correct shape and size, 'the perfect example of its breed'. My certificate simply stated that my rabbit had achieved fourth place for its 'excellent condition'; I was delighted with the congratulatory comment, for which I instantly took credit, putting it down to my good husbandry. I was so proud of that certificate and pinned it up in my little back bedroom where it remained until it was quite faded.

Chapter 15

MY FIRST BUSINESS

One autumn, we were without lodgers. Nan was worried. 'We've got nothing coming in, but the bills don't stop,' she said, sounding distressed. The coalman had just delivered a ton of coal and she had parted with five pounds from her hoard of hidden banknotes. One-hundredweight sacks of coal had been carried on the coalman's back and tipped in a brick-built shed that we called the 'coal cellar'. As a bag was emptied, it was folded and thrown down in our backyard to keep tally of the number delivered. One of the merchant's employees used an empty sack to cushion his back against the uncomfortable load. His method gave him the opportunity, if not observed carefully, to earn his 'beer money' by dropping two sacks on the tally pile once or twice during his visit. The need to watch the man added to Nan's despair, giving her a sad reminder of the hostile world outside.

To keep us afloat temporarily, Nan had already parted with two china figurines that had stood on her dressing table and had some special meaning for her. Before wrapping them in tissue paper, she took a last lingering look. 'These are Wedgwood, 'e made a lot of these,' she said, as if she knew Mr Wedgwood personally but with a warmth that suggested a genuine appreciation of the fineness of the china ornaments. 'Take 'em up to Mr Gooding – make sure 'e knows they're from me – and see 'ow much 'e'll give us for 'em.' Mr Gooding ran a small antique shop in Vine Street, Uxbridge. He examined the figurines, muttering to himself what 'nice' pieces they were and needing a very large magnifying glass to find any minor blemishes. He said he could give thirty shillings for the pair. I knew that was the amount Nan expected and said that I would take it.

Linstan, my friend next door, was about to take on a paper round. He was pleased with what he was going to earn, it would add nicely to his pocket money he said. He wondered if I might want to do the same. I considered it, but the amount I would earn for a paper round was too small to help our present situation.

I had an idea. For some time, I had been going to a local woodworking factory, bringing home sacks of scrap wood and chopping it for our fire. There was a large amount in their waste pile and I had never been refused as much as I could carry away. How about, I wondered, if I chopped wood for other people at a small cost? I was sure it was a chore that a lot of householders would be glad to give up and that I had, therefore, found a 'niche' in the market for something I could produce. I decided to give it a try.

Containers and a means of transport would be needed. The first came in the shape of bright-orange Czechoslovakian onion sacks, from Lane's the greengrocer. Most boxes and sacks had a deposit on them, so they were carefully collected by the greengrocer and returned to the market to reclaim his money. The 'CZ' sacks (as he called them) had no deposit, and I could have as many as I wanted.

Providing the means of transporting the filled sacks would start with finding some pram wheels. Prams must have been changed frequently, as we boys never seemed to have any difficulty in finding wheels for our soap-box trolleys. Wood for the cart came from the pile at the end of the garden. Some good planks were produced by cutting broken raggedy ends from long pieces. Cross pieces, nailed underneath, held them together and a thick piece supported the axle, which was held by nails bent over it. A headboard across the front of the cart, fixed by a pair of not-too-rusty shelf brackets, was ideal to keep the filled sacks upright. I reckoned I could get about ten on to make a full load.

Next, I needed to find a way to balance the cart on its two wheels and connect it to the back of my bike. Uncle Fred suggested that I should go to the blacksmith and get him to make something up for me. The blacksmith's shop was in St Stephen's Road, on a bend next to the Grand Union Canal. In those days, barges still passed up and down pulled by a heavy horse. The smithy was conveniently placed to deal with a loose shoe on a barge horse as well as oblige the local people, as I hoped he could me on that particular day. The blacksmith looked at my cart and thought for a moment. He took, from a rack, a long length of mild steel, about one inch wide, and bent it this way and that until it fitted the requirement. He drilled several holes in the metal and showed me how to bolt it to my cart. Back at home, I could only find wood screws but, although different sizes, they were not too rusty and did the job quite well.

Eager to try my new equipment, I made several trips to the factory and amassed a large pile of wood. It came in a wide variety of shapes and sizes, which needed to be brought under control to produce kindling of a more consistent length and thickness. The only means I had to achieve this was with Nan's old 'chopper'; an ugly oversized brute, much damaged and with no cutting edge to be found. It proved to be too heavy and caused me a few aches and pains.

On odd occasions, I would find myself looking into the window of Smith & Haynes, the hardware and tool shop on Yiewsley High Street ('the ironmongers' as Nan preferred to call it). I would gaze longingly at a display of small axes, so beautifully finished with shiny blades and curvy handles that I thought made them look like the ones in cowboy and Indian films. More likely, they were ergonomically designed to fit the human hand so well as to make the work easier. I had the discussion with myself that 'businessmen' must have had throughout time. Do I go into debt at this early stage to buy this tool that will more than earn its keep, or do I play safe? As is my nature, I played safe, and struggled on with Nan's old chopper until I had filled ten sacks.

Bright and early on Saturday morning, I loaded up. All the sacks went on the cart and a piece of rope held them in place.

My First Business

I knew where I was going because I had already asked those in the know (mostly Uncle Fred) where the money was. The Garden City, West Drayton, was to be my rich hunting ground. 'Research' had been done also into how much to ask for a bag of firewood, so the first house I came to that looked prosperous and worth a call, I knocked at the front door and asked, 'Would you like a bag of firewood for a shilling?' The answer was yes. I took the money and handed over the bright-orange CZ sack filled with waste wood, chopped and broken into raggedy pieces by my own fair hand – or rather Nan's oversized chopper. I was excessively polite, thanking my new customer as I looked at the shiny new coin in my hand. I walked back down the garden path, carefully closing the front gate, and realizing I had forgotten to ask if another sack would be required next Saturday. It didn't matter, I was going to call anyway. The name of the road and the number were written in a notebook, which I had in my pocket for the very purpose. 'One sack' was noted alongside the number of the house. The book would be consulted many times in the coming months; I called it my 'round book', and it would be the key to wealth in my new business.

Encouraged, I went to the next house and the next and worked my way along the road. It was not difficult to find ten people who said 'yes', so, very soon I had no more wood, but I did have ten shillings in my pocket. One person had offered me two shillings for a sack but I had insisted the price was only one. I was not offended by his offer and he was not offended by my refusal. We parted on excellent terms and I had remembered to ask if he would like another sack next Saturday, he said he would, so I reckoned I had found another good customer. When I got home, I handed my takings over to Nan with great pride. She took it eagerly, it would allay some of her worries about the bills that would be arriving at that time of year with the winter coming on.

It was difficult to get on with ordinary chores that Saturday afternoon, I was still excited about my success of the morning. My mind raced on about ways in which I could improve my new business. It was clear that I could make more than one trip to the Garden City.

The problem was finding enough time to chop more wood. I had spent quite a long while going to the factory to collect the waste wood and I could only bring home relatively small amounts. I decided to explore the possibility of having some delivered.

At the factory, they said they would bring a lorry load for five pounds. To me, that was a lot of money; it was equal to the weekly wage of the average adult worker of those days. I told Nan about it and about my fear of risking our money. She recited one of her many sayings, 'You've gotta speculate before you can accumulate.' That was her way of encouraging me to try a load. Any scheme that sounded as if it might result in a profit would be financed from Nan's reserve, and the morning's 'ten bob' was proof enough on that occasion.

I came home from school one day to find a mountain of scrap wood on the road in front of our house. I moved wheelbarrow loads down our alley, through the backyard and half way down our seventy-yard garden to a shed that seemed to be the centre of my existence through my school days and a little beyond. For a garden shed, it was very large, it took hours to clear the road of wood and it was dark as the last barrow loads were squeezed in, filling every corner, floor to ceiling. As soon as I got home from school each day, chopping and bagging would begin. Not having to collect the wood made it possible to fill many more sacks, giving me great encouragement.

Over the coming weeks, with more sacks of wood available, I was able to knock on more doors and expand my Saturday round. I was soon making three trips and delivering thirty sacks. Once a customer had bought a sack, they were keen to have another the next week. I rarely carried one up a garden path and had to carry it back. Several people told me they liked my wood because it had raggedy ends and caught alight easily. 'Kindling from the shop', they told me, had square-cut ends that were difficult to get burning. I accepted the compliment but did not confess that when I watched 'professionals' cutting wood on a circular saw I longed to be able to do the job as quickly and as easily – square ends or not.

Knowing my 'product' had its superior features made me content to continue subduing the waste wood, which seemed to come in ever greater varieties of shapes and sizes as I worked my way deeper into my stock towards the back of the shed. Nan's heavy chopper, I found, had its benefits, as my arm gained strength to take advantage of them. I worked on happily through the winter and enjoyed the fruits of my labours. I was proud to add thirty shillings each week to Nan's pension of ten and to see her less worried. We had our house to ourselves, which meant that I could have my own little back bedroom again, and I was sent 'up' to Mr Ellis, the butcher, more frequently for 'two of them sixpenny chops' – special price or black market I never asked, but just enjoyed them.

It had been exciting thinking up my firewood business, bringing it into being, building it up and running it, but now my stock of scrap wood had been cleared almost to the last piece and I was again bringing home loads behind my bike as I had done in the beginning. Having to collect wood made it difficult to keep up the thirty-sack round. It seemed that the time had arrived to make a decision, either to have another delivery of wood or begin to run the business down.

Recently, my friend Linstan, from next door, had begun to take a great interest in my wood business. Previously, he had wanted to play in the garden, becoming impatient with me for preferring to continue my work. Lately, he was content to sit and talk as I chopped and filled sacks. I told him I was thinking of having a change, and he spoke of his discontent with his newspaper round, having to get up so early for such a small reward. He had gathered, little by little, that my business was profitable and was obviously giving serious thought to trying something similar himself.

At first, I could not imagine that Linstan would be capable of knocking on doors and canvassing for customers; he was not the sort of boy fitted to the coarseness of that kind of life. Besides, his school demanded homework, which would surely keep him busy most evenings. He was slightly built, a little timid and a highly intelligent lad, far more suited to the academic world of his teacher parents, and, no doubt, to their desires for him. Nevertheless, he persisted in questioning me and finally convincing me that he would not be put off. He had come to the conclusion that it would be his choice to have a business that was already set up, and if I was really going to give-up he would like to buy my business. In very formal terms he said that the only thing that remained was how much would I want to let him take over, 'lock, stock and barrel'. I do not think he understood the full meaning of the last phrase, any more than I did, but he added it for affect anyway.

That I could sell my firewood round quite took me by surprise; there was nothing I could imagine that could have any value. There were no premises or equipment. I was not even going to part with the cart that I pulled behind my bicycle. Linstan would not want our old chopper, he had one of those curvy pretty axes that I coveted so. But, of course, the value was in the 'connection'. I had heard, many times, conversations about the value of a well-established business, a good round or a shop that had a respected trading record. Linstan's question had drawn my attention to the fact that my firewood round was a 'business', with all the features that had worth. I began to feel pleased with myself, I told myself that, after all, I had built it up from nothing and it was successful. The investment of five pounds had been paid back to Nan over and over again. I had not given up, had I done so and neglected my customers, we would have been left with an unusable shed stuffed full with enough wood to light our fires for years to come. If Linstan wanted to buy my ready-to-go well-run business with loyal customers, carefully selected over the past months, I decided it must be worth at least one week's takings. I would ask him for thirty shillings. On his next visit to sit with me, it was clear he had remained firm in his resolve. I told him the price. He raided his savings, and our deal was done.

In the following days, free of my afternoon work and a little at a loose-end for the moment, I would hear, from over the fence, the sound of chopping. Usually, the period was brief and followed by the sound of voices, Linstan sounding somewhat under pressure; his parents a little louder than usual. A few ominously silent days went by when one afternoon there was a definite knocking on our back gate. I hurried to open it to find Linstan's mother standing there, with a fierce look on her face. Her arm was thrust out in front of her with my round book in her hand. In no uncertain terms, she was demanding the return of her son's thirty shillings.

I ran indoors to ask for the money and returned to hand it over with the least possible delay. I had never seen Linstan's mother look so severe; usually, she was so pleasant to me and so gentle and loving with Linstan that I felt a longing for her kind of softness that I did not understand. On that day, she took the money and, with only a terse thank you in my direction, she pulled her son away homeward.

With the round book back in my possession, I considered I might as well continue my wood business. I had lost a week and had to make a lot of apologies, but my excellent product was in demand so I was soon forgiven. My brief holiday had given me fresh interest and energy, but having to collect wood again had made the larger round a lot more work and difficult to keep up, so I was pleased when the spring came and business tailed off quite naturally. My little red book was put away for the time being and could be called upon next winter. If not used, the information enclosed would become out of date but the experience and knowledge I had gained would remain and give me the confidence to know that, at anytime it became necessary, I could help Nan maintain her independence and the self-sufficient status that she was so proud of.

Chapter 16

A BRIEF HOBBY

While practical activities, with a useful outcome, could be enjoyable and give great satisfaction, I was becoming aware that, perhaps, I should have an interest that was for pleasure alone. I was seduced into trying one particular 'hobby' by a booklet which I had purchased from Mr England's corn shop. There was, in the shop, a display of small books, which I would look through whenever I was sent to buy animal feed or bedding. They were attractive to me because they dealt with subjects familiar to me and were extra appealing as they did not have too many pages to overtax my unpractised reading skills. The titles clearly informed the potential reader of what was to be found inside: 'HOW TO KEEP' was in bold print on each booklet and each dealt with a different animal. I had passed over 'pond fish', as I had no interest in them. I already had the book on rabbits and the one on chickens, which I would read and re-read. Day to day work with the animals helped me understand each reading more deeply. Sometime previously, I had purchased the book on goats and dipped into it many times, resulting in a longing to have a goat, but there was little chance of that, so the idea had to be shelved for the time being. The subject that took my attention on this occasion was homing pigeons, so I bought the booklet. Everything I needed to know was in that little book, from building the loft to caring for the birds and winning races.

I decided to get started straight away, so I went down to the woodpile to find the wood, straightened the nails, bought a roll of tarred felt from the ironmongers, and soon my loft was up. The 'up' was my first error. I had built my loft high, as the booklet instructed, to be visible and easily found by the tired birds arriving home. Unfortunately, it was also clearly visible to the neighbours, who found my craftsmanship less attractive than I did and hoped my pigeons would. My second mistake was to brace my construction by attaching it to a strong fence-post newly erected by Linstan's parents next door

A Brief Hobby

who were such nice people and so pleasant in their manner, that their gentle expression of disapproval failed to register in the mind of a common knave, so my building programme went on unhindered.

Two birds had already been lined up. They belonged to a friend at school whose dad had told him to get rid of them. My friend agreed to swap them for a dirt-track bike, which I had made up from a frame swapped for a catapult and from wheels that had cost me a boat with an electric motor. The pigeons were said to be pure-bred German racing birds; one was blue and one was pink. They were big healthy-looking birds, and so elegant and pleasing to look at as they strutted around my loft.

After a trip to Mr England's corn shop and a few days good feeding, Nan said, 'With all that good grub inside 'em, they ought to know where they're well-off, so it should be safe to let 'em out by now.' I could not wait to see them on their first flight, so I let them out. My worry that they would not return kept me watching them but I was reassured as they remained in view, keeping their flying circle small and close to home. Linstan's mother came out into her garden and took in her washing; she must have been in a hurry that day, as she seemed to rush and did not have time to speak to me.

After school each day, I let my pigeons out for their fly round. While they were flying, I attended to the loft; cleaning it out and putting in fresh food and water. They seemed content with half an hour or so exercise and would then return to the loft and its comforts. Soon, I thought they should be trusted to go further afield. I feared they might get lost but that was a risk that had to be taken, after all, the book said they could find their way home from hundreds of miles away.

I found a strong cardboard box that fitted onto the back of my bike, and made air-holes all around it. The pigeons were becoming tame by that time so I caught them easily and held them (as I had learned from the booklet) before slipping them into the box without ruffling a feather, which they would need in the best possible condition for their speedy flight home. At first I took them only as far as our local recreation ground, then a mile or two more until, on one trip, I went over the border into Buckinghamshire; I was thrilled that my pigeons returned home from the next county and that whether they were released near or far, they always arrived home before me.

One Monday dinnertime, I came home from school in the usual way at midday. Monday was washday, so our backyard was full of laundry equipment. The electric copper stood under the open scullery window, several baths of rinse water were along one side and at the far end an ancient mangle, with large wooden rollers, stood waiting. Nan would have spent the morning lifting boiled clothes from the copper into the first bath of rinse water, on a broom handle worn to half its length by long service in the task. After stirring, the part rinsed wash would be moved to the next bath of clean water and on along the row of baths, finally being left to await the mangle as soon as I was home to turn the handle.

Washday dinner was always the same: left-overs from Sunday fried up into a delicious bubble and squeak. It was always ready as I arrived home and eaten without delay, as there was much to do before I went back to school. Nan would feed the clothes into the mangle saying, 'Faster, faster,' until she almost caught her fingers in the rollers, and then she would say, 'Slower, slower.'

On one particular Monday, Nan seemed worried. I asked her what was the matter. 'Oh, Mrs Howe has been round,' she said. As it was washday, I assumed that the 'Reckitt's Blue war' was continuing. Mrs Howe was proud of the whiteness of her wash and had upset Nan on more than one occasion by telling her that she should not use Reckitt's Blue because it made our wash look 'grey'. But Nan could not give up a lifelong habit learned from the 'gentry' she had worked for, so, to compete with Mrs Howe, she would boil her wash for longer, reducing underclothes to shreds while the electric copper bubbled and bounced and threatened to electrocute us all.

On that particular day, Mrs Howe's visit was about the whiteness of her own wash. She had left instructions that I was not to let my pigeons out until she had got her washing dry and back indoors. Her problems of recent weeks, she was convinced, were caused by my birds. Linstan's mother had had the same trouble, and possibly Mrs

A Brief Hobby

Howe's neighbour on the other side. Nan looked so worried, as if she thought the whole street was going to rise up against her.

It was not many days later that I came home from school to find my pigeon loft empty. I rushed indoors, saying, 'My pigeons have gone.'

'I let 'em out,' said Nan in a dull monotone.

'Oh, that's all right, they'll be back,' I said, and returned to the garden to search the sky. They usually flew over frequently but today there was no sign of them. I went back indoors wondering why.

Nan knew they were not coming back. She could not pretend otherwise, so she blurted out the truth. 'I got Fred to come round and wring their necks,' she said, quickly defending her action by listing the neighbours who had complained.

I was shocked. I ran out to look in the empty loft. Poor birds; this morning they were there and now they are gone, life and death so close. My feelings confused me. I did not feel like that when a rabbit was killed, why are pigeons different? Briefly, I was thinking like a schoolboy; they were my pets, my hobby. I wanted them for their beauty and for an interest in something that was just for pleasure. I remembered how my friend at school had buried his hamster with ceremony, marking the grave with a large white stone. Should I do the same for my pigeons? But where were they? What had Uncle Fred done with them?

My thoughts turned to Nan's worries, it seemed that upsetting the neighbours was a serious matter. I promised myself I would be more careful in future. My practical side took over my reasoning; the pigeons did, after all, need a lot of attention, I was never going to be keen enough to join a club so they would never race, and if I took the loft down, it would please the neighbours, and it would make a great rabbit hutch.

The last thought convinced me that it was all for the best, and I hurried indoors for my dinner. A large soup plate of stew was put in front of me. I asked, 'What kind of stew is it, Nan?'

'Never you mind about that, just be glad you've got it. Mind the bones!'

Chapter 17

THE FISH SHOP

I had saved seven pounds in my Post Office account. While my earnings went to Nan towards our keep, I was allowed to keep money given to me for birthdays and Christmas, which was usually received by way of half-crown or five-shilling postal orders. I had made almost no withdrawal, having been drilled in the value of money and encouraged to save for the important thing I would one day need, and, of course, the rainy day that was always anticipated.

Nan suggested one day that it was about time I had a new bike. She said I looked silly on my old black one, that I had grown out of it a long time ago and now needed a bigger one. At the cycle shop in West Drayton, I found one I liked. It was a green racer with drop handlebars, cable brakes and thin racing tyres. Nan insisted I had a carrier. The only one the shop had was black and clumsy and looked out of place, but I had to have it. I was getting a new bike, so I did not argue.

I knew the bike had cost more than my seven pounds so, when I handed over my savings, I asked how much it was. 'Never you mind. Money and fair words,' said Nan, in one of her often-used dismissive phrases. I insisted, and she showed me the receipt for fourteen pounds, saying, 'You usually pay twice the amount you think you are going to,' – a warning I have often found to be true.

In a day or two, I was informed that I was going to have a chance to try out my racer. One of Nan's many acquaintances had a corgi puppy ready to leave the litter and Nan knew that her brother and his wife wanted a puppy of that breed. Brother Jim and his wife Nell owned a 'wet, dried and fried' fish shop in Bromley in Kent. I was going to deliver the puppy in a cardboard box secured firmly to the clumsy black carrier on the back of my bike. The fact that I was going to have to ride a dozen or so miles into London, cross the great conurbation and exit to the south-east a similar distance concerned

The Fish Shop

Nan not at all, whatever needed to be done she had confidence I could do it, all I had to do was use my common sense she assured me.

Uncle Fred was, of course, consulted and from memory he gave me a list of roads to ask for. I could not go wrong he said. I wrote the names in route order on a sheet of paper that I would take with me. Uxbridge Road to Shepherd's Bush. Holland Park Road to the Chelsea Embankment. Over Vauxhall Bridge to Kennington, on to Camberwell and Peckham Rye. Down the Old Kent Road to Deptford, on to New Cross, Lewisham, Catford and then to the more rural Downham and Bromley.

On the day of departure, the puppy was made comfortable in his cardboard box and I set off on roads familiar to me, only at Shepherd's Bush would I need to begin looking for names and asking the way. After the first few miles, in which I was excited about my new bicycle, the journey was uneventful, apart from the necessary extra mile or two required to circle great junctions to find my road and the need to cope with cobblestones and sunken tramlines with my thin racing tyres.

At Bromley, I was greeted as if I had ridden only from a couple of streets away by 'Uncle' Jim and 'Aunt' Nell, who could not hide their keenness to welcome their new puppy. I had time to look around. The corner shop was large with a white-marble display counter in the front window for fresh and smoked fish. A substantial frying range was situated at the back of the room with a high counter in front for serving. Behind the shop, private accommodation comprised a dining room and a sitting room, which seemed overfilled with large luxurious settees and armchairs, an oversized cocktail cabinet with glass doors displaying decorative glasses and varieties of alcoholic drinks. The centre piece of the room was a walnut cabinet, which, when folding doors at the front were opened wide, revealed an almost circular television screen about six inches across. One evening, we watched a Shakespeare play, in which the scene and our static point of viewing remained unchanged throughout. For moments at a time, we could see costumed actors through a grey fog that appeared to fill the room in which they performed. As the human images disappeared, Uncle Jim would apologize for the bad reception that night, assuring me it was much better usually.

At the back of the building was a kitchen, which opened onto an enclosed yard where fish and potatoes were stored and prepared. One-hundredweight hessian sacks of potatoes were stacked waiting to be washed and chipped in machines that stood nearby. Fish was kept in an icebox true to its name, literally a large wooden box with thick insulated sides into which fresh ice was added regularly. The atmosphere in the yard, the shop and even the luxuriously furnished living rooms was uniform; aromas of fish, fat, brine and woodsmoke hung everywhere, which in view of the business carried on was to be expected, and although strongly memorable, it was not offensive.

Soon, dinner was put on the table. I noticed we were not having fish. Aunt Nell was a large lady with a loud London accent. Uncle Jim was grey-haired and could have been a retired boxer; his nose was misshapen and seemed to be the reason for his particular way of speaking. Damage to his neck caused him to hold his head on one side, which when added to his short stature and a limp gave him the appearance of an actor playing a part-comic, part-sinister character. Any lack in his appearance was compensated for by his constant joking, teasing and laughing – mostly at his own witticisms.

After dinner, I was told that it had been arranged that I could stay a week or two to help out, as their employee had been called-up into the army. I was delighted that I would be learning what went on in a shop business of this kind. I had been to Billingsgate market and felt I knew something about it already. Uncle Jim led me out into the backyard, to one corner where a brick and concrete air-raid shelter had been built. Inside, empty fish boxes were stacked along one side. On the other was a bunk bed. While we stood in the confined space that intensified the smell of fish, he told me this was where I was to sleep. He watched my face to enjoy my reaction, and then burst into laughter, while Aunt Nell chastised him for teasing me, as she led me back into the house and upstairs to a comfortable little bedroom that was to be mine.

In the coming days, I learned how to do the jobs that I was to help with. One of the shop's specialities was their home-smoked haddock and whiting. The fish arrived fresh, and as complete as it had left the sea. I was given the job of heading and gutting, until I had filled a tub of brine with cleaned fish to overflowing. After a long soak, the fish would be 'threaded' onto iron rods, which would hold several on each. The loaded rods would be hung in the 'smoke hole' – a chimney-like brick-built cupboard that would hold three or four dozen fish when filled. Pure oak sawdust would be heaped in the centre of the floor and a fire lit with oak splinters, which burned only until the sawdust began to smoulder and fill the void with the smoke that would cure the fish.

In the mornings, I served customers with fresh cod or haddock or plaice or Dover sole or Scottish kippers or 'my own' smoked haddock and whiting. In the evenings, I scooped up chips adding them to a small, medium or large piece of cod or haddock or rock salmon (which is really dogfish made to sound more appetizing), shaking on salt and vinegar when required. One customer unnerved me by looking at me severely, perhaps wishing he was being served by the proprietor. He asked for a medium-sized piece of cod, which was tenpence, and fourpennith of chips. I almost caused a riot when I added tenpence and fourpence and asked for 'One and fourpence, please sir.' The aggrieved gentleman became quite excited, leaving me uncertain for the moment as to what had gone wrong, until Uncle Jim quelled the situation with his laughter, taking over my station and asking for 'one and tuppence'.

One sunny morning, Uncle Jim thought I could be helpful by taking the dog for a walk, saying that he and Aunt Nell were not so quick on their 'pins' these days and it was a job their employee usually did. The animal in question was, of course, not the corgi puppy, who was not too quick on his pins as yet and was, in any case, receiving the attention due to his 'royal' status – being so much like one of the Queen's own dogs and probably the reason for the corgis' popularity at that time. The dog requiring to be exercised was Patch, who lived in a kennel in the corner of the yard where he slept most of the day, and being turned loose at night to guard the premises, had taken on a nocturnal frame of mind. Patch was a bull terrier. Stocky, short-necked, broad-chested, fifty pounds of muscle and bone. He was friendly enough, especially when the prospect of a walk was in sight. In fact, when his lead was handed to me, his enthusiastic attention required me to regain my balance in order to return an affectionate stroke, which I hoped might establish some rapport before we left the security of the yard.

Out on the street, Patch appeared to know the route that I had been told to take. At first, he seemed to be acting normally for a dog in need of a walk; going ahead with commitment, his sensitive nose examining everything and anything. But, as he found fragrances to his liking, our pace increased. Gentle words of restraint made no difference, I simply had to stride out heavy-footed on the other end of the lead. I began to wonder about my suitability for the task; the employee who usually took Patch for his walk was a heavy-built eighteen-year-old, more man than boy – the army thought so anyway. My own meagre frame created quite a different weight ratio between animal and supposed controller.

Our walk continued at a speed slightly quicker than would have been my choice but otherwise without event, apart from the animal's occasional glance back at me with an eye that I was beginning to think looked quite evil. Patch was almost all white in colour, right down to his stubby tail. The patch that gave him his name was a large black area over his right eye and covering much of that side of his head. The 'evil' eye was his left; ice blue, surrounded by a porcelain white eyeball and accented by a pink eyelid set into an albino pelt of fine short hair. Our pace increased a little more, at the same time as a low-pitched growl came from Patch. His nose went to the ground and a scent that excited him took us faster still.

Shouting from a man and a woman some way ahead of us caused me to look in their direction to see that they were both holding onto the lead of a dog that, apart from minor variation in its marking, was Patch's double, and could even have passed as his twin. The joint effort of the two owners had brought their dog to a standstill and he could only bark viciously in our direction as his master called to me to get back. I dug in my heels, and shouted, 'Stop!' but scent, shouting and barking seemed to encourage Patch and he charged the twenty yards towards his 'opponent' while I hung on to the lead, trying to keep my feet on the ground and maintain my balance.

The two dogs met and were quickly locked in combat, both sinking vicious teeth into the other. I let go the lead and took a few steps back. The two owners let go of their dog's lead. The man rolled up the newspaper he was carrying and began to take his dog's side against Patch. When the paper was shredded, his wife handed him a stick. The stick had no effect, the two dogs continued entwined, snarling and biting, until a householder came with a large bucket of cold water, which he emptied with great accuracy on the wrestling canines. A momentary cessation of hostilities allowed the man and the woman to grab their dog's lead and pull the tiring bloodstained animal away. The resourceful householder managed to secure Patch's lead and pull the still-snarling dog back along the pavement towards the fish shop's yard. Patch's evil eye took on an even more sinister look, now peering out of a face reddened by blood from his left ear, which was more detached from his head than attached.

I shuddered to think what trouble I would be in, returning with the dog damaged so badly. After pounding on the yard gate, we were admitted, the neighbour saying, ''Ere 'are, Mr Poulton, it's your dog again.'

At the same time, Uncle Jim saying, 'Oh, Gord! 'E's bin at it again. Where did this 'appen?'

'Luckily, it was outside my house,' said the neighbour.

Uncle Jim looked at my worried face and, in his jovial way, told me I was not in trouble by appearing to have no difficulty making a joke of the affair, saying, as he winked at me, 'We usually get further than that.' He cursed at Patch as he returned him to his kennel corner, while the animal seemed unperturbed by his slightly less-than-symmetric drooping left ear, which had now ceased bleeding; he lapped up a full bowl of water while wagging his tail vigorously as if his morning had been most enjoyable. He settled to indulge himself in his daily routine of sleeping.

I was not asked again to take Patch for his daily walk but continued to help wherever I could be useful until I was told, one day, that a young man who had just finished his national service was coming to work at the shop and I was free to go home. My few belongings and some fish delicacies that Nan would like, packed in ice and lots of newspaper insulation, were loaded onto the clumsy carrier on the back of my bike and I set off to follow, in reverse route order, the names on my sheet of paper that would guide me back across London. I did not have to rush breakfast and was not late home for supper. I enjoyed seeing our long garden when I was sent down for a 'good handful' of parsley. The sauce it made was poured over generous portions of turbot, which I attacked with a good appetite while Nan extolled the delights of the particular fish and I told her of my adventures.

Chapter 18

JUST BILL

Willy Walker had turned out not to be a cartoon character after all, but a sensitive man who I quickly came to know as 'Uncle Bill'. His visits to see us at Otterfield Road continued over the coming years and were always pleasurable occasions. When I was older he suggested that the familial title of 'Uncle' should be left behind; it took a little while and a little practise but soon, without loss of respect for my senior friend, I could use his name with ease. Now, just Bill, he began to be a greater influence in my life, appearing infrequently, but usually promoting a new idea or an event that would be memorable. Some subjects, introduced in his enthusiastic way, would grow into an interest that would become my own and remain with me for all of my days.

On one occasion that I met Bill, he had a camera that was so different from anything I had ever seen. He looked like a professional photographer with the magnificent object suspended around his neck. He saw my fascination and immediately transferred the strap to my shoulders, saying that it was a Leica and the best miniature camera ever made.

As I nervously handled the Leica, Bill gave me some of the technical details that a photographer needed to have to operate such a precision instrument. Most I would not understand, but his patient explanation gave me at least an introduction to lens apertures and shutter speeds and the affects they would have on the finished picture. With my schoolboy approach, I was more impressed by the simple fact that such a camera could take thirty-six pictures on one loading of film, and that I had to lift it to my eye in the way I had only seen professionals do in films. Bill encouraged me to take a picture. After helping me to select the correct settings and giving me a few more words of advice, he left me to it. The picture I took was, of course, of Bill. He was an easy subject as, true to his nature, he was totally relaxed and leaning back in the perfect pose as he smoked a cigarette.

The result of my 'camerawork' I would not see until I next visited Bill at Masbro Road. For the day of my visit, he had made preparation and was keen to show me. A short walk was suggested, which took us only a few doors along to a closed-down photographic shop, he had a key and let us in. We passed through the front shop of bare shelves, dusty counters and empty cabinets and went through a door to a photographic darkroom, the first I had seen. Bill flicked on a switch and we were bathed in a red glow, which seemed to fill every corner of the room. He pointed out the various items of photographic equipment: enlargers and printing papers on a 'dry bench' along one side of the room, large trays of chemicals and other 'wet' equipment on another.

A roll of 35mm film had been developed and had been hung to dry. It contained the negative of the 'portrait' I had been allowed to take. I was shown how to cut and load the film into the enlarger, which, when switched on, projected a negative image onto a white baseboard. It was exciting to see our tiny negative producing such a large picture. The enlarger light was switched off while light-sensitive paper was put in place. I was allowed to turn on the enlarger light for the required number of seconds, which I counted on a darkroom clock. In my ignorance, I was disappointed that the 'exposure' had not made a picture. Bill chuckled at my reaction. He pointed to a dish of liquid. 'Put it in the developer,' he said, and I marvelled to see the blank paper slowly produce my photograph. I was given the credit for an excellent picture (probably more than I was due), as Bill pointed out all the elements necessary to make a good photograph - which he said had been achieved - words of encouragement that I would remember always.

It was at one of the Sunday afternoon visits that a day out was spoken of. Bill and Jeff were going by train to Goring and Streetly, which they said was a beautiful spot on the Thames. Their plan was to hire a rowing boat and glide down the river through the lovely scenery. They suggested that I might like to go with them, and then went on to enthuse about the outing: we would take a picnic and row on the river as it ran between beautiful meadows where animals grazed, right down to the water's edge. Both men glowed with anticipation as they described their vision.

My enthusiasm was not immediately engaged, as my only knowledge of the Thames was the dirty old river that I saw on my journeys into London. My disinterest was confusingly entangled with the feeling that I would find more satisfaction in staying at home and doing something more useful. However, while the two men talked, I took a moment to remind myself that, of late, I was becoming aware that many of my thoughts were not entirely my own and that I was feeling subject to guidance of an increasing strength. Perhaps I should take the opportunity to open myself to ideas outside of my enclosed environment. I was beginning to like Bill and to feel that I could learn from him. I decided to go with them if I could.

I knew that I would have to deal with Nan; she would make it clear that she did not want me to go and fill me with guilt because I was leaving her alone. Whether it was her loneliness or chores that would not be done, I never understood. There was no problem when I went to school or to do part-time work or an errand that may take hours, but an outing of this kind would be frowned upon and cause a very uncomfortable atmosphere. Although she had shown no disapproval in front of Bill and Jeff, I knew it was there and would remain until I got home. I cared for Nan's wishes, so the guilt was painful but something about such control did not seem right. I decided that I had to live my life and I learned to push the troubled feeling to the back of my mind while I was out, and ride out her sulks when I got home. I knew that matters quickly improved once I was busy again.

The day of the outing was a magnificent summer's day. I met Bill and Jeff at West Drayton railway station, as it had been planned, and we went together by train on this unusual journey. On the way, my companions pointed out features of interest, encouraging me to see things I would not have thought worthy of my attention and would have failed to notice without their enthusiasm. They revelled in the beauty of the countryside and freely shared their appreciation with me. At our planned destination, a rowing boat was hired for the afternoon. We were advised to row upstream, as coming back would be easier when we were tired. Jeff took the oarsman's position and Bill indicated that I should sit next to him in the stern, where he would steer holding the two ropes that controlled the rudder. To keep my interest, or simply because of his thoughtfulness, he said that I would be asked to take my turn at steering later and, for the moment, I should watch how it was done. I was more than happy to observe, as all that I was seeing was new to me: I saw how the boat was handled, and felt secure as the two men seemed to know what they were doing and worked together in a confident calmness. I had time to admire the boat; it had wicker-backed seats with large faded powder-blue cushions, which were so comfortable. The fineness of the craft was pointed out to me; the traditional clinker construction of the hull and the deep varnish finish, built up over many seasons of fresh coats, that gave a richness and feeling of luxury.

    Jeff rowed steadily for half an hour while Bill and I took turns with the rudder ropes. To give Jeff a rest, the two men carefully exchanged places, but Bill's handling of the oars caused more amusement than forward propulsion. Rower and helmsman decided to return to the positions for which they were best suited. Although the return move was undertaken with as much care as the first, laughter rocked the boat and had to be brought under control to avoid capsizing. After another period of rowing, Jeff declared, positively, that it was time for lunch and, shipping the oars, he lay back for a few moments on the comfortable pale-blue cushions as we drifted slowly towards the bank under overhanging willows. A rope was secured to a branch laying at water-level, and we were held, suspended in a paradise of the gently flowing river and dappled shade.

    A basket hamper, the size of a small suitcase, was pulled from under a seat and, while Jeff rested, Bill took out picnic glasses, filled them with fruit squash, cold from an iced container, and handed them round. Packets of carefully-made sandwiches with various fillings, wrapped in greaseproof paper, were decanted onto serving plates. Ready-prepared salad was presented in a bowl and fruit was displayed in a dish. As our picnic progressed, the wicker basket continued to produce delicacies both savoury and sweet until the luxuriously presented lunch was brought to a climax with coffee from a flask, which we sipped from small decorative cups.

After lunch, Jeff was happy to rest from rowing and laid back in well-fed comfort. Bill, who had been reclining so far that day, was content to continue as he had begun. Conversation was to be our after-lunch entertainment; it was to be light and for enjoyment. My knowledgeable companions avoided subjects which they considered might exclude me, but posed questions freely on matters upon which they knew I had experience. To overcome my taciturn nature, questions half answered were left open and manoeuvred gently in my direction. If my answer made good sense, it would be taken as the next step in the discussion, built upon and expanded. If I gave a less good opinion, there was no direct confrontation but an alternative point of view would be thoughtfully proposed. Thus these skilful protagonists carefully managed me, so that, as the afternoon went on, I became bolder and was venturing contributions to the conversation more easily.

As I gained confidence, I was more easily able to assess Bill the man. This enigmatic man, who I was growing to like so much, was no less fascinating in the light of a bright summer's day. In fact, the warmth of the season seemed to suit, so well, his swarthy lined face and crinkled black hair: this cosmopolitan Londoner who could have had Mediterranean or Jewish origins, I would never know. As I continued to observe him, Bill lay back totally at ease with his world, as he smoked another cigarette; completely relaxed except for eyes, alert and intelligent, that seemed to penetrate and understand all that they saw. There was none of the anxiety in Bill that I saw in many of those around me. He was so easy in his friendship with Jeff, who himself was an easy-going and likeable individual. They seemed to be pleasure seekers; they noticed everything that was joyful or of interest and they shared their enjoyment generously. On days such as that, I began to learn that life is not measured by practical achievement alone, and that man's soul has need of pleasure, beauty, comradeship, thought and conversation, to give meaning to it all.

On another occasion, Bill suggested that I might like to go with him and Jeff to that year's Motor Show at Earls Court. By now, he was well aware how possessive Nan was with me and had learned to charm her into letting me go with them. He was always extremely polite, calling her 'Aunt Carrie' in a most flattering manner that seemed to work and he got his way. As usual, I dealt with my guilt while away and kept busy to sweeten the atmosphere more quickly upon my return home.

At the show there were luxury cars, fast cars, big cars, even ostentatious cars, but I remember best the stand that introduced the new Morris Minor Traveller. The small estate car was modest, homely and appeared far more within the reach of the average person. It was eye-catching for the decorative woodwork on its outside, which gave it the appearance of a small version of the station wagons that we saw in American films. It was offered in a range of colours, at a time when Henry Ford's statement that customers could have any colour they wanted as long as it was black still held some truth – children played a game, competing to see the first coloured car as black ones passed by on main arterial roads out of London. The Traveller's presentation display itself was colourful and modern; it showed a family loading their picnic into the car. It promised such pleasure, and for just a moment I wished I could be the boy in this cheerful scene; the mother and father were young, they looked so loving, and happiness shone out from the life-size artist's impression.

It had been arranged that I would stay with Bill that night. First, we had to call at the 'village shops' for some food to take home. Near to Masbro Road there was a post office, grocer's, butcher's, greengrocer's and a public house providing most things needed for day to day existence. Bill was keen to explain to me that London was no more than a group of villages. He said that he knew people who spent most of their lives in an area between their home, their place of work and these shops, just as would have happened in a country village for many years past.

At Bill's flat, a camp bed had already been set up in his sitting room. After some supper, I was keen to try it out and, being a boy who liked his sleep, I remember nothing of the night; the temporary, slightly unstable, bed having no ability to disturb my slumbers, I slept soundly until well into the morning.

I woke to the sounds of, what I would then have called, 'classical music'. By the time I appeared, Bill was in his kitchen, which overlooked the small walled gardens and the backs of houses in the next street. As I wandered in, still bleary-eyed, he pointed to a large mug of tea, which he had poured for me as soon as he heard me moving. 'Have you been up long?' I asked, fearing I had inconvenienced him by keeping him waiting to begin his day.

'Long enough to hear a couple of symphonies and smoke a packet of Player's,' he said in a cheerful voice, which managed to convince me that he was happy to have done so, settling my concern that I might have been inconsiderate. 'Do you like music?' he asked.

'Yes,' I said adding nothing more, wishing to hide my lack of knowledge. He had, after all, just listened to two symphonies and I was not sure what symphonies were.

'What kind of music do you like?' said Bill, working hard to get the conversation going.

Not really knowing any music, I said, 'Oh, what comes on the radio, sometimes that's nice.' I searched my thoughts for anything I could name. Giving up, I said, 'I like the music that goes with films too. Nan likes to go to the pictures on Saturdays and I go with her. Some films have lovely music. I like lots of violins the most, sometimes it's sad and I like that too,' 'sad' being the best description I could come up with but probably meaning emotional or romantic.

We moved, with our tea, to his sitting room. 'Have you ever heard this in a film?' said Bill, putting a record on an old radiogram. 'This is Tchaikovsky, it's been used in a lot of films,' he explained. We listened as we drank our tea. He could see that my reaction was favourable so, concluding he had made a good choice, my breakfast of toast and more tea was accompanied by another equally beautiful piece of music, also carefully selected to suit my novice's ear.

After breakfast, Bill closed down the lid of the radiogram with a deliberateness that said I was free to escape the music and his talk of

139

it, if I chose. He washed our cups and plates. I dutifully stepped-up to dry them while he talked generally about plans for the day. I could leave whenever I thought I ought to get home, or we could walk in the fresh air at one of London's open spaces or through the market, stopping at a coffee shop where we could observe life and its participants. We looked out of the window at a leaden sky, which appeared it might produce rain at any moment, and Bill added that we could listen to some more music if I wanted to. Still under the spell of what we had heard, I failed a direct answer, instead asking if the music we had been listening to was his favourite. I confessed that I was not really sure what a symphony was. I went on to admit that I did not know the name of any music, adding that I liked what he had played and would like to know more about it.

Bill calculated from my garbled response that it was my wish to stay and talk. He began by saying I should not worry about the things I did not know but I should simply enjoy listening to music and the sensations it gave me. He went on to explain that a symphony needed to be listened to all the way through to be understood. Even then, it needed to be heard several times to be properly appreciated. To think that Bill needed to hear a symphony several times gave me encouragement; I could listen and enjoy without expecting so much of myself. We spent our morning listening to music and talking about it. It was clear that Bill favoured romantic music and the Russian composers, who he said 'wore their heart on their sleeve' and were not afraid to show their passion. I left that day with a certainty that Tchaikovsky was my favourite composer too, and knowing a little more about Bill into the bargain.

Throughout my schoolboy years, Bill continued to appear occasionally on Sunday afternoon visits to see 'Aunt Carrie'. Usually he would manage to draw me into a conversation that would introduce some new idea to me. Although his influence was spasmodic, it would be strongly influential on the adult I would become. I shall always remember him as a source of goodness; as someone who enriched my life and showed me the way to better things. Growing up, of course, changes us and, as I went out to make my own way in the world, contact with Bill was gradually lost. It was not until the uncertainties of my own middle years caused me to have need of my roots that I decided to seek out the font from which so much wisdom had sprung so many years before.

On a day of impulse, I found myself at Shepherd's Bush. I drove along streets I had walked before. I remembered, on that visit so long ago, the houses drab and soot-bound, streets empty except for tradesman calling and children playing. Despite the dreary facades, there had been a calmness in the uniformity of the terrace rows, each house with its low brick wall containing a small oasis of garden, brightly polished windows and doorsteps whitened as if in defiance of the London wartime grime. Now, there was a feeling of chaotic rush and agitation. There was no room for children to play; vehicles of all varieties were parked along the pavement's edge. Many of the low walls had been demolished, to produce a cavity in which yet another means of transport could be corralled. Occupants over the years had succeeded where bombs had failed; no house remained intact, with walls breached to provide for the needs of the modern world, an extra room added without regard to aesthetics, or an adornment to claim individuality, over ornate and without taste.

Masbro Road seemed shorter than I remembered. As I walked along, I could see that my memory was not playing tricks, there were, in fact, fewer houses; number twelve and the neglected photography shop at number six were gone. The last dwelling in the terraced row now was numbered twenty. It edged onto a wide paved area that crossed the ends of the mutilated streets and ran beside a new urban freeway, upon which traffic was speeding. Shocked, I walked from the shade of the street out into the afternoon sun that flooded across the new highway. I stopped at the chest-high railings that separated pedestrians from vehicles and stood for a few moments letting the warmth of the sun calm my agitation. I shaded my eyes and counted from the last standing house to a place part-way across the gash in the residential landscape, as I tried to imagine where the scenes of my memories might have taken place.

I allowed myself a few emotional moments as I thought of times spent with Bill. The music he had played to me filled my head, as I remembered boating and picnics and conversations, the subjects he had introduced to me that were new and exciting then and held my fascination still. Suddenly, the folly of my belated sojourn struck me. It was too late: why had I not come this way long before? I condemned myself for neglecting the friend who had made such an impression upon my early years. I reviled myself for acting only then, in my own troubled middle-years, at a time of my own selfish need. I regretted my foolishness in trying to visit a past that had gone forever. My errors could not be put right, I would remember them for all my years.

    A news vendor thrust an afternoon paper at me. In my distraction, I had stumbled into him. I said, 'No thank you,' just managing, 'Sorry,' which I repeated. The incident jarred me awake. The day was cooling. I had a long drive. I hurried away, carrying my regrets and more happy memories than, at that moment, I felt I deserved.

Chapter 19

CHARLIE RICKETTS

Charlie Ricketts held a strange fascination for me. He had been to America. He had worked his passage there on a cargo ship. He wore jeans, when no one else wore jeans. Despite his age, which must have been forty (which was old to me then), he was slim and strong and his blond hair contrasted with his rugged lined face, which, because of his outdoor work, was always tanned. He never spoke to me of his time in America but, as my only knowledge of the country came from cowboy films, I fanaticized about the jobs he might have done in the 'wild west'. When I saw the Hollywood actor Randolph Scott, I found it difficult not to think that he looked like Charlie, or Charlie looked like him.

The object of my grand illusion was, in fact, very different from the Hollywood star. Charlie's tan did not come from the California sunshine and, although he still had the jeans, his Stetson hat and cowboy boots had been left behind a long time ago – if he ever had any. Charlie, in contrast to his glamorous look-alike, was a window cleaner. He lived in an unkempt, rented flat above a local fish and chip shop. Being a purpose-built apartment, its atmosphere contained only the slightest hint of the trade carried on below, regardless that the establishment, which produced Britain's traditional 'fast food', had a bad name for hygiene. The proprietor who rolled his own cigarettes and smoked them as he prepared fish or potatoes for frying, had a careless habit of letting one, half smoked, drop from his lips. After the appropriate time in the deep-fat fryer and served up in a portion of chips, the foreign object was difficult to distinguish from the genuine article! The health inspector was a regular visitor to the shop and it was well known, by way of local gossip, that he had issued frequent 'last warnings'.

Charlie had suggested I might like to work with him and, as I had had successful dealings with him over several years past, I was happy at the prospect. Previously, I had printed 'business' cards for him to drop through his customers' letterboxes to tell them he had cleaned their windows in their absence from home. I thought it odd that he needed to tell his customers that their windows were now clean, but he explained that it was to prepare them for his visit that evening to collect his payment. When he saw a John Bull printing set that I had been given for Christmas, he said I could save him valuable time having to write notes if I printed them for him. I had already been teased by everyone saying I could now 'go into the printing business' and the tease seemed to have come true.

The set I had been given was the smallest of the range with just enough letters for a simple message, so Charlie's suggested words had to be reduced in number. I worked out an alternative that conveyed his message adequately, I thought, and trusted that he would approve. Rubber letters had to be cut from a strip and set individually into a holder. My first attempt held a surprise, which was not revealed until the trial print. The text, quite readable in the holder, took on an oriental appearance, reading from right to left on paper. After conquering the art of back to front print-setting, and giving attention to missing characters, which required tiny pieces of folded newspaper as padding to correct the inconsistency in the thickness of the rubber letters, a successful 'communiqué' was printed.

I bought all the packets of plain white postcards that Mary's Sweet Shop had in stock and began to cut them into four pieces with a large pair of what Nan called her 'dressmaking' scissors. The useful implements were brought out many times to cope with a wide variety of tasks and nothing was considered beyond their capability, but I had never seen them used for dressmaking. In my haste to produce a hundred cards, I managed to exceed the previously known limits of the trusty shears by cutting too many cards at a time, causing overload and a resulting untrue finish.

On each card, I began printing 'WINDOW CLEANER CALLED TODAY THANK YOU'. At first, I thought I could stamp the cards rapidly, as I had seen them do in the Post Office, but found that each application of my stamp would have to be held in place with firm pressure on the centre and then all four corners in order to produce each letter clearly. Aching fingers had to be dealt with frequently.

When the first batch was presented to Charlie, he was delighted. He understood the need for brevity and said that each card would say all that he wanted. He did not mind that the backs contained part of a word put there by the manufacturer of the postcards, or that my cutting lacked the squareness and precision of a machine-cut business card. Charlie paid me handsomely for my customized product and went away happy, leaving me equally content.

The John Bull printing set was never used for any of my childhood games, but, as an educational toy, I considered that it had done its job; I had learnt the tiniest amount of the printer's art and a little business management. The set was put on one side until Charlie placed an order for another hundred cards, which he did from time to time.

On the day of my visit to his flat, I was considering working with Charlie on his window-cleaning round and he wanted to explain what would be required of me. All he had to show me, by way of equipment, was a rusty trailer that he pulled behind his bike, two extending ladders and two short ladders with pointed tops designed to rest on window frames. All the cleaning, he explained, was done with a chamois leather and a piece of scrim, the latter being a coarsely-woven natural material – usually used by tailors as padding inside a garment, he explained. A square yard would be sufficient to make an excellent polishing cloth, once it had been put through a long process of boiling, beating, washing and boiling again. The final product would be a much-prized tool of the trade.

Charlie had several part-time helpers, he told me; a postman, a baker's roundsman and a milkman, who all had early starts and free afternoons, which was when they worked with him. None of them wanted to work on Saturdays, so he was now considering a schoolboy and wanted to give me a tryout. We came to an agreement, so on the very next Saturday I rode my bike to Charlie's flat ready for work.

As we rode together, Charlie pulling the trailer loaded with ladders and buckets, he said we were going to make a start on an estate of ordinary private houses, which would be the easiest for my training.

We leaned our bikes against the kerb and Charlie rung out leathers and a scrim, leaving an amount of moisture that he said was just right for our purpose. He then cleaned a window to show me how it was done. He left me to carry on while he took an extending ladder and began cleaning the upstairs windows. Each time he came down to move his ladder, he checked my work. After a while, he said there was no need to check anymore. We continued on, house to house, around the estate. During the day, Charlie had made up his mind that he was going to take me on, on the same terms as his adult helpers. I was flattered to be treated like the adults and he could see my pleasure, so he went on to tell me that I could work as hard as any of his part-timers and had kept going longer than some.

After trying me out on some upstairs windows, Charlie saw that I could handle an extending ladder, and that I was aware of the dangers of its length and the need for care in balancing, 'a firm grip on the concept of spacial awareness' an academic might have described my new-found skill. 'You can do some of the upstairs now,' he said, and from that day on we would take a house each. I could keep up with him as we worked our way along a row. When Charlie came to my house and cleaned the last window or two, it was proof of the superior stamina of his mature and hardened muscles, for which even my youthful elasticity and enthusiasm were no match.

On some Saturdays, especially if rain was in the air, we would clean shop windows on West Drayton's Station Road. Householders did not like their windows being dirtied by rain immediately after they had been cleaned but shopkeepers did not mind, Charlie explained. Many shops, before modernization, still had coloured leaded glass around the top of their windows and, at infrequent intervals, it would be necessary to clean inside. To get to the leaded panes required climbing onto a shelf created by the window display cabinet, laying on one side and squeezing between shelf and ceiling. Being lightweight and slender, I was built for the task, and Charlie, with careful planning, managed to arrange that the 'infrequent intervals' fell on a Saturday. Most shelves had an inch of dust, impregnated with a great variety of dead insects. I was not keen to roll in the dust but it was part of the job, and I did learn a little entomology when I found out that the six-legged arthropodal animal *Hymenoptera Vespula*, commonly known as the wasp, could still give a painful sting even when it was dead. 'That's how you learn', said Nan, as she got out the green oils that cured everything.

One Saturday, Charlie said we were going to try something more interesting, explaining that he had some large houses on his round and was having difficulty in getting part-timers to help with some of the windows that were not easy to get to. At our first stop, Charlie selected the longer of his two extending ladders, which he needed to cope with the greater dimensions of this superior house. He told me to take his usual extending ladder, as it would be needed even for the downstairs windows. I had to push through established evergreen garden shrubs to get to the large sash windows. Many panes seemed to be as old as the house, the antique glass having a superior clarity and brightness that was satisfying to bring back to life.

When we had cleaned all that we could see, Charlie said, 'Come on, let's tackle some of the awkward ones.' He placed his long ladder against a parapet, which required full extension to reach. He took my ladder and carried it up to the parapet. Once erected, it reached to a third-storey window. He called me up, adding, 'Just a leather and scrim.' I climbed up and stood next to him. 'I'll hold the ladder,' he said, 'you'll be quite safe.' I trusted him and went up, leather in hand and the corner of the scrim tucked into my back pocket. The window was latticed and had obviously not been cleaned for some time. At the top of the firmly-held ladder I was well within reach of my 'quarry', so had no difficulty in removing the weeks, or months, of grime. I carefully dropped the spent leather onto the wide, parapet wall and as I turned my body to reach for the scrim, which was still hanging from my back pocket, the ladder began to twist with me, causing a momentary loss of balance and a word of caution from Charlie down below. I had no fear of heights but quickly learned to have respect for them and, in future, to put my arm around my back and find the scrim without moving my body's weight on the rung of the ladder.

Once my work was done, I took a moment to look across the

rooftops. From the lofty pinnacle of that grand house, I could see other elegant houses, all individual in style, interspersed by mature, comfortable cottages from varying ages past. Most within my view, edged the ancient West Drayton Green, a scene as attractive as any I had realized existed in the area that was my home. For a moment, my thoughts turned away from the ugliness that I saw in so many parts of the county of my birth, where the outward sprawl of London had covered the poppied cornfields and the green meadows of days gone by, and where the insatiable demand for building materials had brought about the ravaging of the rural idyll it had once been.

For just a moment, I had the glimmerings of questions I would ask myself in years to come. Was the environment of my schoolboy rovings responsible for the modest self-perception I had developed? Would my inward view have been kinder had I been the product of a fairytale landscape or if the educators had taught me something of the rich history of the joint villages of my birth? Would I, perhaps, have felt some pride in my home and, indirectly, in myself? But I was unaware that queens, emperors, philosophers, writers, poets, playwrights and actors had been entertained in the grand houses that, at that moment, were under my gaze. I did not know that intellectuals, artists and creative people had chosen to live in this 'centre of culture', as it had once been known, here in the comfort of the countryside so conveniently near to London. I knew nothing of those things; at school it was a closed book, at home it was of no relevance to those busy with matters of immediate need, as on that day I was too, and the grand houses all around me, simply a means of earning my keep. 'Come on,' said Charlie, and we descended carefully, took down our ladders, retreated down the drive and respectfully closed the gate behind us.

I continued working with Charlie for several months more. The cowboy of my childhood fantasy was gradually left behind as a mature friendship grew up between us. Charlie paid me the compliment of suggesting a fully adult arrangement if I would consider working with him once I finished with school. He was not offended by my clumsy rejection and, being a man with an eye to his business, he made sure that any work that needed the attention of us both was tackled and dealt with on the last few Saturdays I spent with him. We parted on the best of terms, Charlie knowing that his work was up to date and his customers satisfied, and me feeling that I knew all about window cleaning and had worked my way to the very top of the ladder in that particular business.

Chapter 20

ARTHUR

Colham Avenue was an unusually wide thoroughfare just a hundred yards from Otterfield Road. Although far apart, the houses on both sides had similarities, being of a more genteel appearance than those in neighbouring streets. Most were modest cottages from a previous era, well maintained and much loved it would seem. The expanse between the houses was furnished with a road on either side of a broad grassed area, which ran the full length of the avenue. Two rows of trees, beech and chestnut mixed, flanked the grassed strip, giving a grandeur in contrast to the modesty of the dwellings.

By its name, the avenue gave no indication of its history or reason why the houses had been built at such a distance from their opposite numbers. In fact, the grassed area that formed the centre piece was once a canal. It was a branch of the Grand Union Canal, and was known as Otter Dock. It was 'cut' about 1876 to connect the brick works of Yiewsley, Hillingdon and Stockley with the main waterway. It is recorded that about five million bricks a year were moulded, fired and transported by barge to Paddington via this seemingly humble canal arm. Much of London was built with the grey-brown bricks from this district. The last brickfield closed in 1935. By that time, Otter Dock had already been filled in and the trees planted to form Colham Avenue.

Mainly older people lived in the avenue and several had dealt with Nan for many years. I would be sent to deliver various items that had been purchased from her and collect payment. On Sundays in the winkle season, even an elderly person living alone would treat themselves to half a pint of winkles or cockles or shrimps to relive, if only the fading memory, the ritual they would have enjoyed with their families in past years. At Christmas they would want to contact old friends, and half-dozen of Nan's pre-printed greeting cards would be purchased. A few weeks earlier, I would have been sent to ask what message the customers wanted to have printed in their cards and to complete the form that Nan would post off to Jones, Williams & Company in one of the midland towns where the cards were produced.

On my way home, I would hear a piano playing in one of the smaller cottages. I stopped many times to listen to the sounds coming from inside and read the name of the music teacher on a brass plate on the outside wall. I had only rare contact with a piano, although we had one at home in our front room. Like many homes of the day, the best front room was only ever entered on special occasions. Ours could have been called a best 'front parlour' as it was truly Victorian in style, having large amounts of red velvet on cushions and curtains, and covering delicately made wooden-framed chairs, which had to be sat upon 'nicely' and were uncomfortable anyway. The fireplace, which had a surround of velvet-matching red-glazed tiles, was only used at Christmas – the only days of the winter when the room was not so cold as to need no 'out of bounds' sign. When an occasion allowed, I would play our piano, with one finger. I liked the sound, and could pick out a few notes of a tune called 'The Dream of Olwyn', which was popular at the time. At carefully selected moments, I would talk about the teacher in Colham Avenue, telling how I had stopped and listened, and say, in the vaguest ways, how I wished I could have piano lessons. But I knew that such things were outside the understanding of our family, and my direct question was never asked, or if begun faded in the making, and the lack of response accepted.

It was on the wide green of Colham Avenue that I first remember noticing Arthur, who would later become my friend. I had joined a group of boys playing there. Soon, we were all riding imaginary horses; one hand out in front holding pretend reins, and making uneven gallops to represent horses' hooves. We were 'knights in armour' and Arthur was telling the story loudly as we trotted about. I was impressed by his knowledge of Lochinvar, Sir Galahad, King Arthur and Guinevere, and by his ability to direct us as we acted out his story. We were probably 'making a film', that would be about the style of Arthur's rich imagination.

I think it was Arthur's creative abilities that attracted me to him. My first impression of him was that he was certainly more artistic than athletic. I once asked him if he would like to go swimming and he looked horrified at the thought. I was amazed that he would not want to on such a hot day. Swimming was a normal part of life for me; I lived only a few doors from Yiewsley Swimming Pool and would queue, waiting for it to open, on the first day of the season to complete my two-minute dip in the near-freezing water of the unheated outdoor pool. My friend and I were so different in many ways, but that did not hinder our sharing of interests that we did have in common.

Arthur had many skills that I did not have. Some impressed me, but left me aware of my own shyness and lack of confidence. From a young age, Arthur would be called out to the front of our class at school to tell a story. As he started to speak, he would snigger – in a way that I would remember always – as if he knew that the story he had just thought up was going to be funny. The whole class would be silent, paying full attention to the storyteller. Quite naturally, without nerves or hesitation, the story of 'Willy the Tiddler' would be told, and would go on with ever more invention until the teacher said, 'Thank you, Arthur, that's enough. Please sit down'.

I had an early lesson in 'love' from Arthur. One day, we were walking along Fairfield Road, between his house and mine. As we came to the sweet shop, he said he was going to get something. We went in, and he bought a couple of ounces of small sweets, Dolly Mixtures or a similar type. I thought they were a strange choice but it became clear when he tucked them into his pocket to take home saying they were for Ronnie, who at that time was about two or three years old. I would always remember the warmth in Arthur's voice as he spoke of his little brother. As a lone child, this expression of sibling love was new to me, and the revelation gave me a respect for my friend.

When we went to secondary school Arthur's house was on my way, and it was agreed I would call in for him so that we could walk to school together. I would go to the back door, which opened into the kitchen. Arthur would hastily be making toast, by laying a slice of bread directly onto the top of a gas cooker. The 'toast', when ready, would be as white as it came from the packet except for a dozen black holes burned into the bread in a perfect circle the exact size of the gas ring. He would spread the toast with National Margarine. Before the margarine was put away, he would rub a small amount into the palms of his hands and slick down his hair with it. His fair straight hair, now a little darker with the addition of the yellow edible concoction, would be combed directly back from his forehead ending well down the back of his neck in a precise line across. It gave him the appearance of an artist and was admired by all who knew him.

The only 'athletic' activity that Arthur and I ever shared was a surprise to both of us. Arthur's imagination was at work, as usual, when, for some reason unknown to me, he tied his left ankle to my right ankle. We put our arms round each other's shoulders and we walked, then ran. Our bodies and limbs seemed to be empathetic and running came as natural as if our legs were not tied at all. Whenever an opportunity arose, we practised our own special sport. We ran faster and seemed not to trip. We could start, go slow, go fast, stop suddenly and not fall. Mind and body were linked and in time.

One day, we were practising our new-found skill on the sports field of Evelyn's Secondary Modern School, which we were both attending. The PT teacher ran across the field and, between panting breaths, rebuked us severely for our foolishness. We could 'fall and break a leg' he said. He clearly did not want any accidents showing up on his record.

Arthur and I were astonished when the irate PT teacher came to us, a week or so later, in quite a different mood and asked us, in appealing tones, if he could put us down for the three-legged race to represent our school at an inter-school sports day. We cautiously said he could. We warmed to the idea in the coming days and now, having free range of the sports field, shackled ourselves together on every opportunity to take full advantage.

The sports day was a wonderful day for us both. We won by yards from our nearest rival while others fell by the wayside littering the whole length of the track, some not far from the starting line. Our school had not had many winners that year so we were hailed as heroes next day when results were announced in assembly, albeit with some condescending laughter from those who thought the three-legged race more comic than heroic. But then perhaps they had a point, we had not won a marathon or achieved the four-minute mile, it was just the three-legged race.

Arthur and I cemented our friendship that summer. Our matched physical capabilities gave us a feeling of closeness and comradeship. For my part, I would never have put myself forward to compete, so I was grateful to my artistic friend whose imagination had given us both something to remember. At school, we were in the same class and sat together when, one day, the headmaster entered the room with a man we did not know. They came over to our desk and asked Arthur to draw for them. First he drew a horse and then a footballer, both of which he did with ease, forming the outlines almost without taking his pencil from the paper. It was shortly after this that Arthur told me he was going to art school.

Although our paths had diverged we remained friends, keeping in touch at weekends at Arthur's house, which was near to Colham Avenue where I first joined his games. Arthur lived with his mother, father and two brothers. The family house was not beautiful outside, and the inside, at first glance, had no visible signs of luxury. Regardless of first impressions, or perhaps because of them, the house was filled with love, a relaxed almost unnoticing kind of love that allowed maximum freedom of spirit. The three boys grew up in an unfettered atmosphere with the solid foundation of caring parents who would not hinder but would be there when needed. They were free to create, and their creativity was encouraged by their parents' simple admiration and pride. All the boys could draw without effort. They drew, they painted, they re-designed their clothes, and they made music. No music was too loud or too late as far as their parents were concerned.

A room with a small serving hatch to the kitchen, which in other houses might have been called the dining room, was in Arthur's house known as the 'music room'. Through the hatch would come cups of tea or Camp coffee or, on special occasions, fizzy non-alcoholic drinks or, after closing time on a Saturday as their parents arrived home, bottles of Whiteway's sweet cider. The room was given over to the three boys and their friends. There was a shelf loaded with gramophone records, full of what I came to think of as wonderful music. All the classics of early jazz were there; the sounds of so many of the famous New Orleans players such as Kid Ory, George Lewis, Jack Teagarden, Bunk Johnson and, of course, Louis Armstrong. We compared the different sound of the Chicago-style of jazz, with players like Bix Beiderbecke, and were excited by the 'Hot Club' of France and the soprano sax playing of Sidney Bechet accompanied by the three-fingered guitarist Django Reinhardt.

Both Arthur and his brother Ted, who was two years younger, were very knowledgeable on the history of jazz. They talked of the early Negro bands who would not only improvise music but, because of poverty, improvise instruments too. So-called 'jug bands' not only included empty liquor jugs, which would act as resonators when blown into, but guitars made of cigar boxes, washboards for tapping out a rhythm, tea-chest basses, kazoos or comb and paper, and any real instrument that could be found.

Soon, we were wanting to try it all for ourselves. Arthur acquired a battered trombone. Ted had a side-drum and some sticks. Willy, a friend from school, had a banjo, which on many occasions even had a full set of strings. I made myself a bass out of a tea chest, a piece of nylon cord and a broom handle, with which I could produce a reasonable range of notes. Little Ron, aged four, provided good rhythm with brushes on a suitcase.

A knowledgeable musician was invited to hear us on one occasion, to give his opinion on our playing. He listened with a fixed grin that gave us no indication as to his feelings so, after our performance, we asked directly, putting him embarrassingly on the spot. He hesitated briefly, and then we understood the words 'very enthusiastic'. I always think of him when I hear that particularly ambiguous accolade. At the time, we took it as a compliment and continued our 'enthusiastic' playing with even more vigour than before. Our ambition was to play New Orleans jazz and we were convinced that one day we would play like the band in *Pete Kelly's Blues* or like Louis Armstrong in the film *High Society*, which we went as a group to see at our local cinema.

I enjoyed my attempts to copy the sounds of the double bass. My ear became attuned to the lower range of notes. Eventually, my desire to have a real instrument led me to explore the possibilities. The ambition was quickly abandoned when I found that the cost would be so far out of my reach. I looked around at other instruments that I might take-to and could afford. The decision was made for me one day when I saw a clarinet in a second-hand furniture shop. What I was doing peering into that particular window in the backstreets of Hounslow I cannot remember but, so beguiled was I by the beautiful thing, that I undertook a long bus-ride home to ask for the money, and the same journey back to the shop to claim my prize that very afternoon.

After, what must be, the usual painful process of learning to extract a sound of any kind from a clarinet, I could produce a few notes. With a beginner's tutor book, I could name and recognize them when written on a music stave. This achievement, however, did not help me when I joined my friends in the music room. My individual practise had taken me to a point of division in the process of learning and I had, unknowingly, made a choice. I had abandoned learning to play as our jazz heroes played; from then onward I would need written music to help me find the notes that they found by ear. I had taken the first step that would eventually separate me from my old school friend.

By the time I left school and started work, Arthur and I were experiencing life in very different ways. While he was a student, and later a commercial artist in a London advertising office, I had become a farm worker. After a week at the art college, or the office, Arthur would exchange his smart clothes and relax into weekend casuals, mostly of his own design and becoming more 'artistic' as time went on. He was surrounded by friends and colleagues whose lives, interests and appearance matched his well. For me, the weekend was a time to throw off muddy clothes and, as working class people did then, don a very conventional Sunday best. I continued to play the tea-chest bass on Saturday evenings but my traditional attire and the imaginative clothes of Arthur, his brothers and his friends were becoming noticeably different.

As well as the superficial variation, our physical selves were also undergoing change. While Arthur and his brothers were pursuing indoor careers, they were becoming pale, even sallow, in complexion. I was following an outdoor life, looking weathered and acquiring a roughness and a ruddiness. The contrast was broadcast in an innocent game played by Ronnie, by then aged about five. He liked to press his fingers onto the back of my hand until the pressure drained the blood and left white imprints. When his fingers were removed, blood and redness returned slowly, amusing Ronnie and causing him to produce the same giggles that I had heard from Arthur. I shared Ronnie's amusement, but awareness of my differences from my friends was sharpened at the same time.

Our taste in music began to go in separate directions too. I remained determined to learn to play an instrument, but Arthur's trombone had dropped by the wayside in preference for what I thought he considered to be a quicker route to success. He had formed a guitar group as their lead singer, and they were already performing locally. My influences were coming from other directions. I was beginning to come under the spell of orchestral music, which went along well with my efforts to learn to read music and play what I read. I also preferred the sound of natural instruments, with their harmonic richness, and was not attracted to what I considered to be the thin lifelessness of electronic amplification. Perhaps the musical ear, which I felt had let me down, had an agenda all its own and simply needed to be nourished in its own special way.

The friendship between my school friend Arthur and me did not end but we did continue to grow apart. Outside experiences, our own tastes and choices, and, finally, 'the call to arms', when national service separated us, taking us to extreme ends of the country and keeping us busy with ever wider and more varied occupations.

Arthur had one last lesson in 'love' to show me, which I shall always remember and be grateful for. In those days, if we wanted to make a telephone call we would take pencil and paper and coins to our local telephone box, which was situated next to the Town Hall on Yiewsley High Street. The box was a ten-minute walk from Arthur's house, nevertheless, he went there one day and made an expensive long-distance call to me while I was on basic training with the army in North Wales. I had been called-up a few months before him and he was aware that it was the first time I had been away from home. The rich imagination I knew him for told him how I might be feeling. A little of the thoughtfulness I had once glimpsed in his concern for his little brother he now turned in my direction, thinking, so rightly, that a familiar voice from home might be a comfort. It was not our intention to say our last goodbyes during that telephone call but in the general rush of life it turned out to be so, and any contact after that day was rare.

Chapter 21

SENIOR SCHOOL

In 1948, I failed the Eleven Plus examination. At that time in the twentieth century, the word 'fail' was still in full circulation; if we failed, we were told so. We were informed that we would not be going to 'the grammar school' but, instead, to a secondary modern school. There was no attempt to say that the new school had been selected for a curriculum more suitable to our needs; the British 'stiff upper lip' was still in command, we were failures and it was made known to us without dubiety.

On the morning of the new term, I made my way to Evelyn's Secondary Modern School. The vast building enclosed three sides of a large playground, and its many spacious well-lit classrooms provided teaching space for 900 boys and girls between the ages of eleven and fifteen years. At the heart of the school, there was a double-sized assembly hall, each end having its own performance stage with backstage facilities. The great hall doubled as a gymnasium, so wall bars were always in view while other necessary equipment was stored under the stages. Central dividing partitions, once in place, allowed two classes to exercise independently. The school had been opened in 1936 and local dignitaries had dubbed it 'an educational palace'.

Our days began with morning assembly, at which time a full complement of pupils and staff packed the great hall from end to end. The headmaster read the morning prayers, with their messages of love and forgiveness and turning the other cheek. His words could be heard comfortably by the first dozen rows and beyond that they were amplified by teachers distributed evenly throughout the congregation, who mumbled as closely in synchronization with the senior man as could be achieved. After prayers, we sung with gusto hymns that included phrases like 'Bring me my bow of burning gold. Bring me my arrows of desire. Bring me my chariot of fire', (the word 'fire' being the loudest and most raucous as we boys tried to raise the roof).

Next, we sung 'Onward, Christian soldiers, marching as to war', and something about not letting 'my sword sleep in my hand'. Our singing seemed to contradict the prayers we had just listened to and confused anyone who thought about it.

Regardless of the doubtful introduction my school had, and a misunderstanding of the description of 'secondary', which many of us took to mean second class, Evelyn's Secondary Modern could not have been better selected for my own individual needs; the emphasis on practical teaching and learning suited me well, bringing school closer to my home life and experiences. I was happy to be introduced to skills that could help me earn my living and I grew to appreciate the broad curriculum, which gave me at least the beginnings of an understanding of a wide range of subjects that might later help me steer my life out of any preordained rut my early years had prepared for me.

As I settled and began to feel a desire to fit with my contemporaries, I made an attempt to conform that was given short shrift by Nan when, one day, I combed my hair in a different style from usual. When asked why, I answered that all the boys at my new school were doing it, to which the retort came as decisive as a falling butcher's cleaver, 'If they put their fingers in the fire, would you?' My new hairstyle remained, but the response was remembered and considered when less innocent influences came my way.

School discipline was strict and at that time corporal punishment was not questioned as a necessary aid to teaching. A bundle of mass-produced canes could be seen in the headmaster's office and one would be available in each classroom – swishy flexible sticks about the thickness of a large man's finger.

Some teachers exhibited their canes freely. Our mathematics teacher, Mr Kilburn, was never parted from his, using it as a pointer all the time he talked loudly to the class and hanging it on his forearm when he wrote on the blackboard. Any boy daring to interrupt Mr Kilburn's flow was quickly checked when called out to the front of the class and ordered to bend over to feel just a sample of what the cane could do. A troublesome girl would hold out the hand not needed for writing high in view of the class for her feel of the stick. The uncompromising Mr Kilburn quickly became known as 'Killer Kilburn', and certainly put fear into all but the roughest and toughest in his charge. We were, after all, not the grammar school selection, so our class contained more than its fair share of back-row rabble-rousers. Fortunately, our tutor dispensed his implement of authority with great wisdom, so we, the more biddable and quiet listeners of the middle ground, benefited from the environment for learning he created.

Mr Edwicker, our woodwork teacher, was an equal disciplinarian. When a boy cut his finger on one of the sharp tools, which was a frequent happening, Mr Edwicker would raise his voice, with his arm held high pointing in the direction of the headmaster's office, as he threatened to send the damaged child to be caned for 'misusing school property'. While continuing to reprimand the 'culprit', Mr Edwicker would bring out a well-stocked first-aid kit and tend the wound with skill, applying cream and bandages with great care and concern for the individual.

The woodwork classroom was large and well equipped. We were instructed in the carpentry and cabinetmaking techniques of the day. All we were shown was put into practice when we began work on a greenhouse that our class was to help make for the gardening department. We were each given a small section to complete. My contribution to the finished structure was to be one of the opening window frames. The project gave purpose to our work, and great satisfaction when we saw the result erected, glazed, painted and providing a place of horticultural instruction for our friends, and for ourselves when our turn came.

Apart from the upright piano in the assembly hall that thumped out morning hymns, there were no musical instruments to be seen around the school apart from the occasional modern plastic recorder. It was my own fault that I missed the opportunity to join the recorder class, so that, once again, I missed the gentle introduction to written music that might have helped me in future years. The name 'recorder' was not familiar to me, and my lack of attention left me imagining that a 'recorder' class listened to 'records'. I remembered Vera, our lodgers' daughter, winding up her portable gramophone and putting on records by the Henry Hall 'orchestra' playing foxtrots and quicksteps and 'The Teddy Bears' Picnic', and I had no wish to stay after school to do that..

What I missed in the recorder group was more than made up for in a class that remains vivid in my memory. I shall always be grateful to a teacher who engaged our attention with his love of poetry and music. Mr Tom Gittings worked tirelessly to give us a glimpse into a treasure trove of the finer things that raise man above the animals, and could lift us, too, out of the daily struggle to fulfil our basic needs. He showed us that the world was an exciting place when he read to us John Masefield's poem that spoke of stately Spanish galleons laden with diamonds, emeralds, amethysts and cinnamon, and quinquiremes from Nineveh with cargoes of apes and peacocks, sandalwood, cedarwood and sweet white wine. He told us how privileged we were to speak such a wonderful language, rich with so many words of subtle variation. He demonstrated the use of strong and dramatic words in William Blake's 'Tyger! Tyger! Burning bright in the forests of the night', and contrasted them with the smooth gentle description found in Thomas Gray's 'Elegy' where no other order of words could say as well 'The ploughman homeward plods his weary way'.

To my special delight, Mr Gittings talked about orchestral music and played us records on a modern electric machine he had brought from home. He shared with us his enthusiasm for the three orchestral sketches of *La mer* by Claude Debussy, which he considered to be the 'most descriptive music ever written'. He played us small sections and asked us if we thought the music matched the titles. He brought the music closer to us by saying that the sea being described was our own English Channel. Debussy, he said, was staying at a hotel in Eastbourne and was looking out to sea as he composed.

We sang 'Linden Lea' to music by Vaughan Williams, and classical songs from earlier centuries. Mr Gittings played us the famous record of Manchester schoolchildren singing with the Hallé orchestra and taught us 'Nymphs and Shepherds' from the record. On one occasion, the forbearance of some of our classmates was exceeded when he tried to teach us the words sung by the character 'Ariel' in Shakespeare's play *The Tempest*. The front row entered into the spirit of the experience, but when some of the macho lads of the back row were asked to sings words like 'Where the bee sucks, there suck I' they rebelled, creating a pandemonium that had to be quelled with a strictness Mr Gittings rarely needed to apply. Co-operation was quickly restored without need to resort to the cane, demonstrating another of Mr Gittings's strengths as a teacher.

Apart from the brief time I was strapped to my friend Arthur when we shared the limelight as winners of the interschool three-legged race, my prowess on the sports field was sadly lacking, regardless of a good choice of sport offered. Rugby, I decided, was far too rough, and I quickly learned to stand well back when a team was being chosen. I was safe from having to play football as, after my first game, the captain picked a full team before he turned his eyes in my direction. Cricket was only played by boys with white trousers. We half-dozen still grey-legged and surplus to needs for both football and cricket, made up our own game in the corner of the sports field, managing to ignore the 'flannelled fools at the wicket and the muddied oafs at the goals' as the poet advised. In the gym, I never found out what we were supposed to do on the wall bars, and for climbing the ropes or vaulting the box or the horse I practised my 'technique' of remaining at the end of the queue.

During the years I was at Evelyn's School, the number of pupils was in excess of that for which the building had been designed. Extra places were provided by 'huts' at the rear of the school. I have memories of two of them. One accommodated our metalwork class, where I practised my blacksmithing skills. The second housed Madame Jacqueline Boulanger, an eccentric motorcycling French lady who attempted to teach us her language. I liked the subject and could recite JU SUIS, TU ES, IL EST, NOUS SOMMES, VOUS ETES, ILS SONT with great confidence. I thought I might make headway with the French language, but Madame Boulanger, who quickly became known as 'Crusty' (translation, no doubt, by one of the high flyers of the front row) had other ideas. Madame put me to work each week cleaning her motorcycle, which she parked in a secluded spot near her hut. I immediately forgot my aspirations to learn her language and, instead, fell in love with the beautiful little green BSA Bantam motorcycle, and decided that, when I was old enough, I would like to have one just like it. Madame Boulanger appeared in our lives for one term only, her sudden departure caused one or two imaginative stories but we really did not know the truth of her going. French lessons were not encountered by us again.

Regardless of my plan to get through school unnoticed, I managed to improve my previous average scores and moved up in subjects that matter most, such as mathematics, English, geography and history. It troubled me not at all that others of my own age were learning Latin and Greek at a grammar school nearby; my school had good facilities and good teachers. Corporal punishment did not seem unreasonable, after all, being a troublemaker was optional; the cane, I considered, was an aid to those who wanted to learn as well as to teachers. Whether Evelyn's Secondary Modern School had been selected for me, or I had been selected for it, became of no importance, and I remain grateful to the school for the things I learned there.

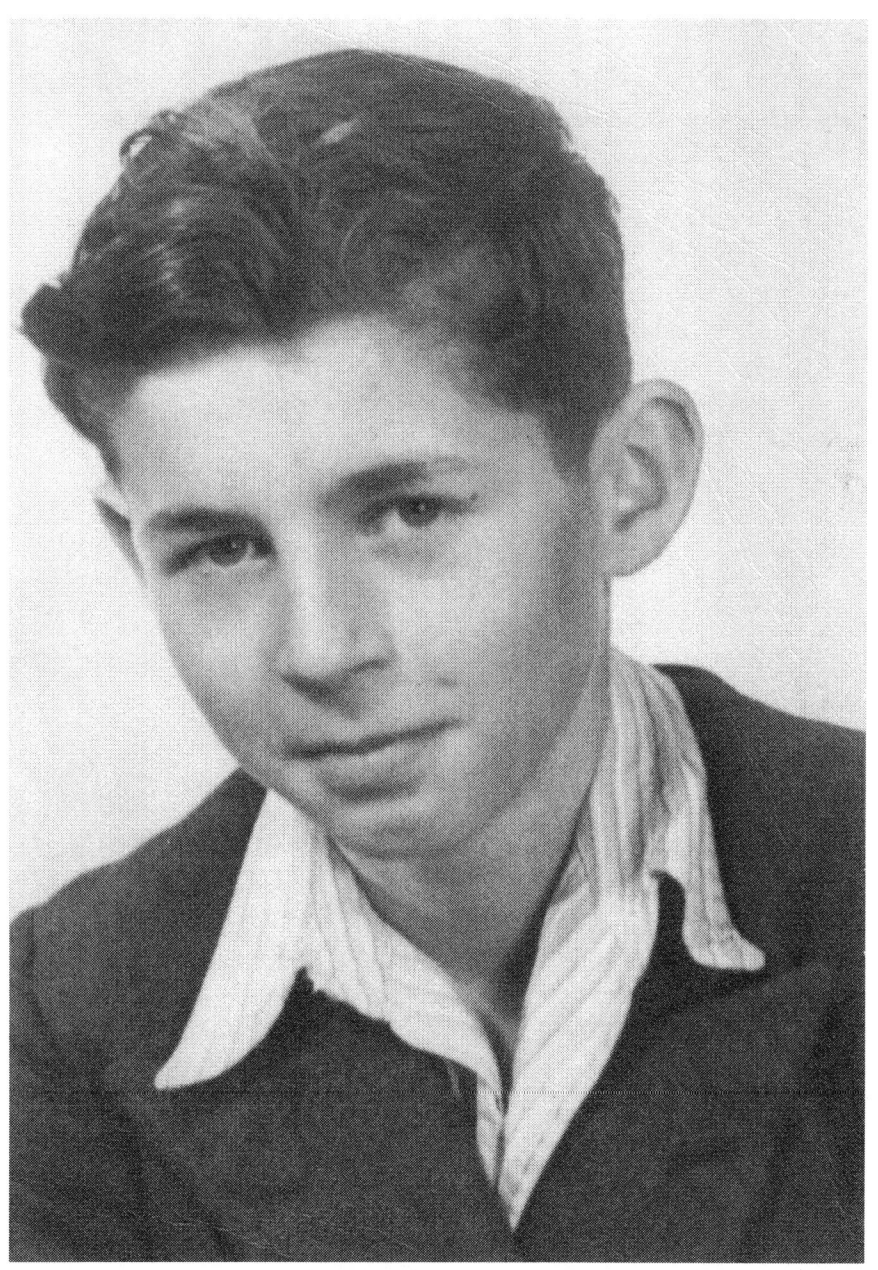

About 1950

Chapter 22

LEAVING SCHOOL

When the time for me to leave school was in sight, Nan argued that I should be allowed to leave at Christmas. She insisted that she could no longer afford my keep and I would have to start work and bring in a much needed wage. Officially, I should have continued until the end of the summer term, the school protested, but, giving consideration to Nan's demands, a compromise was reached and I was allowed to leave at Easter. So, it was arranged that I would start my working life at age fourteen years and eleven months.

It was up to me to find a job. For a brief while, the freedom, so sudden and so new, overtook reason and I was seduced to explore horizons as far as I could imagine. My attention was taken by advertisements, which seemed to be everywhere at that time, proclaiming that Australia wanted Northern European immigrants to increase its population, and telling me I could get there for just ten pounds. Publicity images romanticized open spaces and busy farming scenes. Adventure, and perhaps release from my restricted life, attracted and excited me. Only gradually did reality return with the realization that the giant step was beyond me, if only for the time being. I resolved to prepare myself for the day when I might take-up such an opportunity. The 'open space' of a local farm might be the place to begin.

One Sunday morning, several weeks before I was released from school, I rode off on my bike to keep an appointment for an interview at a dairy farm situated over the border in Buckinghamshire. The county name sounded appealing, there were fewer houses and I loved the rural scenery. I liked the farm and the idea of working with animals. I got on well in my interview and the farmer said I would be suitable. He went on to enquire how I could get to work at the very early hour in the morning that would be required, but when he understood how far away I lived he said he thought the distance was too great to cycle. I was sent away to rethink and contact him again if I could obtain some speeder form of transport, such as an autocycle, he suggested. There was no chance of that, so I did not return.

Much nearer was Wild & Robbins' farm. I knew them mainly as vegetable growers, as I had been with Bobby to buy for his greengrocery round. Working on a market garden would be less exciting, but they had a large herd of pigs and at least four working horses, so I told myself it was still a farm. I was offered the job of field hand, which I accepted, and the day of my starting was agreed. I left school on the Friday, a week before Easter, and I started on the Monday following the same weekend.

On the appointed day, I rode my bike to Sipson, which was a couple of miles from my home and almost to London Airport (or 'Heathrow' as it was known then). The village was quite rural with the usual complement of public houses, church, chapel and general store. Rows of workers' cottages, all built of local grey-brown brick, lined the main road either side of Wild & Robbins' yard; the farm owned many of the cottages, which were occupied by employees. I entered through the heavy-gated entrance into the yard, which was surrounded by workshops, offices, stables and warehouses. Every building was of the same drab brick, brightened by yellow and green painted woodwork.

I was directed to the estate office, where on payday, I would learn in the coming weeks, workers would queue, rising slowly up stone steps to present themselves at a window on the second floor of the building. They would say their name and be handed a note or two and some coins. Once recompensed for their week's labours, they would touch their caps and descend quickly down the other side of the pyramid staircase.

On the day of my arrival, the yard was empty and the office appeared closed. I climbed the steps and tapped nervously on the window, which flew open to reveal a grinning man with tortoiseshell-framed glasses and thinning ginger hair. In as far as the small aperture allowed, he looked me up and down while I attempted to introduce myself. He told me I needed to see the field manager, Mr Williams, and slammed the window shut.

Back in the yard, I wondered how to find Mr Williams. The doors of one building were open, so I cautiously went towards them. It was the tractor garage. I could see several machines of the day, grey Ferguson and orange Allis-Chalmers, all of them looking new and carefully tended. The tractor drivers were strutting around with a tool or greasy rag in their hands preparing for the day's work, it appeared. They told me to wait in the yard and the field manager would find me. 'You'll see him on his bike in a minute when he comes to give us our orders,' one told me.

Old hands frequently want to give new arrivals advice and the tractor drivers were no exception. 'What's yer job,' the same man asked.

'Field hand,' I said. 'But I'd like to work with the horses.'

Another of the men stepped forward wagging his finger. 'Take my advice,' he said, 'you don't wanna work with 'orses. 'Orses have 'ad their day, they're a thing of the past. As soon as you can, apply to get on the tractors, that's where the future is.'

I was thanking the tractor driver for his advice when Mr Williams came riding into the yard. I waited while he gave the men their instructions for the day. He turned to me, saying, 'You're the new boy, follow me.' I trotted behind him as he rode out to one of the near fields, which was muddy and slippery and still showing signs of the snowstorm that had struck freakishly late in the winter of 1952, cutting off Sipson village only a short while before. A gang of men, about a dozen, were cutting cabbages. The field manager stopped and spent several minutes speaking to one who appeared to be the leader. The remainder of the gang continued working, giving me an opportunity to learn what would be expected of me in my new capacity of field hand. Regardless of recent weather conditions, the crop had fared well through its growing period and produced large heavy cabbages, creating difficulty in packing the required number into a bushel box. Sometimes more outer leaves would be hacked off, sometimes a cabbage would be crushed and spoilt by a heavy hand in an attempt to force it into the available space, or the sides of a wooden box would give way causing extra work repacking. These minor accidents were dealt with, and cursing under the breath faded harmlessly into the cold air of the morning. Overall, calmness, good language and good manners prevailed as the gang persisted in filling boxes, which were left in stacks to be collected by the carter.

Scenes such as this must have endured for many generations, the dignity of labour giving each man equal status to one in any other occupation, profession or calling as he stood stiff-legged, bending from the waist to reach the ground and his work. Every member of the gang in that field, where winter was still in command, secured against the cold as warmly as his well-worn clothes would allow. Wool-cloth overcoats or gabardine raincoats, which had once been Sunday's best, were pulled tightly around the waist by the garment's own belt or a piece of farm twine. Corners of the long coats dragged in the mud about their feet. Some wore wellington boots but most swore by the comfort of tough leather boots and protected their legs with strips cut from hessian sacking, wrapped around and tied with the rough twine.

Either plans had already been made for me, or the gang leader, who was a large man himself, thought that I would not be strong enough to pull my weight in his team, I did not know. I was ordered to trot on behind the bicycle and was led to another gang of about a dozen women cutting lettuces, most, I learned later, were wives of the men who I thought might have just rejected me. There was no hesitation, I was told to join them, and Mr Williams rode off.

''Ere, bring some of them boxes over 'ere,' said one of the women, and my working life began. When the boxes were in place, the same woman handed me a knife, and said, 'Look, like this.' She slashed at the base of a growing lettuce, and it separated from its root. She turned the crisp green herb over, enfolding its roundness in the palm of her hand, so that her fingers could guide it, now inverted, into the half-bushel box. I started cutting and soon learned how to control the rosette of leaves to enable packing. After half an hour, I needed to take a moment to stand up straight to rest my unseasoned back.

I took the opportunity to look around to find my bearings. The field in which I had begun my working life was next to the road from Sipson to West Drayton, along which I had cycled many times. Evelyn's Secondary Modern School, which I had attended until just a day or two ago, stood silent on the other side of West Drayton. When the pupils returned after the holidays, I would not be going with them. Suddenly, the full meaning of leaving school struck me. As a schoolboy, I knew the day of finishing was only a few years away. Now, I was an employed person, and this would be forever; there would be no release from this new phase of my life in which I suddenly found myself. This was adult life, I was no more than any other working man now, and working life went on until sixty-five years of age. To be more than four times older than I was at that moment was unimaginable; it was a life sentence – the thought sent a cold shiver through my body. 'Come on,' shouted the woman who had taken over my education, 'What's the matter?' I hastily had to put my aching back and my worries from my mind.

We moved on through the lettuce crop leaving filled boxes behind us, stacked on the now exposed mud and leafy rubbish. As we worked, I was able to continue observing my surroundings and the people nearby. The women seemed older than their years. Their faces were weathered. Their hands were red and rough. The hands of the oldest women were misshapen. Like the men, Sunday best overcoats of a previous time now dragged in the mud as the garment served its owner still. Some wore a scarf around their neck or head, some wore mittens, hand-knitted from the remnants of their wool-basket, in unmatching colours, but now giving a welcome flash of brightness to otherwise colourless raiment.

Soon it was time for 'breakfast'. The women pulled up empty boxes and sat around within speaking or shouting distance of one another. From an odd assortment of bags, they took containers or small parcels of food brought from home. Pieces of bread with small amounts of cheese. Some had an onion from which they cut slices, passing them directly to their mouth on the back of the knife or offering them to a friend. All had flasks of warm drinks. I was not properly prepared on that first morning but, soon, an unused cup was found and I was offered as much tea as could be spared. As sips of tea were taken and cold throats eased, talking began. Mostly banter, as one woman called across to another some joking or teasing question or statement that created a little amusement and light relief for the group as a whole. A mildly probing question or two was aimed at me. A new arrival and a young lad amongst so many women, of course, some teasing was due. I probably blushed. I tried to keep smiling to hide my shyness as I attempted an answer. Perhaps my answer was too hesitant, too soft or much too polite. Whatever I said or however it was delivered it brought laughter, for this was the time for the women to relax, to forget the stress of cold hands and aching backs. The teasing was gentle and no hurt was meant.

The woman who had earlier told me what to do, and the one who did most of the talking, joking and teasing, I learned was called Molly Pert. Whether or not she was the appointed gang leader, I did not know. If the women were spoken to, she was the one who would be addressed, and if an answer was needed, she would give it. Molly was not afraid of any man and, in fact, flirted with any who came near. No man, however, allowed himself to flirt with Molly, probably for the same reason that gave her the confidence to speak as boldly as she did to them. Daniel Pert, her husband, was head of the men's' gang. Often working nearby, he would raise his head and look in his wife's direction whenever her voice rang-out across the field.

From time to time during the day, the field manager would ride up and look around. He would nod to Molly but seemed to say very little, everything must have been going along to his satisfaction. As he rode off, there was time to observe him and his ancient black bicycle, which he rode in an extremely upright position, grasping the high-set handlebars with hands close together and held straight out in front of him. As he leaned forward, putting weight on the pedals to get his machine up to speed, his elbows protruded backward behind the line of his back. Across a field, in silhouette against the sky, he appeared as a cartoon character passing across a cinema screen. The image did not, in any way, diminish respect for him; everyone who spoke to him was polite in a way that suggested genuine warmth, as well as the deference due to his rank. He, in return, was quiet-spoken and treated field workers as his equal. Friendly exchanges kept the work progressing as the masters required.

There were other distractions from the repetitive work, which could, no doubt, become tedious after long periods. Prince, a shire horse, would pass close-by several times during the day pulling a large two-wheeled wooden farm cart. Sitting high on the front of the cart was, in contrast to the size of the horse he controlled, a diminutive man. I was told his name was Harry Clarke. He was on his way to the field in which the men were working, where the heavy bushel boxes of cabbage would be loaded onto the cart to be taken to the packing shed.

To transport our lighter lettuce crop, a more compact vehicle would be sufficient. This would arrive at intervals as the stacks of filled boxes mounted. A young rough-mannered boy shouted and cussed as he drove up, jumped down and backed his horse close to the stack. This smaller cart required only a cob to pull it. This was to be my first sight of Queenie. She was about half the size of Prince but clearly a working horse, too rounded and too stocky to be a riding horse. The cart was similar in style to the one pulled by Prince but was of lighter construction. It was used only in winter for Queenie, I would learn. Its balloon tyres, being less likely to sink into winter mud, and having only two wheels, it would move with less resistance on the heavy ground. Briefly, I saw myself in the rough boy's place, convinced I could do his job better and enjoy it more

Towards the end of the day, the field manager told me that I would be on 'potato riddling' tomorrow and, at 8 a.m., I should report to Mr Jim Frewin in the big packing shed.

With two older friends, c.1951

Nan and her bother, Jim, devour newspapers

Chapter 23

THE PACKING SHED

I made sure to be early next morning and, as instructed, went directly to the packing shed. The building was enormous; high and spacious enough for market lorries to drive in for loading. At one end, a wing of the building housed the old apple store below and a corn store above. Access to both was gained by way of a large opening, the height of the two floors. Corn sacks were raised and lowered by a rope hoist.

As I entered, it was not difficult to see who was in charge; while others were quietly attending to their work, a dapper little man in a pinstripe suit moved importantly back and forth across the great building. Each traverse commenced at a desk, fixed, at his chest height, to the whitewashed wall adjacent to the apple and corn store. There he donned a pair of dark-rimmed glasses and read his orders for the day, before turning smartly on his heel and speeding-off to give instructions to a subordinate.

My arrival was noticed, causing the man so clearly in charge to change direction smartly in order to approach and challenge who ever had dared enter his domain. His black eyes were made the more piercing by his sallow indoor complexion, framed by the dark-rimmed glasses. 'I'm Mr Frewin the manager. Who are you?' he announced and demanded in the same breath – his voice as sharp as his movements.

'Mr Williams told me to report to you,' I responded submissively.

'The others are not here yet. Wait there,' he snapped, and, taking no more of his valuable time to enquire which of the expected three I might be, he veered off to undertake another important task.

Along one wall of the vast shed were large metal sinks for washing vegetables and salad crops. A machine in front of the sinks had a wooden slatted cylinder partly submerged in water. Boxes of root vegetables were tipped onto a conveyor belt that guided them into the revolving cylinder where they were tumbled in the water and regurgitated at the further end, clean and ready for packing. Vegetable washing was undertaken by George, a man close to retirement age, assisted by a young man in his mid-twenties who worked cheerfully with his older colleague.

My observation ceased abruptly when my working companions of the day entered the shed loudly. The taller, a local man, about thirty years of age, had a jovial country bearing; his outdoor face was ruddy and smiled easily. The other was a lad of eighteen or twenty who fitted his surroundings less well, perhaps travelling from a nearby town to give farm work a try. He was the shorter of the two but had a strong stocky build. He was the source of the excess noise, as he freely dispensed his self-proclaimed superior knowledge, which, when combined with a nervous mocking laugh, was of sufficient decibels to fill the building that we were presently occupying.

The new arrivals aroused the manager's attention and he moved over smartly to take control. 'Right! You're on potato riddling today,' he said, and led us to one end of the building where potatoes lay on the concrete floor and rose ten or twelve feet high across the full width of the end wall. 'I want six tons today,' he said, conveying his orders from the office that had told him what was to be loaded onto the market lorries. 'Start off with you over there and you over there and you over there, an' change round later. You should get a couple of tons done before breakfast,' he added. The noisy lad began to laugh, but stopped quickly when he received a steely look from the manager whose statement was not for amusement.

The handle of the stationary engine was spun a few times, then a few turns more and the chuff chuff of the motor commenced. A long flat belt started to move and the riddling machine rattled into life. Potatoes were carefully forked onto the machine. They travelled across an oscillating sieve onto a short conveyor that dropped them into a waiting sack, which was then weighed to ensure a full one-hundredweight and laced with rough twine. The manager's advice to change round was taken up eagerly as backs and arms demanded a change of task. The process continued until forty sacks had been dragged from the scales and breakfast was declared.

After our break, we worked on, and as completion of the full quota came closer, our stops to count them became more frequent, giving us the tally but, more importantly, stolen moments of rest. Finally, we were there – six tons; 120 sacks of potatoes. We threw ourselves down on the heaps of sacks, full or empty we did not care. Our relaxation was brief, the shed manager came striding over as a market lorry was seen reversing into the shed. 'Get these on and you're done,' he said.

To load the lorry, we were going to have to lift the sacks to chest height, which until now we had only moved a short way at a little above floor level. The noisy lad was keen to show off his strength and wrestled with a sack, finally getting it up onto the lorry. Only one did he try this way. Then he and the local man took a sack ear in one hand and a bottom corner in the other and found that together they could swing it up to the required height. The manager brought a pickaxe handle over and offered an end to me. We took an ear each and laid the sack back on the stick, which aided our swing. Thankfully, several workers came to help and soon our potatoes were loaded.

One of those who came to help was the young vegetable washing man. He was different from the other workers and seemed out of place; his voice was soft and cultured in a way that was new to me. He was warm and friendly to all he met and he had a gentle enquiring manner that gave him an unusual kind of superiority. I was aware that when I spoke I did not sound as he sounded, and was drawn to spend time in his company just to hear his voice. In his desire to be accepted he would greet all who came near, attempting to engage them with some polite remark or enquiry, and if a brief conversation was enjoyed he would ask if he might take a photograph. If authorized he would produce a 'Polaroid' camera and in a few moments hand over an image of his new friend, pleasing him and beguiling him with the wonders of science. I would learn that he was a graduate who had been allowed to complete his degree at university before fulfilling his time of national service by working on a farm.

Without exception Mr Frewin, with acid in his voice, referred to the young man as 'the conchie'. In the coming days, I would hear that 'conchies' were shirkers who refused to enter the armed forces. They were lazy cowardly degenerates who only wanted to benefit from the sacrifice of others. The conversations with the young man that I desired were fewer than I would have wished, for, like other workers, I avoided contact with him when under the gaze of the manager.

As the days went by, whenever the 'conchie' was talked about, I would hear varying opinions, some as scathing as the manager's but others that threw quite a different light on the matter. 'Conscientious objectors', as they were known by those of a more benign opinion, refused to carry arms because they were thinking people who could see that it was wrong to kill their fellow man and wanted to resist nature's urge that told them to do so. They were not cowards and, in fact, needed great courage to proclaim their beliefs in the face of hostility from the authorities and less questioning individuals. They would have to withstand insult and contempt, even imprisonment, punishment, and cruel treatment. Without abandoning their beliefs, many elected to help their countrymen in time of war by entering the services without carrying arms, as doctors, ambulance drivers or stretcher bearers, and, proving they were not cowards, as bomb disposal officers.

So why then was the manager so hostile to the young conscientious objector? It took the wisdom of George, the senior vegetable washing man, to begin to unravel the mystery. While he befriended, respected and worked cheerfully alongside his young colleague, he also had sympathy and great understanding for his old friend, the packing shed manager. He would explain to anyone who spoke out of turn or showed a simple curiosity that, at about the same time as the conscientious objector came to work on the farm, Mr Frewin's son, Tom, had been called-up to do his national service. Immediately after his basic training young Tom had been posted abroad, and his whereabouts in the world was unknown to his father. At that time, the Korean War was at its worst and Mr Frewin was reading daily, in his newspaper, of the deaths of national servicemen, expecting at any time that young Tom might be listed amongst the dead. As George finished his explanation, his listener would become silent and appear to begin rethinking his assessment of the 'cowardly' conscientious objector, and also of the 'embittered' packing shed manager.

There was no time to stand and wonder about the little I knew as the second market lorry was seen reversing into the shed. By the end of the day, both lorries would be fully loaded with our potatoes and any vegetable in season at that time of year. Cabbage, cauliflower, kale, spinach, lettuce, carrots, parsnips, turnips and beetroot were all grown naturally in the rich soil of south-west Middlesex. They would be transported on their night-time journey along the Great West Road to the London markets. Drivers of similarly laden vehicles, from the Heathrow farms and beyond, would acknowledge one another as they went about their nocturnal ritual. From the crack of dawn onward, shopkeepers would be able to purchase fresh vegetables and by mid-morning the produce could be in the shopping basket of the housewife.

Over the next few weeks, I was sent to help anywhere an extra hand was needed. It was the employers' policy to move young workers around, providing them with variety while giving them knowledge of the farm. I enjoyed the experience and seeing the different activities gave me a respect for a business that earned its 'keep' in such a wholesome and useful way. Employees were loyal, seemed content, and paid attention to their work. Many had specialist skills and were proud of their 'craftsman' status, and they were friendly and helpful to a new arrival who was keen to learn.

Chapter 24

THE HORSES

The tractor driver's advice, as to where the future of farming lay, made no impression upon my schoolboy wish to work with horses. My desire outweighed any attraction to call in at the tractor garage, where shiny new machines could be found. Neither was it of any consequence to me that only a mile or two away the Comet jet airliner was coming into service at an airport where already the new world had entered into a battle with the old. I was seeking the past rather than the future and to work with a form of motive power that had endured for centuries past. It was, therefore, at any opportunity that could be connived, that I would wander into the stable yard. The only occupation I could assign myself there was to run the tap over the drinking trough until accumulated debris on the surface was removed by the overflowing water. I then imagined the horses returning after their work to a long cool drink of my clear sparkling water.

Hearing the sound of running water and curious as to what might be going on, the foreman of the horses would step out of the furthest of the two stable doors in the opposite corner of the yard. He would say nothing but simply look for a moment or two. He was known as Jonter Evans, I had been told. While he watched me, I was able to observe him. He was a character from the past, a countryman without doubt, with his round red face, the cut of his coarse twill jacket and breeches, his shiny brown calf-length leather gaiters above leather boots, which themselves had once been brown. The appearance of Jonter Evans was no distraction to my ambition, and was perhaps even an enticement.

The door from which the foreman had emerged led to two stalls, in which two greys were stabled. The foreman worked with the larger of the two, pulling a flat-backed two-wheel cart when absolutely necessary, but when fieldwork was required he assigned it to himself. On his way to and from a field of ploughing, he could be seen sitting high on the bare back of his grey with both legs together on one side of the animal, as if he were sitting on a comfortable over-stuffed sofa. The stablemate of the foreman's horse was a slightly lighter-built animal; an otherwise matching grey that looked well when paired on field work under the foreman's control.

The second door enclosed two stalls. In one, Prince, the young shire, spent his resting hours. Whenever he was looked in upon, he appeared content, passively but noisily munching chaff, which had been cut from straw by an ancient hand-turned machine. Harry Clarke, the oldest of the carters, would be in attendance, fussing around to provide for Prince's every need, slapping the horse's rump, saying, 'Gid over,' as he pushed his charge to one side of the stall while he forked in clean straw to cover the cobbled floor. More chaff was put into the manger to ensure no shortage through the night and another bucket of water wedged into a holder at one end to quench the animal's night-time thirst. Harry would then take a curry comb in one hand and a brush in the other and begin to groom Prince dutifully, and some suspected even lovingly.

Harry, being small in stature, would lift onto his toes to reach Prince's withers. As he worked at full stretch, creases in his suit opened to reveal fillings of dust, which were accented by shafts of light from the open door. When he stood down at normal height to clean hair from the curry comb, blowing as if attempting to whistle but in truth blowing dust away from his face, the creases of his suit fell back into place hiding the soiled folds once again. The turn-up bottoms of his trousers returned low around his boots, giving his rough tweed suit the appearance of a tiredness, brought about no doubt by long hard wear, which was confirmed by a tear in the waistcoat pocket where his fob watch chain had worn through. Harry's ensemble was completed by a white-spotted red cotton handkerchief, which he wore around his neck and never removed.

Prince's stablemate was Queenie, the stocky black Cob, who in the summer months would pull a flat trotting van, bringing in the lighter produce from the fields, but who, at that moment, pulled the winter cart in the charge of the shouting cursing boy.

One Clear Morn

Very soon after taking up employment on the farm, I let it be known that I wanted to work with the horses. I had been dissuaded by the tractor drivers and discouraged by the office manager, who told me I would not be allowed to do so until I was fifteen. Although that event was only weeks away, the impatience of youth considered it to be forever and, in any case, I could see that there were only four horses and a full complement of carters. The matter seemed without hope.

I was surprised, therefore, when hopefulness was rekindled by reports of an incident, which might have had some affect on the existing state of affairs. It was the subject of conversation between fieldworkers as they sat having their breakfast one morning. The less sensitive of the group were laughing. The women were mostly feeling sorry for the animal involved in the occurrence, some were revealing their dislike of the loud shouting boy, who was the other participant in the event. 'He's been sacked, you know,' said one of the men.

'Good,' said one of the women. Several had examples of the culprit's mistreatment of the horses. 'I've seen him hit 'is 'orse round the head,' said one, and others gave similar reports.

On the only occasion I had encountered the boy closely, he was telling a group of fieldworkers how experienced he was with horses and how much he knew about them. He was in charge of Queenie at the time, who, I would learn later, was a 'biter' and the self-professed knowledgeable horseman was relating how he dealt with such an animal, which, even with my lack of knowledge, sounded to be quite the wrong corrective treatment, as well as being cruel.

The incident that brought the matter of the boy's cruelty to the notice of management had taken place when he had been assigned to work with the lighter of the two greys. He had been warned that the animal had certain unstable ways. He had chosen, however, not to manage the horse sensitively to avoid trouble but, instead, to exploit its weaknesses, for reasons known only to himself. He had discovered that he could provoke a violent reaction from the horse, and did so frequently and, finally, once too often. From his position high on the cart, he could make a noise with his lips (a noise that one child might make to another in a junior school playground) and the horse would throw up its back legs, kicking out to where the sound came from. It was a cowardly thing for the boy to do, as he was well out of reach of the hooves and protected by the front of the cart. It was also potentially hazardous to the welfare of the animal.

'An' this went on for some time, I believe,' said one of the men.

'Ah, it did,' said another.

From the conversation that morning, I learned that the foolish behaviour went on until one day, moving downhill, the cart had rolled closer to the horse when it kicked and the animal's hooves broke through the front of the cart. With its hind legs entangled, standing on forelegs alone, the animal lost balance and fell into a confused heap, which needed several helpers to unravel. The horse was unhurt but there was damage to the cart and valuable leather harness, which had to be cut to free the horse. The incident gave the management the opportunity to sack the boy who had for some time had his misdeeds mounting up against him.

I had soaked up the gossip and, now aware of the new situation, I made sure to wander into the stable yard at the first opportunity. The diligent foreman quickly appeared to see who had entered the territory under his control. 'Ahoy there,' he called across the yard in an impersonal way. He walked towards me speaking as if addressing someone above my head. Without looking into my eyes, he said, 'I hear you want to work with the 'osses.' His manner reduced me to the schoolboy I had just ceased to be; I was certain that if I said that I did, he would laugh and send me away. I would need experience of life before I would understand that the fearsome Jonter Evans was employing the defensive mechanism of a shy and nervous man and that I had no need to turn his anxieties upon myself.

Unnerved but full of desire, I screwed up my courage, and said, 'Yes, I do.'

'When are you fifteen?' he asked the person above my head.

'Last Friday,' I said.

'Well, you're old enough to apply for the pony boy's job, if you want it,' he said.

'I'd like to,' I said, gaining a little confidence.

'Well, go an' see 'Arry Clarke, he'll show you how to get Queenie ready,' he said.

'What! I start now?' I said, totally surprised by the change in my prospects.

'Yes,' he said. 'The field foreman knows, so go an' see 'Arry.' And he turned and walked off.

Harry Clarke had heard all that was said so that when, still dazed, I went into the stable, he said, without ceremony, introduction or even hello, 'Ned's gettin' her ready. You can 'elp 'im.' So it was, I met Ned Larkin. He was twice my age and could have considered himself my immediate superior. Instead, he gave me a broad impish grin and from that moment he treated me as an equal. Ned was not tall and his lack of height was exacerbated by the manner in which he held his body in a partial stoop. When viewed in his usual attire of a dusty serge suit, he appeared to have the demeanour of a subservient Victorian railway porter. He was friendly and helpful to me, I was grateful, and liked him instantly.

'Come 'ere,' Ned said. 'We'll get Queenie ready to go out, 'ere y' ar', put her collar on.'

He handed me the collar. I held it for a moment and moved towards Queenie's head.

'Not that way,' Ned said without rebuke. 'Turn it upside down.'

I turned the collar so that the widest aperture was at the top and would go over the broadest part of the animal's forehead without hurting her eyes. The collar, once on the narrowest part of the neck and revolved half a turn, would settle down onto the shoulders where it would remain for the period of work. Ned went on to show me how to put on the saddle that would take the weight of the shafts, then the breeching and the crupper strap and, finally, the bridle, which would hold the bit in the horse's mouth.

My first experience of dealing so closely with a horse began in me a lifelong wondering as to what went on inside an animal's head. Surely a horse could not enjoy the iron bit in its mouth or the whip of the jockey or spurs of the huntsman, and yet they seem to remain good natured and have no desire to wreak revenge once the 'abuse' has stopped. I had just experienced the strange feeling that Queenie had even co-operated with me as I harnessed her ready for work and I felt humbled in the knowledge that without her acquiescence I would have not succeeded.

Ned said, 'Come on,' and showed me how to take the bridle so that Queenie would turn in the stall and clop clop over the cobbles out of the stable. She went over to the water trough and sunk her muzzle in, but appeared to decide a drink was not required, she simply wanted to remind us of her right to do so, and looked back as if to say so.

In the main yard, in front of the tractor garage, the trotting van was being worked on by the farm engineer. It was going to be mine to use every day. I admired its dark-green woodwork and its red wheels and thought it looked so special, so different from the heavy two-wheeled farm carts. I walked Queenie towards the van, but Ned said, 'No, this way, the harness you've put on is for the cart.' I followed him, still leading Queenie, to an open-fronted barn next to the packing shed. Queenie was backed up to the cart and the shafts brought down so that the chain between them rested on the saddle. A broad leather strap that Ned called a 'wanty', was passed under her chest, the ends were attached to the shafts and would stop the cart tipping up if too much weight was put at the back. 'Keep weight on the saddle when you load up,' said Ned, 'The wanty gives 'em a headache.' Tug chains to the collar and short chains to the breeching were connected. Queenie's rug was thrown over her back.

'Come an' 'ave yer breakfast,' said Ned.

Reluctantly, I left Queenie standing. I was too excited to think about breakfast and looked back at her as we walked across the yard. I worried about her; would she mind waiting? Ned saw my distraction and assured me that once her rug was on her back she would be happy to stand resting. We joined some fieldworkers who were having their breakfast in Siddy's box-mending shop. The title, 'box-mending shop', was rather grand for the end of an open-fronted barn, closed in only by an endless number of unrepairable boxes that Siddy had used to improvise walls. He must have suffered many cold winters, motivating him to add so many odd-shaped pieces and discarded packaging capable of keeping out the wind.

Siddy Clarke was the brother of Harry, the senior carter. He was even smaller than Harry but as talkative as Harry was taciturn. His voice was more cultured than the other workers and his words were delivered at a slightly higher pitch, which fitted quite naturally with his diminutive stature. His pinstriped suit was of a finer material and superior cut, so that when appearance was added to conversational ability, he would not have been out of place had he been encountered in the farm office. He chose, however, to wear the usual workers' black leather boots, coloured cotton scarf around his neck and flat tweed cap, the colour and design having no matching connection with any other item of his apparel.

I joined the group but could eat little breakfast, so great was my wish to return to Queenie. I tried to hide my excitement from the group, acting casually as if this was just another day for me. My performance must have slipped in places and drew gentle teasing about my promotion. Soon, Ned said he must get back to the stables. He was going to be working with the smaller of the two greys from now on. He reminded me where I had to go with Queenie, and said I was on my own now.

I could not wait to get started but managed to walk casually across the yard, although my mind raced with the joy of my promotion. At last, I had a place on the farm; I was not just the boy helping out anywhere he was needed. I was a carter now, a craftsman. I was proud; I had been accepted as a full employee. To prove my new grade, my wages had gone up from eight-pence an hour to ten-pence, I had been informed that very morning.

Before I reached Queenie, a sudden awareness of my new responsibilities fell upon me. I told myself Queenie was a living animal, only recently she had been mistreated, I must make up for that and care for her with extra concern. I wanted her to know I was kind so that we could work together and enjoy our days. I thought about the iron bit in her tender mouth and told myself I would be gentle. But I must not forget that a horse is a powerful animal, I must take care and

The Horses

learn all that I need to know.

By the time I got to Queenie, I knew what I must do and that I could do it. I took the bridle gently but positively and led her directly forward out of the barn, noting how wide the cart was and how far the horse had to travel out in a straight line before turning to avoid hitting the support post of the barn with one of the two large rubber-tyred wheels. Not wishing to make any mistakes within the view of the workers, who were still milling about, I decided to lead Queenie out of the yard.

Once out of sight, on a long stretch of farm track that commenced behind the pig sheds, I pulled Queenie up and got up onto the cart. She had walked so placidly and now stood so still that I judged it was safe. I knew that in the tip cart we could only proceed at walking pace, so this would be good practice. I carefully picked up the reins, and said, 'Walk on,' but, for some reason, Queenie lurched forward and went off at a terrific pace. Not trotting, cantering or galloping but running, in a strange way that, to my inexperienced eye, seemed unnatural. Her back sunk low as she took long paces forward. I had never seen a horse from the high position I now occupied. The animal's haunches looked so powerful as they broadened and lowered with the great strides. The power that caused us to rush forward at such great speed was frightening, my heart thumped and the cart, intended only to travel at walking pace, rattled and vibrated, almost shaking my heart out of my mouth.

Locked in fear, I could only manage to hold on to the reins and, with feet wide apart, keep my standing position in the lurching cart. I had promised myself I would be gentle with the reins that controlled the iron bit in the animal's sensitive mouth. I pulled them back carefully. I called, 'Whoa! Whoa! Whoa, Queenie!' Neither reins nor command had any effect. I pulled harder and called louder, still without response. I leaned back until the reins were taking much of my weight. I remembered my wish to be gentle but this was a runaway horse and the end of the farm track was in sight, and so was the open field gate to the passing traffic on the main road. I leaned back further until I could pull no harder, my feet edging up higher on the front of the cart to throw more of my weight onto the reins and through them onto the iron bit in the animal's tender mouth. Suddenly, the expression 'Getting the bit between your teeth' popped into my head. Immediately followed by the realization that Queenie might have done just that. What had only been a saying could now be real life. If the iron bit was no longer in her tender mouth but instead between her teeth, then I had no control over the situation. ('That's the way you learn' I could hear Nan's voice saying.) I clung onto the reins and concentrated on keeping my standing position as the cart pitched and rolled, moving ever closer to the main road and speeding traffic, certain that disaster was only seconds away.

For some reason known only to Queenie, she stopped, scarcely a few yards from the open field gate, and stood stiff-legged, as if rooted in the grassed trackway. Her body alone moved, heaving like bellows as she gained her breath. For a minute, she stood firm and blew steam from her nostrils like the black dragon I was beginning to think she might be. I climbed down from the cart on trembling legs and was pleased to feel solid ground under my feet. I wondered what had just happened to me. Did I do something wrong? Was it Queenie's idea alone? Did she know I was new and thought I needed a lesson? Did she simply want to let me know that she had some say in our new partnership?

Once I had composed my shaking body, I led Queenie onto the field where a load waited. As soon as I was in sight of the women, the teasing began. Molly, of course, was first, 'Look who's pony boy now,' she called, and another said, 'I bet you're pleased with yourself.' I could feel myself blush but I knew the taunts were the women's way of congratulating me. Dealing with my shyness helped me forget the fright I had just undergone. Once loaded, I led Queenie off the field onto the track and climbed up on the cart. A little nervous, I bid her, 'Walk on,' which she did as if the earlier event had never taken place. At the packing shed, the load was quickly removed and I was told to hurry and get back to the field. As the day went on my fright of the morning faded in importance, after all, no damage had been done. I had been given a good shake-up but I had been more in fear for my pride than for my life, so perhaps I should consider the incident as an initiation to my new position of pony boy.

Age 15 (with Queenie)

Prince

Loading for market

Chapter 25

THE STRAWBERRY VAN

As the heavy weather of winter receded and the fields became drier and easier going, it was time to bring out the four-wheeled trotting van. I had been shown the harness, which was lighter and smarter than that for the cart, and had brought from home Cherry Blossom shoe polish to blacken and shine the leather, and Bluebell brass polish to make the brass glitter. I had stayed late to work on my project. Harry was bedding down his charges for the night in his usual caring way. He looked at my tins of polish and at what I was doing and laughed. He said I was wasting my time and would never get a shine, as the only treatment the leather ever had was a dab of used motor oil to keep it supple. He was right about the leather; the Cherry Blossom blackened but never shone. The brass looked good and gained a few slightly condescending compliments; nods of approval with a smirk from the tractor drivers. Mr Williams was more generous, and Mr Tom Wild, the boss, showed pleasure without hesitation; he noticed I was the new boy and stopped to pass a few pleasant words.

Queenie seemed to be happy now, as if she knew that she was not going to be held back at a walking pace in the heavy winter cart; in the lightweight trotting van she could have her head and move at her own pace. While the shafts were lowered onto the narrow saddle, she stood placidly and appeared to be enjoying the sun on her back. She made tiny heaving movements that I did not understand, but which brought knowing grins from Ned, Harry and the foreman when I asked them what was she doing and was something wrong with her.

The ginger office manager had come down from his upstairs viewpoint to inspect my smart newly-prepared vehicle more closely. He had heard my questions and, as usual whenever I encountered him, he seemed to want to be playful. On this occasion, he began to speak as if performing on the stage, as he took it upon himself to provide an answer to my query, 'Spring sunshine penetrates all living things, creating the desire to bask in its warmth, to live anew and regenerate its own species.' His references went over my head, and his desire to be friendly felt as menacing as it always did.

Instructions had been given that horses leaving the main yard onto the Sipson Road had to be led and not driven; motor vehicles passing at speed were still few but increasing. Once again I was happy to lead Queenie out of sight of any fellow employee who might observe my first attempts to use the long reins to control the animal whilst riding on the van. Once across the main road, still close at Queenie's head, we passed The King William public house; a building that had started life in the fifteenth century as a thatched Weald house, the home of some well-to-do family. We were on our way to one of Wild & Robbins' fields at Harmondsworth, a mile or so away. The last cutting of a field of cauliflower was ready to be brought into the packing shed and we were going to collect it.

When we were clear of the public house and the few cottages in the lane, I stopped Queenie and checked that all the harness was adjusted correctly and would be comfortable for her. Queenie's dark coat shone, and my polished brass contrasted pleasingly. I admired the summer vehicle, and proudly jumped aboard. A quiet word and Queenie walked on, a gentle word of encouragement, and she moved into a leisurely trot. Morning sun and birdsong filled the lane. I mused as we went along as to how the strawberry van had got its name, after all, it was just a flat-backed cart with a low headboard. We hummed along on rubber tyres, which had come with the wheels from a scrapped Riley car that had been owned by one of the Wild family, I had been told. The empty differential gearbox from the car could be seen situated centrally between the rear wheels of the horse-drawn vehicle, as it would have been on the motorcar. Now, it was painted red, matching wheels and all underparts, as befitted its new role on the smartly turned-out van.

The strawberry van, I would learn, was more than entitled to its name. Had I travelled this very lane in previous times, I would have seen strawberry fields in all directions. Until the early twentieth century, much of south-west Middlesex was given over to fruit-growing; many orchards but, in particular, strawberries and other soft fruits for the markets, local shops and Sipson's own jam and preserves factory. Women from the industrial towns of the Midlands came to take on the seasonal work at strawberry-picking time, treating their visit as a summer holiday with pay. The strawberry van would have been ideal for bringing the shallow trays of fruit.

I would learn too that, by the 1920s, fruit-growing had given way to vegetables, and a wide range has been grown ever since. The cauliflowers I was going to collect on that day was one of those crops; 'a cabbage with a college education', as Mark Twain called them. There was a good load and Queenie seemed to know how to deal with it. It was clear that a walking pace was necessary for the rise back up the main road towards Harmondsworth village. As we turned into the lane to Sipson, Queenie stopped for a breather. I let her show me the ropes and was happy to jump down to check the load while she rested. She snorted and sounded as if she was ready to go on, so I mounted the van and picked up the reins, which was signal enough for her to move on. First a walk and then, as the downhill slope helped, as she seemed to know it would, quickly into her relaxed trot, which she maintained until a few hundred yards from Sipson and home. I led her across the main road into the yard and round to the packing shed, where our load was removed rapidly from our care.

The farm was soon entering a busy time of year. Fresh vegetables were in demand in the London markets, requiring both of the farm lorries to be fully laden on the nightly run. Local shop proprietors were arriving in vehicles of all shapes and sizes and leaving with full loads. Fields of spinach, lettuce, salad onions, marrow, field beans, Swiss chard, turnips and carrots were all being harvested daily to fulfil orders. Harry with Prince, and Ned with the grey, would plod in with the heaviest root vegetables, while I was directed to the lighter more-perishable crops needing swifter removal to safety.

I was getting plenty of practice and learning much that I needed to know; I could harness Queenie confidently and had learned how to handle her to avoid her tendency to bite. I was misguidedly convinced that kindness would cure her habit, and fed her apples from home and small white turnips, which she liked, from the fields. I only succeeded in giving her the scourers and gaining a telling-off from Harry. I came to the conclusion that I would never cure her of her biting habit; the demons in her head were not under her control and surprised us both when they struck, I felt sure. I continued to speak to her softly as we worked and was pleased that the violent incidents became fewer. At least with all the trotting she was doing she seemed to have no 'wish' to bolt again.

At the very time harvesting was in full swing and days were at their busiest, crops to follow on still needed to be sown or planted. Ground had to be prepared, keeping the tractors occupied throughout the daylight hours ploughing and cultivating. Once they had done their work, a finer tilth would be needed to form a successful seedbed, and the gentle step of a light horse was considered best to pull a fine harrow or a light roller. Queenie and I could only be spared on Saturday afternoons, once the morning's orders had been fulfilled and the fieldworkers had finished for the weekend. I was happy to take on the overtime, as what I had been asked to do was different and sounded interesting. Queenie had done the work many times and she cared not that I was a novice; she showed me how it was done, stepping forward to take up the slack in the long chains attached to the harrow, then leaning into the collar until the implement moved in the soft soil. She could then continue at an easy pace that she could maintain for the hours asked of her. At the end of the field, a touch on the long rope reins to tell her turn this way or that, and she would be best left to navigate the wide circle she knew was needed to avoid entanglement with chains and ropes. Only if I offered assistance, by way of the reins, would disaster strike. Even then, Queenie would stand placidly, resisting saying 'I told you so', as I lifted each hoof to return chain or rein to its rightful place.

While I traversed the empty fields, workers, then at home, would be free for a brief time from the demands of their employer. Men might be attending to a job that had waited until the weekend to be completed, perhaps mending a pair of the family's shoes; cutting the leather, driving in brads and finishing with a rasp and dubbing.

Perhaps helping a neighbour with a task too great for one, while their wives shopped and made preparation for Sunday, the traditional day of rest.

Sunday was the one day of the week that workers could indulge themselves and put their own desires first. The only day that allowed time for a cooked breakfast, time to read the Sunday newspapers, and for the men to meet their friends at the public house to share a pint or two before the family gathered for the Sunday roast at home. Full of breakfast, beer and dinner, a lie down on the bed might be necessary, and a man might call his wife to bring up the Sunday papers, and, knowing he had already read them from cover to cover, she might take them to him.

Feasting would continue following the afternoon's rest, as there was also time on Sunday for the ritual of 'high tea'. It was the meal to which a friend or prospective sweetheart of the son or daughter of the house might be invited, so the best china would be brought out. After tea, the lovers might walk in the country. The children might ride their bicycles around the village, shouting and calling to their friends as they invented games. Mum and Dad might listen to the radio or just sit, enjoying the last hours of their day of rest, before preparing for work next morning.

Some more overtime came my way, slightly less attractive as it meant getting to work an hour earlier each morning. A number of fields were ready to receive leek sets, which were waiting in the greenhouse yard. One of the fields to be planted was at Harmondsworth, from where I had brought the last cutting of cauliflower. It had since been ploughed and had received all the further attention needed to create a suitable tilth. It was there I was to go, at that unearthly starting hour. The strawberry van had been loaded the previous evening and stood ready. Harry was already attending Queenie and Prince. 'Come on,' he said. 'They'll be waiting.' Soon we were on our way. The morning was moist and fresh and promising to turn into a warm day, Queenie's step was more brisk than her years would expect. She was a good age for a horse and, as I had begun, I continued letting her find her own pace. We whirred along Harmondsworth Lane and I had time to enjoy the sweet air and perfumes of leafy crops from the fields on either side.

As we arrived at the Harmondsworth field, the men pounced on the load, carrying boxes to where they were going to start work. Some were planting by hand and began immediately. With a short hand-dibber, they punched a hole in the soil and dropped in a leek set. A second thrust of the dibber pushed soil into contact with the set. With feet wide apart and bending from the waist the men moved forward, planting leeks at the required spacing as they worked their way across the field.

Another group had been assigned to plant the leeks mechanically. It was clearly going to take some time to set up the machine, but, no doubt, they would catch the hand-planters and overtake them. Each leek set had to be put into jaws, which travelled around a belt inverting the set 180 degrees before pushing it into the ground. Providing the operators placed the leek in the jaws of the machine correctly, it would end up in the ground the right way up – mostly, they kept their wits about them and all was well. It did, however, take five men to operate the machine and, when it finally got going, it was only planting three rows. The hand-planters, managing a row each, were by that time out of sight; far away on the other side of the field. (It could have been concluded that the Luddites of 1811 need not have worried about this invention throwing men out of work.)

There was no time to continue my time-and-motion study. I had other fields to deal with, so Queenie and I trotted off.

Chapter 26

THE OAT HARVEST

A field of oats was grown to provide feed and bedding for pigs and horses. When the crop was ready to be cut, the foreman of the horses took his usual role, assigning the most skilled fieldwork to himself. He led out the two greys, hitched up a finger mower, which he rode like a charioteer, and went round the field in an ever decreasing square. The mower, powered by two heavy horses, felled the corn with ease, cutting it a few inches above the ground and laying it neatly in rows as straight and untangled as it had grown.

As many workers as could be spared helped in gathering up the crop. Armfuls were tied into bundles of varying sizes, according to the man's or woman's dimensions of reach, producing sheaves, which they stood upright in heaps of ten or a dozen to form stooks. The corn, now separated from its roots, remained in the position it had grown, with its head in the air and sun, while it continued to ripen and mature.

Later, the gangs of fieldworkers returned to plunder the stooks, carrying the sheaves to a part of the field, chosen for its dryness, where a corn rick was to be built. Sheaves were laid in a circle on the ground, seed heads protected in the centre with straw pointing to the outer circumference where wind and weather would come. Layer after layer was added in similar fashion until it was necessary for several of the men to remain on top of the stack to position the sheaves while others used the full length of their pitchforks in order to elevate the bundles of straw and corn heads to sufficient height. Always, more sheaves were laid in the centre of the stack so that, when all the stooks were gone from the field, the rick formed a conical shape, which, when covered, would throw off the rain.

That year the weather had been kind to the corn, so when the mower had been ordered the grain was ripe and its moisture content low. Every man on the farm considered himself an expert on the subject, and would take an ear and rub it in the palms of his hands to release the grain. He would gaze at the grain, commenting on its colour, smell it, bite it, taste it and, finally, spit it out, declaring that it was either ready or required just a bit longer to ripen. In any case, it would be a few weeks before the contractor arrived with the threshing machine, so the rick would be tidied up and, this year, covered only with a tarpaulin as, it was hoped, it would be for just a short time.

On the day the corn was to be threshed, I arrived at the stable to find all four stalls empty. 'It's all right,' said Harry. 'They're having an extra day's holiday, we're 'elpin' with the threshing.' The four horses were in the paddock, where they had been over the weekend. When we had finished work on Saturday, we had led them there and turned them out, as happened through the more pleasant weather from late spring to autumn and as long as warmer days and nights went on.

The first 'turning out' that I had assisted in, Harry was full of warnings for my safety. 'Watch me and when you let Qucenie go, do exactly as I do.' I wondered what could be as dangerous as his serious voice suggested, but told myself I would watch carefully. We arrived at the paddock, its condition had been planned for this day and was so attractive to the anticipant animals. It had been mowed at just the right time and left long enough to produce a rich sward of succulent young grasses. The horses knew it, and the placid workers of the morning began an agitated dance as their nostrils took in the smell of the fresh green delights that awaited them.

'Stead-dy,' said Harry, as he held firmly on to Prince's bridle. I did the same with Queenie. Harry led Prince into the paddock, well clear of the gate he had just entered. He turned Prince as if to return, but then stopped and moved round to face the great shire. He unbuckled the bridle, loosening the straps that rested behind the animal's ears and held the bit in place. Harry then held the bit, his hands either side of Prince's mouth, as he gently pushed the horse back, keeping control with the help of the bit and the command that Prince had heard many times in his working hours, 'Whoa! Back Prince. Whoa! Back.' As Prince moved back, the bit was allowed to fall slowly from his mouth and Harry stepped back several paces with the bridle in his hand, giving Prince plenty of room to show his joy at being released into

The Oat Harvest

that lush green field.

It was suddenly made clear to me why Harry had taken so much care. Once free, Prince became as nimble as a frolicking lamb; he spun on the spot, kicking his heels in the air and turning at the same time, creating a spiral of potential death to anyone within reach of the animal's hind hooves as they travelled in an arc reaching seven or eight feet high. Prince was a young horse and showed his youth. To see this gentle giant on that day gave me just a little understanding as to why Harry held back Prince's ration of oats, passing more than her share to Queenie. The oat-straw chaff that Harry cut so lovingly for Prince, had all the nutrition that the animal needed for good health but was lower in carbohydrates, which provide only energy. The aging Queenie was grateful for the extra energy that oats could provide and trotted any surplus off during the course of her working day.

I followed Harry's example carefully, when turning Queenie loose. Her actions were the same as Prince's but slightly more sedate, as befitted her age. The two horses ran off to join the greys and they all ran around kicking at one another and biting each other's necks (as horses do to establish a pecking order until it is decided who is boss and where the others fit into the hierarchy of the herd). It was good to see that an animal under man's daily domination could still contain, deep inside, nature's driving force, which even the bit, the whip and the spur could not subdue.

While the horses holidayed, we were free to help with the threshing. The foreman and Harry had jobs to do around the stable yard for an hour or so, they claimed, but Ned and I were told to 'get on down' to the field. The contractor had arrived early, having towed his machine from a nearby farm where his last job had been completed, and was set up ready to begin. The threshing machine had the appearance of a great timber-built farm cart. It was as high as the rick it stood next to. A flat belt, as wide as the span of a man's hand, went round a large iron wheel on the thresher, flying through the air many yards to a tractor, which was stationary with its engine running and was the power source for the day.

The Field-Marshall tractor had unique statistics: a five-litre two-stroke single-cylinder engine. It ran on diesel oil and was started with an explosive cartridge, which was placed in the side of the cylinder and hit with a hammer. The engine was left to run all day rather than go through the starting procedure again, or perhaps it was to save the cost of another cartridge. The contractor's involvement was no more than attending his machinery, he was occasionally to be seen carrying an oilcan and an oily rag.

The fieldworkers had already removed the tarpaulin covering from the rick and would undertake the work of threshing. A ladder was placed at the side of the rick and three men took their place on the top, from where, with pitchforks, they passed sheaves to a further two men on the top of the thresher, one cutting the binding and the other feeding each sheaf into the top of the machine.

Down on the ground, two men carried away sacks of the threshed grain, and two more removed straw. Another man was fully occupied clearing chaff and rubbish from under the heavy toothed threshing drum, which revolved at great speed and needed to be free of any impediment.

As the work began, sheaves were passed across the top of the rick to the feeders on the thresher. As the day went on and the rick reduced in height, it became necessary to lift each sheaf higher until, at the time arms and backs were beginning to ache, pitchforks would need to be pushed upward using their full length to reach the top of the thresher. The enthusiastic uninitiated suffered, while the experienced had paced themselves in preparation.

With the rick now being so much reduced in height, there soon would be an event that would give a few moments of respite to everyone of a coarse sporting nature. An air of agitation could be felt, mysterious to me as I had no idea what might be about to happen. Ned was tying more twine around his ankles, and others were doing the same. I was encouraged to check my own, and I did so without knowing why. We worked on until another layer of sheaves had been removed from the stack. Then, several men shouted excitedly, 'There they go!' Rats, mice and corn-loving rodents of all kinds had decided, all at once, that the game was up, their warm dry tenement with so much food on hand was no longer the place to be. In all directions across the field and away from the stack they scampered as fast as they could go.

One man who had not taken care when tying his trousers around his ankles, enlightened newcomers as to why the operation was necessary as he beat his own leg with his cap to remove one of the fleeing rodents. Aching backs were forgotten briefly as the afternoon exploded into mayhem, any weapon close at hand was used to pursue the dismayed rodents; shovels and pitchforks were wielded dangerously.

It was not widely known that the contractor was accompanied by a pair of terriers, who had remained under the master's tractor snoozing away the warm day. However, their apparently sleepy animal senses were in tune with the temporary tenants of the corn rick, whose growing fear of eviction had communicated itself so thoroughly to each and every one of their number. The small dogs were more than ready when the moment came, adding to the excitement and chaos by barking and growling, seemingly from all directions at once, as their tiny legs carried them so rapidly hither and thither.

Men and women fieldworkers from across the field had been drawn to the rick in anticipation of the event now in progress. Mostly, men took up arms and, mostly, women looked on, some expressing dislike of the barbarity. But it was not a clear division of feeling, some men preferred to stand back and some women surpassed the men in the wielding of a shovel or a spade or a piece of scrap wood previously selected. Some women were frighteningly accurate with a pitchfork.

By the end of the day, the threshed grain had filled enough sacks to be counted as a good harvest, it had been carted back to the grain store in the main yard where it would remain until it was needed. It would be rolled to feed the horses or ground into meal to feed the pigs. The soft oat-straw, ideal as bedding for horses and pigs, had been transported throughout the day to the rickyard, where by now a good-sized straw stack would be ready for thatching.

The contractor had by that time packed up his travelling circus and was ready to move on to the next farm that required his services. The field would be cleared of machinery. The workers, men and women, would make wearily for home.

Chapter 27

THE MANGOLD FIELD

As the summer days cooled into autumn and light perishable crops were finishing, root vegetables came to their harvest time. The days became wetter and the fields muddier. The strawberry van was put away and it was time for Queenie to go back into the winter cart.

I was still being directed to the lighter crops or smaller loads. One of these was the Jerusalem artichoke, the name having nothing to do with that religious city but a corruption of 'girasole', the Italian word for sunflower. Like its relative, the artichoke grows to ten feet high or more, so I was surprised to see that it was only the knobbly tubers that were harvested and eaten as an up-market alternative to potatoes.

When the artichoke crop was finished, I found myself being paired up with Ned. One day, we were sent where tractors could not go. After days of rain, the fields had become too slippery for a light tractor to venture on; horses, once again, came into their own. Ned and I were sent to collect mangolds; the large beets would be chopped to make a valuable addition to the diet of the pig herd. Ned had the smaller of the two greys. We both had the short tip carts. The oversized tyres almost floated on the slippery surface of the field and the horses' hooves were able to grip where other means of propulsion would have failed.

As we were preparing to leave the cover of the open barn, where the carts were kept overnight, it came on to rain, not a sharp shower that might cease at any moment but a constant drizzle, fine and penetrating. Ned had collected up a few of the newest hessian sacks before we left the yard and I wondered why. By the time we got to the field, the rain appeared to be set in for the day, and the days were getting colder. Ned folded one of the sacks so that one corner remained prominent. ''Ere, put this over yer 'ed,' he said, handing the sack to me. He folded another and put it on himself. The sack corner acted like a pixie hat and the length of the sack covered our backs and shoulders. We wrapped more sacks around our legs like gaiters and tied them on with twine.

We covered the horses' backs; they would be moving only a pace or two at a time as we worked our way across the field. We started picking up the giant beets, which lay on the surface of the field, and throwing them into our carts. The first few were noisy as they hit the empty cart floor, making the horses throw back their ears in a fearful alertness. The noise was ignored after the first few and soon the thumps of the arriving roots became muffled as the bottom of the cart was covered and beet landed on beet.

The rain neither increased nor decreased but remained gentle and fine, in a way that seems to penetrate in such an insidious way. Within a short time, the sacks on our backs became heavier and soon the feeling of dampness around our collars travelled down inside our shirts to our backs and chests and arms. The sacks dripped onto our trousers and penetrated to the back of our legs. The rain fell onto the front of our trousers and penetrated to the front of our legs.

When our carts were fully loaded, we led the horses off of the field. Our boots slipped under us but the horses dealt easily with the mud and the load. We continued to lead the horses, crouching as we walked to remain low on their dry side and away from the rain, as we travelled the short distance along the main road back to the village and the rickyard, where we were to deposit our loads.

At the rickyard, two men were building storage clamps, elongated heaps of root vegetables built up by successive cart loads tipping and adding to their length. One man was packing and shaping the heap to a point and the other, a skilled man, was thatching the sloping sides to a weather-proof ridge with a sufficient thickness of straw to withstand and protect from winter rain and frost. We tipped our loads and returned to the field.

When it was time to open our flasks for a hot drink, we huddled by the side of a cart. We took the briefest time to enjoy our breakfast; by this early hour we were already wet and cold and needed to keep moving to keep warm.

We completed several more journeys, working side by side,

helping one another with the last few roots to complete a load. We continued like that until dinnertime, when we were able to return to the main yard. The horses were sheltered under the open barn and rugged while we huddled around Siddy's fire of scrap wood in his box-mending shop. We were soaked through and there would be no chance of getting dry, we could only hope to feel the warmth of the fire on our hands and faces while we ate our sandwiches. We managed to find more sacks, not quite as new as the ones Ned had found in the morning but they were dry and afforded a little warmth and protection from the rain, which had no intention of ceasing that day. We kept our break short for, although it was difficult to leave Siddy's fire, we considered it best to continue working to keep our bodies moving.

We worked on through the afternoon, leading horses at all times, not wanting to expose ourselves to the weather high on the carts. The mangolds became more slippery and our wet cold hands became sore. The horses' hooves began to slip and backing the cart in the rickyard became more difficult; the horse, losing its footing, would fall back into its breaching causing the cart to reverse too far, stopping only when it rammed into the heap. The beets of the previous load would be damaged and curses would be heard from the stacker whose work had been disturbed.

At last, in the fading afternoon, the field was cleared and we could return to the yard. Once our concentration on the task was eased, the wet and cold filled the place in our minds where determination to complete the job had been.

'You all right?' said Ned. 'You're shivering.'

'So are you,' I said, trying to be cheeky in a comradely way.

'Cold, in' it?' said Ned, returning my cheek with a grin and a giggle. 'Come on, let's get finished,' he added in a caring way.

We laughed at our own comments and with the relief of finishing the job. Still leading the horses, we went through the main yard to the open barn where the carts would remain. We still had to lead the horses to the stables, unharness them and bed them down for the night.

Many years later, I was reminded of our day in the mangold field when I read Gilbert White's observation, written in 1788, of farm workers in his parish of Selbourne who he said 'have a good life and can expect to live to the age of about forty years'. I was saddened by the thought of such short lives, but my experience of a cold rain-soaked day helped me understand at least one contributory factor.

Ned said goodnight and walked off up the village home. I got on my bike and rode a cold wet couple of miles, and was pleased to get in to a warm fireside and a good hot dinner.

Chapter 28

WINTER

Ned and I continued to be paired up through the winter. My respect for my companion had grown over the months we had worked together. Ned was a simple man; unspoiled by sophistication. He was without bias or a prejudice that tainted his opinion or an ego that needed to be proven. When Ned spoke, his words were sincere. They were, on occasions, delivered with a grin that was, by some, considered foolish. He may have been a simple man, but he was not foolish.

One morning, we were told that we were 'on dung-cart today'. Ned looked as happy as if we had been given the day off. I wondered why. 'We'll be all right while this job lasts, we'll be in the pig sheds where it's warm and dry.' When I remembered wet cold days out in the fields, I could understand his joy. Ned must have had many days like that in the fifteen or twenty years in which he had built up seniority over me.

We made our way to the pig unit. It was my first opportunity to see inside. The 'sheds' were indeed warm; they were superior modern buildings, well insulated and spacious. The pigs looked healthy, clean and boisterous. Ned had an interest in pigs and chatted on about them. They were farrowed from sows of pedigree stock, he told me, and weaned and fattened on the premises, thereby avoiding the stress of transportation and markets. They were fed on vegetables and meal from home-grown produce. When piglets had first occupied the vast open shed that we were about to begin clearing, soft oat-straw had been spread to cover the floor. Soon it would have been necessary to add a fresh layer, to keep the young animals in the same comfort as they had begun. As piglet became pig, many more layers of straw were added, causing the floor surface and pigs to rise. While bedding remained wholesome, as winter came on it had the advantage of warmth created by the microbic activity deep below.

One Clear Morn

We slid back the doors of the shed, now empty of pigs. 'Their ears must have been touching the roof,' said Ned, in a way that sounded as if it was for my amusement, for, in truth, he had seen it all many times before and knew what to expect. We were greeted with a wall of dung covering an area greater than we could see. My heart sank; I could not imagine that we would ever finish this job, the fork in my hand feeling, at that moment, like a teaspoon. The doors were wide enough that we could both back our carts in side by side, allowing us to continue our conversation. Ned chatted generally, always cheerfully, always optimistically, about his work or the farm or fellow workers, but never of his life outside work, and he asked me nothing of mine.

After a while, we were silent and, as we forked on, I was able to sink into my own thoughts. I wondered about the man I was working with, his apparent acceptance of life, his contentment, his deference to all those with authority over him. Was the image that Ned projected true, or was it simply acquiescence to what nature had designed for him? Was he really as happy as he seemed? Or did he begin life full of plans that failed, and were his hopes crushed, reducing him to the accepting sole that he was now? My thoughts turned to my own life. What about my future? I was not Ned. I could not be content with what he had settled for. Where was my life going? I had enjoyed collecting crops from the fields during the summer, my job was individual, I had felt special, I was proud of what I did, but this was not the same, being warm and dry was not enough.

We continued until we could get no more on our carts. Our first loads made little impression, but the journey to the dung heap brought a brief respite. It was good, after only a short spell in the confined space, to see across the fields, even the damp air was welcome. Our work of that day, although tedious, was nevertheless a small part in the natural cycle of life. This year's waste product, once weathered, would become next year's soil enrichment, as has happened since plants and animals first inhabited the land. At our destination, we backed our carts into position and pulled a rod from across the front of the cart to release the tipping mechanism. The load shot onto the ground with a force that shook the vehicle through to the shafts,

Winter

causing the horses to move their feet to maintain their balance. The day went on, load after load, forked on painfully, and released effortlessly. We were dry, we were warm, and Ned was satisfied.

Clearing the sheds took days, but when it was at last finished Ned and I were, for the first time in several weeks, sent on separate jobs. When the morning break came, I found myself alone in the yard. Siddy, the box mender, called me over to his workshop, saying I should have my breakfast by his fire. The fieldworkers were spread far and wide that day, so I was his only company. As we made ourselves comfortable, Siddy began to speak as if he knew all that I had been thinking in recent days. 'You'll be wanting a better job soon,' he said. I was shocked; had he some super-natural ability to look into the mind of another person. For a few moments I stared at Siddy in astonishment. I had heard him several times taking an advisory role in some discussion, and had wondered why this man, who sounded so wise, was mending boxes in a workshop made of scrap wood. I must have shown my surprise. 'Don't worry,' said Siddy, 'your secret is safe with me.' I tried to smile, but said nothing intelligible, wanting to keep my thoughts to myself. 'Of course you'll be wanting a better job. You've got your life ahead of you. At your age you can be anything you want to be, if you put your mind to it.' Siddy paused to assure himself that I was giving him full attention. Then he went on, 'You've done well since you've been here. The bosses are pleased with you. But that means they'll try to keep you here, they don't like to let good workers go.'

I was pleased to hear that I had 'done well' and let a small smile escape.

Siddy came back firmly, 'They'll want to keep you here because it's good for their business, but it may not be the best thing for you, you'll need to make up your own mind, what's right for you. People will try to give you advice but you'll have to decide for yourself.' A wry smile on Siddy's face suggested that he realized he was one of the people giving advice. Hoping to correct the matter, he said, 'Everyone will have a different opinion, and you can't please them all, so you'll have to make your own mind up in the end.' There was another brief moment while Siddy thought up a compliment or two as if to apologize for his outspoken remarks, and to perhaps soften his words, 'You seem to have common sense, you'll need to use that, and I can see you are a cautious lad, a little caution never hurt either.'

Siddy's words of advice had been rather direct, but he had the wisdom not to point out the direction I should take and left me to act on my own feelings, using the common sense he had complimented me on having. Such advice, clearly free of self-interest, was welcome, as I was finding that I needed to take responsibility for my own life. I longed to have conversations with a close family member about my struggle with the problems that every teenager encounters, but such a luxury was not available; some I could not ask, and some I would not. My guardian would, I knew, proffer a gem of potted wisdom, which many years later I would realize was shrewdness itself, but it would not, at the time, help me, step by step, up the ladder to the promised nirvana. One person I would not ask was Uncle Fred; his guidance had always been unhelpful, confirmed recently when he put pressure on his older sister to dissuade me from taking up a mortgage that had been offered to me now that I was working. For less than the cost of our rent, we could have owned our house, which would have given Nan security and me roots in future years. No doubt Uncle Fred considered that some responsibility might fall upon him, so he gave his usual negative advice. As there was no one else I could ask I had learned to consider advice from wherever it came. I was able to thank Siddy and assure him I would think about all that he had said.

Siddy, satisfied that I had listened, began to speak more generally and, after a little while, about himself. He told me he liked to read. It was clear that he was proud of the ability, saying that he was unable to do so when he left school and had taught himself later. He admitted that he still read slowly and, because of the effort it took, he always chose to read things that might teach him something. 'Do you like to read?' he asked.

'I read about things I want to know about,' I said hesitantly.

Siddy responded immediately, 'You mean practical books about how things work?'

'Yes, and how to look after animals,' I said, gaining confidence as I remembered the little books from the corn shop.

'Do you read stories or any other kind of books?' Siddy asked.

'I haven't read any stories,' I admitted, feeling a little ashamed.

'I expect sitting down reading is thought to be lazy then, is it?' said Siddy.

'Yes. There's always something more important to be done,' I said.

'Oh yes, there's always something else to be done,' Siddy said. 'That was always the way when I was young. But now, when I'm working, I remember what I have read, then my mind is free and I can think about the world outside my workshop.'

As I listened, I was thinking about Siddy's advice on my future but, still wanting to keep my thoughts to myself, I was pleased he was now speaking more generally.

'I was reading about the airport the other day,' Siddy said.

'Heathrow airport?' I asked as brightly and with as much interest as I could summon up, hoping to encourage him to continue on matters other than my own.

'Yes, the one just up the road,' Siddy confirmed, and went on, 'Heathrow was just a village once, you know?'

'Was it?' I said.

'Yes,' Siddy lamented, 'until in the war, when they said they needed an aerodrome for the RAF. Heathrow was a village, just like Sipson, with houses, pubs, a shop and farms all around.' Siddy paused, he stared blankly for a moment and then, his voice hardening a little, he continued, 'The Government doesn't ask. If they say they want something, they take it, and the war was on and they needed it for the RAF they said. The buildings were knocked down and the farms taken over to make runways, and that was that, they had their aerodrome.' Knitting his brow and wagging a finger, Siddy said, 'According to what I read, the RAF didn't really need it.' After a thoughtful pause, he continued, 'When the war was over, they didn't put it back as it was, the aerodrome became an airport, and now people can go on holiday from there.'

I felt a rush of confidence, 'I know,' I said. 'Our class at school was taken to see the new Comet jet airliner.'

My sudden enthusiasm must have been interpreted as approval of the airport and its aeroplanes, as, for a fleeting moment, Siddy looked at me as if I would not understand his objections and perhaps he was wasting his breath. Nevertheless, he was determined to try to make me a convert to his cause, so he went on to tell the story of what he thought was a dreadful thing to have happened and how in years to come it would be considered the cruellest of ironies. 'Do you know,' he said, 'they have started bringing fruit, and even vegetables in by plane? It seems funny to me to concrete over good growing land and then have to bring vegetables in noisy smelly planes from goodness knows where.'

'It does, doesn't it,' I said in an uncertain way, trying to be agreeable but not feeling as troubled about it as Siddy, after all, I had grown up with the airport and, as young people do, had accepted the world as I had found it.

Siddy saw my lack of empathy for his narration but must have thought I was worth the effort of an explanation. 'You drove the strawberry van didn't you?' he said. 'You must have wondered where it got its name?'

I retorted confidently, 'There were strawberry fields here, weren't there?'

Siddy came back in controlled excitement, 'There were strawberry fields for miles, and lots of other fruit too in the early days, nowadays, of course, it's all vegetables. The whole of south-west Middlesex was blessed with the best Grade One growing land, and only the richest soil is good enough to grow vegetables year in, year out, you know,' Siddy emphasized with a building passion. He went on, 'Not only Heathrow but all the villages around, like Harmondsworth, Harlington, Hatton, Bedfont, Stanwell and Cranford. All, like Sipson, with farms around them like ours, growing tons of good fresh vegetables.'

'There's lots of farms still though, aren't there?' I said pleadingly.

'There are, but that airport is getting bigger, every year there's more concrete and more tarmac and more roads, and they're talking about special hotels now. It all takes space, and it's not only the farms that are disappearing,' Siddy said, repeating himself in his fervour, 'it's the villages too. Each one of them was different and a complete community; friends, neighbours and workmates depending on each other. A whole way of life is being lost.'

Siddy pulled the cork from his flask and poured himself more tea, and offered me some too. The inactivity of sitting while we had our breakfast caused us both to shiver, so Siddy dropped a handful of wood scraps into his oil-drum fire and, as it burned up, we drew in to warm ourselves once more while we sipped our flask-worn tea. As we looked into the flames, Siddy bemoaned, 'The farms are going one by one. Farms, like this one, that have done nothing but good for everyone for hundreds of years, growing good natural food. Any muck we make goes back in the ground, as nature intended. And we don't make any noise, not like them planes that frighten the life out of you when they go over. That airport will cover us all up one day.'

Siddy's narration was interrupted abruptly as Ned appeared in the doorway, 'Come on, they're waiting for you down the field,' he said. I drained my last sip of tea and, with matters that affected me personally still uppermost in my mind, thanked Siddy for his advice and said I would think about all he had said. We got up and Siddy gave me a knowing smile as he patted my arm lightly, and said, 'You'll know what to do.' As he turned towards his bench, he said, almost to himself, 'And you mark my words about that airport.'

Chapter 29

THE DECISION

Through the winter months, I had come to the conclusion that working on a farm in south-west Middlesex could not be compared to the Australian farming scene the posters had promised. So it was that the bold plan, which sudden freedom from school had encouraged in a foolish boy's mind, had faded during the days of mud and cold and wet, and was almost forgotten by the time spring came round again. Without knowing how it could be achieved, I decided that I must 'improve my position in life'. I would have to hold on tightly to my resolve, because I was enjoying my work now that the strawberry van was out again. I would also have to build up courage to take the leap into the unknown, and to overcome my nervousness at having to tell my employer I wanted to leave his employ.

As it happened, an event was about to unfold that would speed matters along, when one morning Queenie was reluctant to trot and, at her walking pace, it was easy to see she was lame. I pulled her up and got down from the van. I ran my hand down her ailing leg to let her know I wanted to lift her foot. A stone chipping, the size of a small walnut, was wedged up into her hoof. I was not a Boy Scout with one of those special folding knives that has a 'thing for getting stones out of horses' hooves', so I had to hunt around to find an improvised tool. A piece of broken box helped me carefully coax the stone back down the path by which it had entered and out of the hoof.

Removal of the stone did not cure the problem; she was lame and clearly suffering. I decided that Queenie could do no more work that day. I led her to the stables to report her plight. Before I could find Harry or the foreman, Mr Williams came up on his bicycle and said I should be at the field now, a load of spinach was spoiling. I told him I could not go, explaining the reason.

'Well, just get this load and after that you can put her in the stable,' Mr Williams compromised.

The Decision

I protested politely, but he insisted firmly. I knew that the crop would be ruined by the sun, so I felt I had to obey. Reluctantly, I put Queenie back into the van and led her out of the yard into the lane. Her left foreleg was very lame and each sound of her hoof on the hard stony surface hurt me as much as I thought it must be hurting her. I felt cruel. Our pace was slow as I led Queenie painfully along the lane. I kept my head close to hers, whispering apologies as we went. I began sobbing quietly as I felt her pain, and my own. Mr Williams came along on his bicycle to hurry me up. As he pulled level with me, I turned my face towards Queenie so that the field manager could not see my tears. I felt foolish; I had not expected to be found out.

Seeing my distress and speaking in a soft caring voice, Mr Williams asked, 'What's the matter?'

Protesting, between sobs, I said forcefully, 'I'm hurting her. She shouldn't have to do this. Look at how bad she's limping.'

I feared that I had raised my voice and that my attitude would be taken as insolence, but Mr Williams continued in a soothing manner, his previous order was softened once again, this time to a kindly suggestion, 'Take her to the stable immediately you get back with this load.' His order was unchanged but had been put even more kindly; his gentleness combined with firmness was perhaps the reason for the esteem in which he was held by the fieldworkers. He had dismounted his bicycle by now and was walking beside me pushing his machine as he continued to coax me towards the load in need of rescue.

Nothing was said for a short while. I sunk into my thoughts: I still had to go all the way to the field and all the way back with each lame step hurting Queenie. I could not stop sobbing. That made me feel more foolish still, and in my confusion I told myself that having raised my voice I was now in 'conflict with management'. I was sure I would be dismissed for disobedience, and as I had come to the conclusion that I wanted to move in another direction with my life anyway, I took the opportunity to tell the manager that I wanted to leave. I would only have to get up courage another day to speak to him, so I might as well say it now.

'Don't get yourself all upset,' said Mr Williams, his voice full of sympathy. 'She'll be all right. I'll ring the farrier when I get back to the office. I'll get him to come in the morning.'

I continued walking beside Queenie's head, suffering each time her foot touched the lane, until we reached the field. 'Where you been?' one of the women shouted. 'Stay on the cart, we'll chuck it up to yer.' Boxes of Victoria spinach came at me from all sides, which I stacked as quickly as I could. I made sure to keep my reddened face turned away when Molly came near; she would so enjoy teasing me and I did not feel that I could take it just then.

Once the load was in the packing shed, I led Queenie to her stall and unharnessed her while she snorted into her manger to blow away any dust. She found chaff and oats to occupy herself, and showed no distress or even any great interest in the events of the day; she was so completely placid as to suggest that she had no memory of the happenings and would not even be aware of her disability until she next put her hooves, one before the other, on a hard stoned tarmacadam road.

Next morning, the farrier came on his motorcycle, which had a great wooden sidecar loaded with the tools of his trade: a forge, already glowing and needing only a pump or two on its bellows to bring it to life, an anvil, hammers, pinchers, nippers, hoof knives, clinchers, rasps of various sizes and even a pot of Stockholm Tar with a brush already in place, to paint the hoof to finish and protect. On that morning, the farrier carried in his kit something that he did not always need on his day to day rounds of ungulate maintenance. He had been warned of the special need and had a thick piece of leather, from which he cut a round, a little larger than Queenie's troubled hoof. As he worked, he explained that the stone had bruised the animal's frog, the tender part in the centre of the foot. The old shoe would be removed and replaced with a built-up one, which would take weight off the affected area. The leather would go between hoof and shoe, to further protect the frog, and would remain there until the next shoeing when bruising should have healed.

Once the farrier had done his work, I led Queenie for an hour or so until I assured myself that she was walking without pain. I mounted

The Decision

the van, and bid her, 'Walk on,' which she did with ease. When we were on a homeward journey, as horses do, she became enlivened, in the sure knowledge that the comforts of the stable awaited, although, being early in the day, on that occasion her expectation would not be immediately gratified. The brisk trot that she seemed to manage so easily, did however assure me that the farrier's work was successful and that all was now well with Queenie.

As we purred along the lane, my thoughts turned to my statement to the field manager; I had declared my desire to leave the farm and, although in my distress I had let my intentions be known in haste and without preparation, it was, after all, what I had decided to do. I must now continue and see it through. As we arrived at the main yard, the boss, Mr Wild, was standing talking to the field manager, who I imagined was telling him about the silly boy who had made a fool of himself and was then ungrateful enough to reject the good job he had, and wanted to leave. I decided to make myself scarce for the time being.

At the end of the working day, I led Queenie to the stable yard. She was having a long cool drink from the trough while I fussed around her, slackening straps and buckles ready to unharness her, when Mr Wild came across from the office indicating that he wanted to speak to me. I had learned, during the course of the past year, that a lowly worker like myself was usually dealt with by a manager or a foreman; only an exceptional matter would warrant the direct attention of the boss. Jonter Evans appeared at the far stable door, he gave a quizzical look and quickly disappeared back inside. For my part, the vision of the farm owner himself striding across the yard towards me filled me with trepidation; my worst fears had come to pass and I was in for a telling off.

'How is Queenie?' said Mr Wild, with an unexpected kindly gaze and gentle voice that sounded as if his concern was as much for me as it was for one of his animals.

'She seems all right now,' I said hesitantly, a little perplexed and still anxious about what might follow.

'You mustn't worry, you know. It's common enough for a horse to pick up a stone. The farrier can usually put it right straight away. Mr Williams told me how upset you were and there's no need.'

I curled with embarrassment.

'Do you still want to leave us?' asked Mr Wild.

'Er, yes,' I said, unable to think of any words that might soften my abrupt response.

'We-ll,' said Mr Wild, the 'well' drawn out as if filling in the time I might have taken with a more courteous answer. 'We shall be sorry to see you go, we've been very pleased with your work. It's commendable that you want to make progress in your life, and at your age, of course, you should. You could progress here on the farm if you wanted to; once you have learned about the business, you could become a foreman or a manager. But, naturally, you will have to make up your own mind about that.'

Siddy's words about making my own mind up rang in my ears.

Mr Wild patted me lightly on the shoulder, his eyes smiling directly into mine. 'You'll need to think it all over, and if you decide to leave us we shall wish you lots of good luck. But if you change your mind, or if you ever want a job, come and see me personally,' he said, and he turned and walked off, leaving me a little shocked but with feelings of warmth and pride to have had such important confirmation that I had done well and would be welcomed back. It was a great relief, also, to know that I had not provoked the boss's anger and that my desire to do better things with my life seemed to have been given an understanding approval. All I had to do now was show that I was up to the challenge I had set myself.

Chapter 30

THE INTERVIEWS

Once I had made up my mind to leave the farm, I began looking in the local newspaper for employment that would progress my ambition towards self-improvement.

The first job that attracted my attention sounded as if it had a science connection and might be interesting. The firm carried out electroplating, which I felt I knew 'all about' as I had seen it done at school, where our teaching being practical rather than academic required the science master to perform, like a conjurer, experiments that would prove the validity of a scientific theory to even the most resistant to enlightenment in our class.

My application to the plating company resulted in an invitation to visit the factory for an interview and to be shown what would be involved in the work. Unfortunately, the classroom introduction to the subject was no match for the real world; the factory was, of course, operating on an industrial scale. Vast tanks of chemicals sloshed about menacingly, metal fabrications waiting to be plated cluttered every corner, and slippery muddle and mess was everywhere. Workers were covered by heavy rubber aprons down to their feet, on which they wore wellington boots. Hands and arms were protected by rubber gloves, stiff enough to stand free of forearms, to elbow height. Two boys who had just been taken on were dressed in this fashion, looking very out of place, not quite knowing what was expected of them and clearly feeling some embarrassment. Despite their unintended disguises, I recognized them as two local lads who were widely known to be troublemakers.

After an enlightening half-hour, I was sent away to think about the job I had been offered. It was clear that dangerous chemicals and untrustworthy colleagues would surely be a lethal combination, so I wanted no part of that. Neither would I consider that I had made any progress in such a job and felt sure I could do better for myself.

I feared that refusing the offer of a job would cause a break in our income and Nan would be worried and become cross, but my future was important too, so I decided to weather the storm but waste no time in looking again at the employment section of the newspaper. There I read 'Young man wanted to train as assistant to Managing Director of new company. The position entails world travel'. Momentarily possessed by the thought of 'world travel', I decided to telephone immediately.

A secretary passed me to Mr Bond, the managing director, who sounded pleased that I did not want to miss any working days at my present job. He said that he was just about to leave for America but would be returning by next weekend and would be in his office on Saturday afternoon. I could call to see him then. My interview was brief, a few words only passed between us, leaving me with little impression of my employer-to-be other than he was a smartly dressed man of perhaps thirty years. I was told I could start for a trial period on the first Monday I was free to do so.

When that day came, I put on my Sunday best and made sure my shoes were polished. The premises I was to attend were on the edge of Heathrow airport, which meant I would need to cycle through the village of Sipson, passing directly by the main gates of the farm I had worked on until two days before. As I approached the village, I was filled with mixed feelings that unnerved me: embarrassment that I might be seen and laughed at in my best clothes, the unease of my changed situation, and fear of the unknown that I was about to confront. I kept my head down and rode on.

I arrived promptly and entered a brightly lit workshop. I had been told that the company was involved in advertising world travel. The explanation was sufficient to sound exciting but not enough to give me much idea of what to expect. I was greeted by sights and smells that created an environment so different from the one I was leaving behind. Broad benches were covered with tools, equipment and materials all strange to me, appearing to be for fine or artistic work. There were sheets of plastic and celluloid, rolls of adhesive, opened and half-empty packets, pots, jars and tubs of diverse concoctions of

The Interviews

resinous, vinyl, plastic or acrylic nature. Unfamiliar, intoxicating and, I imagined, explosive gases filled the air.

Amidst the confusion stood models of jet airliners in various stages of completion, some two feet long, some three or four. Two men, wearing long brown overall coats, were working quietly on separate sides of the room. One man was using a steel rule and scalpel, painstakingly cutting shapes from a sheet of plastic, while the second was applying adhesive with an artist's brush and fixing parts to a model early in its construction. I hoped I would not be expected to do this kind of work, it was too intricate for my liking and not an occupation I would enjoy.

I stumbled out that I had been told to meet Mr Bond here this morning, in a manner that attempted to befit the fact that I was now his assistant. 'He's not here today,' muttered one of the men, barely looking up. He did not ask me who I was, or introduce himself or his colleague, or acknowledge that he knew anything or nothing about my arrival. After an uncomfortable pause, he said, 'I don't know what he thinks you are going to do.' I had been given no indication during my interview with Mr Bond, so I was unable to enlighten the brown-coated man. There was another silence. Both men continued with their work. I tried to look around 'intelligently'. I began to feel embarrassment, after completing a full circuit of the workshop and finding myself back at the side of the muttering man. 'Perhaps you could sweep up,' he said, pointing to a well-worn soft broom. It was not what I had come to do, or had dressed for, but I was not yet in a position to have an opinion on the matter, so I picked up the broom and began to sweep. When I paused for a moment, the second man lifted his eyes from his model and gave me a blank stare. I took the opportunity to ask, 'What are the models for?'

'Advertising,' he said flatly, as he continued working.

'Are they Comets? I went with the school to see the Comet at the airport,' I tried to enthuse in hope of gaining a few words of conversation.

The man made no response but nodded towards a small room at the end of the workshop. 'You could make a cup of tea,' he said. I hunted out the teapot, tea, milk and sugar and made the tea. I took it for granted that I was included, so at least there was small compensation in the second demeaning job I had been given.

Through the rest of the morning, both men gave full concentration to the models they were working on. There was no conversation between them, and if I asked a question no response was given satisfactorily, so I learned nothing about the position I was hoping to fill. I could obtain no indication as to when, or even if, Mr Bond would appear in the days ahead. I was left to occupy or amuse myself in any way I chose. The morning was long and as it dragged by, in my youthful impatience, I began to think that these model aeroplanes were as near as I would get to the world travel that had sounded so exciting.

Just before one o' clock, I was asked, 'Are you going out to lunch?' Not knowing what to expect of my first day, I had made no plans but took the opportunity to say, without hesitation, that I was. I got on my bike and rode home, and, seeing no point in repeating the embarrassing situation, I did not return. For a few days, I worried that I might hear from the firm in some uncomfortable way, but I never did.

Having found that the modern world of plastic was not to my liking, I was attracted by an advertisement that offered the chance to learn 'the ancient craft of woodturning'. I rang, and agreed to meet Mr Dennis White at a farm in Harlington. At the farm, I was directed to a large corrugated iron building across a field. In front, on either side, were rusting farm implements. The shed and the apparently discarded machinery formed the boundary of a work space that had at its centre an iron monster of a circular saw. As I arrived, the saw was whirring noisily but, suddenly, the power went off and the revolving blade slowed and stopped. Through double doors, I could see that most of the inside of the building was taken up with timber, almost to roof height. Planks of various lengths were the full width of the tree, so that bark and uneven edges, as the tree had grown, remained on either side. Some were two feet wide, some were three feet or more, from rough edge to rough edge.

The Interviews

Mr White appeared, climbing over and around the timber, shielding his eyes as he stepped out into the bright sunlight. 'I 'ave to go 'alf way to Yiewsley to turn the saw off!' He laughed and, with a broad grin that remained while he enjoyed his own joke, he put a cupped hand behind his ear in case I wanted to say something (I would learn later that a bomb blast in the war had shattered his hearing). Without even appearing to look me up and down, he assured me he could teach me to 'turn'. 'Do you know anything about turning?' he asked.

'No,' I said as politely as I could, trying not to sound dismissive.

Neither my answer nor its brevity mattered, he was going to give me a demonstration anyway. There was just room for his lathe on one side of the building that was timber store and workshop combined; space not occupied by lathe or timber was taken up with woodchips, waist-deep in some places, and only the smallest area of floor was clear where the turner needed to stand. Fortunately, Mr White did not need much space as he was slightly built and quite nimble. He would have spent much of his time indoors, which accounted for his sallow complexion. His deafness affected his speech and immediate comprehension, all of which aged him to the uninitiated observer. Once he was known better, his energy, his love of life and his sense of humour would tell a truer story.

''Ere y' are, look,' said Mr White, sounding as enthusiastic as a keen young apprentice, as he picked up a piece of wood about nine inches long and put it into his lathe. The wood was rough-sawn walnut, about two and a half inches square, with corners that looked lethal when revolving two thousand times each minute. The master turner took a wide gouge and stroked it a few times with a slip of fine Indian stone to ensure a keen edge. His actions were as casual as a billiard player chalking his cue, but with the precision of a barber stropping a razor, his exactness contrasting with the chaos around him. He then held the gouge firmly, the right hand low down the handle to control the angle of attack, the left pressing the blade firmly on the tool-rest, palm cupped to deflect the flying woodchips. The sharp edge buzzed on the corners of the wood until the rough exterior was removed to reveal a smooth cylinder of walnut and its attractive grain.

The master turner fondled the revolving wood as if it was stationary, his hardened hands appearing to feel no discomfort from friction. He picked up an inch-wide chisel, which required only a few strokes on an oilstone fixed at the end of the lathe. A demonstration of correct use was, of course, forthcoming.

The lesson was on the difference between turning and 'scraping', the latter term I would hear many times uttered with vehement disapproval. The correct use of the chisel required cutting to be done with the centre only of the sharpened edge, which meant that the tool was held at a frightening angle across the work. Disaster was threatened if an unsteady hand should allow a corner to impale the revolving hardwood. In Mr White's hands, the chisel began to cut as he intended. A curl of wood spiralled down towards the floor, adding to the already abundant collection of chippings. 'A "scraper" only makes dust,' said the master turner, with a glow of satisfaction at his own skill.

My teacher then stopped the lathe, using his hand as a brake on the flywheel, the seemingly perilous operation distracting my concentration for a moment. Drawing my attention back to the piece of wood, now stationary, he pointed out the smoothness that had been achieved by a sharp tool used correctly. 'You'll need an accurate eye, too,' said Mr White, and to show how accurate his own eye was, he delved into a foot of woodchips that lay on the bench in front of him. With a pair of callipers, which had taken a few moments to find, he showed me how precisely he had produced a uniform diameter along the length of the work, measuring the middle and both ends and being clearly delighted with the result.

The demonstration had to stop. 'I've gotta get on,' said Mr White. 'I've gotta get out enough wood to make a couple of dozen ten-inch.' I had no idea what 'ten-inch' were. While I was wondering, my prospective employer appeared to reconsider and decided to continue his interviewing role a little longer. 'I'd better tell you a bit about the job', he said, and went on, 'Me and some other people are going to make pepper mills. I'm moving from here. I'm going to teach you to turn.' Mr White was not as eloquent with words as he was with a well-honed chisel, but it did not matter, my attention had been taken by the term 'pepper mill'.

I wondered what they were. I liked the name. 'What are pepper mills?' I asked.

A brief absence, and Mr White returned with an example. 'This is a Number One,' he announced, handing me a small pepper pot of polished walnut. 'They are called 'mills' because they grind the pepper. They are going to be hand-turned in traditional styles.' In truth, very little of the aesthetic qualities of the turner's art did I appreciate on that first day, but I said I thought the pepper mill was 'nice', and I really did like the feel of the polished wood and the naturalness of its attractive grain. I was sure I wanted to learn woodturning.

My strongest memory of that first day can be conjured up by the aroma of black peppercorns, which increases immensely when the mill has done its work and turned whole corns into fresh ground pepper. 'Cooks on the Continent like their pepper fresh and grind it as it is wanted. We are going to try pepper mills over here,' explained Mr White. I was given a 'Number One' to take home, it was displayed on our mantelpiece with other 'novelties'. It was never used in the kitchen, so all the relish it might have added to so many dishes of the day was never explored and its potential remained unknown. It was commented on, without enthusiasm, from time to time by friends and neighbours and its unusual smell noted. Its fate was to remain on sad display until the aroma of the contents faded, and even became a little rancid.

Once again, Mr White said he must get on, but then he remembered another piece of information I would need. 'We are taking over our new factory at Hanwell tomorrow,' he said. 'You'll have to come there.' He gave me the address, and told me how to get there and what time I was wanted. 'Right! I must get this wood out. You don't have to stay, but you can if you want to.' Half afraid to say I would go, instead, wanting to show my keenness, I said I could stay. 'Good,' said Mr White, obviously pleased. 'Let's find a plank.' Some planks were two inches thick, some were three and a few were four.

'We need a three,' he said. 'We'd better find a not-too-big one as there's only two of us, and neither of us is Charles Atlas!' he added, which I took to be a comradely remark and encouraging. We hunted round and found one we could lift. Out in the yard, I was left to balance the plank on the sawbench while Mr White went 'half way to Yiewsley' to drop down the mains switch to provide the power.

To the woodturner of many years, one end of the plank had a special attraction. A piece, longer than we required, was cut off the plank. 'That'll make a nice bowl,' said Mr White, putting the oversized piece in a 'safe place'. The rest of the plank was cut at the ten inch mark until all the pieces, still the full width of the plank, lay on the ground. A guide was then set three inches from the blade. The pieces were going to be cut down the grain to produce blocks ten inches long by three inches square. Mr White took a strong stick in his right hand to push the timber that would pass down between the blade and the guide. He supported the remaining tree-wide piece with his left hand. I was instructed not to put my hand nearer to the blade than the place he could reach with the stick, where he would leave the blocks for me to pick up and remove. All began well, several pieces were cut and pushed well clear of the blade.

As we worked on, I considered my own part in this potentially dangerous operation into which I had suddenly been thrust. Mr White was experienced, so I could trust that he would be accurate and precise in all that he did. Nothing would go wrong then if I paid full attention and removed the cut pieces as I had been told. Each finished piece was heavy, it was, after all, solid walnut, just separated from a block as heavy as a man could lift. The circular blade, which was cutting with comparative ease, did so by means of coarse teeth that were revolving rapidly in the direction of the operator. In my self-enforced alertness, I considered the consequence of one of the oversized teeth catching the finished block before I could remove it; I had noticed how vibrations of the sawbench caused them to move, so it seemed entirely possible that one could vibrate back towards the blade and be snatched up. I wanted to make my thoughts known to the master and suggest that he pushed the pieces further away from the blade, but surely he would know better than me. In fact, he was, by this time, tending to push them less far from the blade, so I concluded that I was worrying about something that could not happen.

'How many you got over there?' called Mr White. I told him. 'Oh, we need a few more yet then.' He lifted another full-width piece onto the sawbench and began cutting again. After trimming the rough edge and cutting a couple of pieces, the next piece came through and I positioned myself to pick it up. I could hear Mr White saying, 'That's a hard piece, that'll have some lovely grain.' As I went to pick it up, it disappeared, I did not see it go. The only indication that anything had happened was a sound from the revolving blade, a 'ding' like the bell on a shop door. My worst fears had come true, the newly cut block had been snatched up by the teeth on the speeding blade and hurled back in the direction of the sawyer.

The wood about to be cut, in Mr White's left hand, fell to the ground, causing me to look across the saw. My prospective employer was staggering backwards. He sank down, blood pouring from his forehead above his right eye. The amount of blood frightened me; I had never seen anything like that. In spite of the shock he had just received and his obvious situation of distress, Mr White seemed to remain composed. 'Better get some help,' he said calmly. Regardless of his unemotional request, I ran furiously to the farmhouse and banged on the door. The farmer and his wife came with me to Mr White. The farmer's wife ran back to their house and when she returned she appeared to have gathered up all the tea towels that were currently in use in her kitchen.

The wound was moped and held, to stop the flow of blood. It was examined, moped and held again, until the tea towels were red with blood. Fresh tea towels, appearing to be straight from the linen cupboard, were brought and the procedure repeated. The farmer said, 'This is no good, 'e's going to bleed to death. I'm going to phone for an ambulance.' By the time the ambulance arrived, all the tea towels were sodden red and Mr White was looking very ill, and was so weak as to be content to lie back on the grass bank where he had managed to stagger a short while before.

'He's going to need a transfusion,' the farmer's wife said with great concern.

The ambulance driver agreed, and said, 'We need to get him to hospital.' Driver and attendant carefully lifted the patient onto a stretcher and made him as comfortable as they could.

Until now, the master woodturner's attention had been fully focused on the subject he knew best, and my presence had been a secondary matter. At that moment, when he could have been forgiven for forgetting that I ever existed, he turned his thoughts to my welfare. He began rather tongue-in-cheek, 'Sorry to leave you like this.' But then, in full sincerity, he went on, 'You've got your bike, you can get home all right, can't you? You'd better give me a ring to find out when to come to Hanwell now.'

My prospective boss, tutor, mentor or whatever he was going to be, won my respect with his unselfish and considerate words. He went on to begin in me a lasting affection too, when he turned a wicked sense of humour in my direction. Even with a blood-drained face he could produce mischievous eyes and deliver the kind of line I would remember him for, when, from half way into the ambulance, he called, 'Don't worry, you've got the job!'

Chapter 31

THE HANWELL FACTORY

The day after the sawing accident, I went to Mr White's house to see how he was. He lived near to us, on Falling Lane, which crossed the top of Otterfield Road. His wife told me he was sleeping. He had been sent home from hospital after a few hours yesterday and had been told to rest. He had left a message for me that I was to meet him at the Hanwell factory at nine o' clock on Monday morning, ready to start work. Even through the sincere delivery of the message, an old friend of Dennis White would have detected bravado.

I had been concerned that my inexperience may have contributed to the accident, so it was good to hear that Mr White would be well enough to go to work after the weekend, and a relief to find that Mrs White did not come after me with a rolling pin; I was nervous when she had opened the door to me, and surprised that she had been so pleasant. I came away worrying, just a little, that she, perhaps, had not yet heard the full story.

I was impatient to start work because I was going to learn something new. On Monday morning, I left home in good time to find the address I had been given, a journey which I estimated to be six or seven miles. As my nervous nature demanded, I arrived much too early. After confirming that I was waiting at the correct place, I had time to look around. The main building appeared to be a converted, once private residence with outbuildings enclosing a small gravelled yard. I peered into windows without learning a great deal, and found a corner where I could leave my bicycle.

Just then, also early, a car arrived with Mr White in the passenger seat. He got out cautiously, as befitted the man I had last seen, but, seeing me, he enlivened himself in order to give me a cheery greeting loaded with message, which said without words, 'You didn't expect to see me here did you?' He was clearly pleased with himself for his own toughness, and he wore the bandages on his head like a crowning badge of honour. Any tension I had, in anticipation of this meeting, subsided.

By contrast, the driver was without humour, perhaps more concerned with his own status and the seriousness of his position in this newly-formed company. Once out of the car, it could be seen that he was a tall man. He was dressed, in what proved to be his own unvarying way, in a smart sports jacket, plain tie and, as if worn as a trademark, a plain dark-coloured trilby hat, which he was never seen without. He turned and walked across the yard and up some steps to a room that was his office, which, once inside, he rarely left and few people were ever invited into.

'Thank you, Mr Peters,' my new boss called cheerily, partially raising a hand in thankful salute as the two men parted. I was beckoned to follow and we entered one of the outbuildings on the opposite side of the yard to the main building. Inside, one lathe had been set up and, from the depth of woodchips underneath, it could be seen that it was in full use. 'This is where the turners will work,' said Mr White. 'New lathes are on order, but today you can use mine and see how you get on turning.'

A piece of wood, with corners intact, was put into the lathe. It was smaller than had been demonstrated on at Harlington and the reduced size was comforting, but only slightly less frightening when revolving at full speed. I remembered how I had seen the wide gouge held and copied the actions. 'That's good,' said my tutor, 'If it looks right, you're doing it right.' As the gouge travelled across the tool-rest, chippings from the square corners cut into the palm of my cupped hand like a thousand needles. I tried, secretly, to rub my hand on my trousers to take away the sting. Mr White laughed. 'Don't worry,' he said, 'your hand will soon harden up,' and, to help it do so, I was left with several dozen pieces that I could 'rough out', as the terminology went. To complete this stage, I was shown how to taper one end of the finished round to fit a hollow chuck. I was given callipers to help me find the right diameter but assured that I would soon be able to do it by eye. A hollow chuck was left on the bench in front of me to help me test my work.

The Hanwell Factory

When it was time to take a break, Mr White went over to the main building. I took the opportunity to step outside into the yard. It was good to escape the enclosed space and the dust-filled air. I looked up at the sky, which had been my natural ceiling during my time on the farm. I took a deep breath and enjoyed the sun on my face. I was going to miss the outdoors, but, remembering wet days and cold days, I told myself there were compensations. I thought of the excitement of learning, and I knew this was what I wanted to do. Mr White returned with two large mugs of tea. He did not consider, or even appear to notice, the sunny spot I had found but beckoned me inside, keen to continue telling me about the various styles of pepper mill we were going to make.

Our attention was taken by Mr Peters, who descended the stairs from his office, jumped into his car and disappeared, prompting Mr White to tell me a little more about the new company and to take me across to give me a brief glimpse of the old house. He said that the buildings, yard and workshop had belonged to Mr Peters. He had run a small precision-engineering business here for many years. Under a new arrangement, his business and property had been merged in an agreement with a Mr Edwin, who appeared from time to time only and was one of the rare visitors to Mr Peters's private retreat.

By rumour and chance remark, it was generally believed by employees (to whom such information was not formally available) that Mr Edwin had been left a sum of several thousand pounds. Whether on impulse or by some long-standing desire, it was not known, he decided to start a company specializing in the manufacture of pepper mills. Some staff sounded to be in full support of Mr Edwin's plans, and even deemed them admirable. A few, however, thought the venture risky and their future employment not completely secure. The doubters considered that while freshly ground pepper was perhaps a culinary necessity in some countries, it was not widely appreciated here, and the pepper mills, a mystery to most British cooks, would be difficult to market and would not bring in the revenue upon which their wages relied.

During the years of the engineering works, Mr Peters had

employed two machine operators who produced a wide range of precision parts. Under the present arrangement, they would be making parts for pepper mill mechanisms and nothing more. Sid would spend his working day maintaining his machine while it chugged away cutting teeth on the outer part of a pepper mill grinder. Walter, in similar fashion, would cut teeth on the inner half of the grinder. Each tooth, whether inner or outer, was cut individually and the completed grinder, after being sent away for hardening, was no less a piece of toolmakers' art than the best precision engineers could make.

The two skilled men, loyal employees for many years, were close to retirement age, if not a little beyond. Without affecting the quality of their work or quantity of output, they both moved so slowly as to fit the role of old retainers admirably. Sid had the accent of a working class Londoner and a cautious but dry sense of humour. Walter was more reserved. He was a dapper man with a thin black moustache, who, in a genteel accent, spoke of cars he had experienced, as if he had been in the motor trade in his early life or was an enthusiast undaunted by time.

The engineers took up two rooms on the ground floor of the main building. Other operations were carried out on the upper floor, where partition walls had been removed to create larger working spaces. Grinding mechanisms were assembled and fitted into the newly-turned bodies and the mill filled with whole black peppercorns, from a sack the size of a stuffed armchair, before being passed to the packing bench.

After our break, my work was checked. 'That won't hold. That won't do.' Those pieces were tossed aside. 'This is better. That's all right,' and those pieces were placed separately. The tutor took over the lathe and fitted the hollow chuck. As he worked, he chuckled all the time in a joking pretend-mocking way, so that even when he said 'That's rubbish. That's no good' the pupil knew he was not so displeased and was not discouraged. A contemporary of the master may have understood the insecure amusement he found in seeing the work, sacred to himself alone, now being attempted by another with whom he was sharing his most guarded secrets.

The hollow chuck and a small club hammer were as far as technology had penetrated the woodturning world at that time; more sophisticated methods of holding the piece of wood about to be turned came later. One of my 'roughed' pieces was offered up to the chuck, the size was correct and the taper not too steep or too shallow, it was given a tap to lodge it and a few more to centre it, to ensure true running, and it was ready for the next operation, which would be boring and recessing, the subject of another lesson on another day.

A response to the company's advertisement for a second young man to learn woodturning had been received. The news was pleasing to hear, for although my time as sole pupil had been enjoyable, to share the experience with a fellow could add so much. If he was as keen as me, then we had something in common already. I looked forward to his arrival.

'He'll be here in the morning,' said Mr White. 'His name is Robert Bun.'

Next morning, when Robert Bun appeared he announced himself as 'Max'. Now, Maxi Bun I knew of straight away, he had been something of a celebrity and sporting hero at school. Our paths had not crossed before; I had only known his name. We were very different people; Maxi taking naturally to the notoriety and limelight of the sports field, while I (apart from being 'half-winner' of a three-legged race) was never attracted to competition.

Maxi was a champion javelin thrower, he had represented Middlesex County. He was still 'at the top of his game' and full of ambition. He was in every sense a 'modern' young man, he wore sports clothes with ease at a time when it was not common to do so. He was a much loved son, all that he wore was new and smartly turned out. When he carried an oversized sports bag on his training nights, he could easily have passed as a graduate on an athletic scholarship at Harvard or Yale.

Instead of coming between us, our many differences seemed to cement our friendship and, over the coming weeks and months, we built up a mutual respect. For my part, I admired Max for his sporting abilities and his bounce and confidence in everyday life, some of which may have been a cover for a modesty and a sensitivity that made him the likeable person he was. For his own reasons, he always treated me as senior boy, although, in truth, I had only arrived a few weeks ahead of him and he had been quick to learn.

From the day Mr White introduced Maxi Bun, he called him Robert, never changing a syllable from that day onward. Whether deafness or preference guided the boss's choice was not known. In conversation with several people, Max was 'Robert' to Mr White and 'Max' or 'Maxi' to everyone else, sometimes alternating in confusing ping-pong quickness. No one ever corrected anyone else and Max/Robert took it in his stride.

Max himself enjoyed playing with names and, despite his college-boy appearance, he liked to affect a local cockney form of speech. When he was first introduced to me, he said, ''Ello Moulder,' and I was 'Moulder' from then on. I was never quite certain of the meaning of the name, apart from a vague suggestion that the head man in a foundry was addressed that way, which I assumed Max knew something about. The name was always used in a teasing way, but said with a warmth that conveyed a certain regard, so that I grew to like it. Maxi's name for Mr White, by contrast, had no mystery and some might say lacked imagination, but with equal affection he became, what else but, 'Chalky', at all times except in his presence.

Soon our new lathes were installed. Brand new but old-fashioned in style, with heavy cast-iron benches, solid headstocks and fittings. 'Lathes for professionals' Mr White called them, 'You won't be afraid they'll break,' he proudly announced, as he admired what was undoubtedly his choice of machinery. We thought of the club hammer, which he occasionally used with enthusiasm, and knew what he meant. Max and I selected our 'beast' and, as we settled in, became full members of the new organization. Eventually, as many pepper mills as we could make would be wanted, but from rough square block to the finished article there were many stages of production, each needing a particular skill, so we had much to learn.

The Hanwell Factory

While we learned, our teacher needed to make changes, too. Previously, he had produced items individually or in small numbers, now he was charged to produce a simple item but in large quantities. His methods would need to be modernized in order to speed up each operation. For example, our first attempts to bore the cavity in which the peppercorns would be stored inside the mill were positively primitive. We were grudgingly allowed to use an auger that Mr White said had been handed down to him, and which he swore was a hundred years old at least and quite irreplaceable. By chance, the tool had a cutting diameter of seven-eighths of an inch. The master considered that 'about right' for the purpose. His judgement proved to be correct, as the dimension has been adopted by thousands of pepper mills ever since.

To control the two-foot long antique, we turned a rough handle, which we needed to hold tightly into our shoulder ('like a shotgun suspected of having a nasty kick,' the master said – impressing us, although we had never fired a shotgun). The cutting edge of the auger was offered up to the wood, which was held in the hollow chuck and revolving at full speed. Pressure on the tool seemed to have no affect, the auger would not drill. After several attempts, when perhaps the tiring operator had changed the angle of approach, or maybe the time had been selected by the tool itself, we never knew, suddenly the auger 'bit'. A roar brought terror to the fledgling woodturner as the museum piece ripped through end grain of hardwood and removed seven-eighths of an inch of it in a perfect pepper-containing cylindrical tube.

The difficulty in starting the boring was only equalled by the problem of stopping the process once it had begun. The operator could only hang on until the end of the wood was reached. Even then, on the odd occasion, the relic with a mind of its own would continue its journey, pulling the one supposed to be in control with it. When the metal of the lathe was reached, damage to the 'man-eating ogre', as we were beginning to call it, would have to be shown to the maestro, and that needed courage. Mr White would visibly sink at the knees to see his old friend damaged, and declare that the regrinding necessary would represent ten years normal wear. His teasing style of criticism would be suspended temporarily while he affected the most serious voice he could muster. The rarity of his reprimand made it near impossible to bear, but in three minutes all was forgiven. Forgotten? We never knew.

Luckily, the master's years of knowledge and an inventive mind thought up speedier and potentially less hazardous methods of completing the relatively unskilled operations. Free of the stress, Max and I could progress to bring hand tools under our control. Soon, we were putting the sharpest possible edge on our chisels and turning beads, hollows and fillets on hard and beautifully grained walnut wood. We boasted a finish so smooth as to need almost no further attention before adding a 'French polish' finish. As the days went by, we worked on side by side, eyeing one another's production in gentle rivalry but in greater amounts of co-operation and comradeship.

Chapter 32

THE TRIO

In pure Homeric terms, our woodturning mentor was a 'true and trusted adviser'. In modern parlance, he was a mother hen with a couple of overgrown chicks. 'Chalky', as Max referred to him without exception (except in his presence), grew, over the weeks, into his new role of tutoring. The old man was, inside, a youthful rebel. His association with two young disciples added to his already endearing mischievous enjoyment of life, which only a man who had experienced its dark side, as well as its many joys, could display.

The trio of master and pupils spent a considerable amount of time together outside of the workshop, invariably with an educational theme but always with pleasure not far behind. Even the long cycle ride to work, which could have been tedious, leaves me with happy memories so many years later. Like lads going to school, I would call for Mr White and we would meet Max a little further on. We would all ride together, our leader teaching as we went, in mechanized peripatetic style.

In good weather, we would take the 'country route'; riding along the towpath of the Grand Union Canal where it coincided with our journey. The magnificence of trees growing on adjoining land would be pointed out to us. We were shown how to recognize the different species and our attention was drawn to the particular natural splendour of each variety. Of course, the character and merit of the timber was talked about, its uses to mankind, the beauty of the grain patterns that we might find inside, and the hazards that a woodturner may have to overcome to bring out the best the timber had to offer.

If out tutor had found something of interest to show us, our midday lunch break would be spent in the town. An expensive china shop was sometimes our place of learning. We were directed to examine superior bowls, lamps or vases with classic features; shapes that we should remember. Aesthetically pleasing lines that ran from one element to another were pointed out: the curve of a bead reflected, in inverted form, in an adjacent hollow, or a fillet that added suspense without disturbing the eye as it followed the flow of the pattern. We would leave via the 'bargain basement', where the master would display his revulsion (quietly in our direction) of cheap mass-produced items that visibly jarred his sensibilities.

On other days we would go to a specialist tool shop. We would pass-by the sets of woodturning tools, our tutor having explained that they were made of carbon steel and that we needed something harder now that we were verging on mass-production. We moved to the engineers supplies department where the shelves were full of tool steel used by metal-turners. Maxi had grasped the master's meaning, and said excitedly, 'This is what they cut metal with, it must be very hard.' Maxi's enthusiastic outburst demonstrated the self-confidence I admired in him. While I was quietly accepting what I was being told, he was racing ahead and wanted everyone to know that he had received the message.

We made our way to shelves of small boxes that contained a single piece of steel in each. 'These are what we want,' said Mr White. 'If we can find the right size, we can make our own tools.' We discovered there were many kinds of steel. Some, under the general name of 'high-speed steel', seemed to have been the metal machinists' choice for many years, while one or two modern brands sounded quite unworldly. 'Corona', the technical data informed us, had been created from a combination of cobalt, tungsten, molybdenum, boron, manganese, phosphorus, sulphur, silicon and titanium, and compounded in electric kilns that could produce temperatures hotter than the surface of the sun. Maxi just had to have 'Corona', while I settled for a safer, tried and tested well-known make of high-speed steel.

In the coming days, we worked on the tools of our choice. We learned that metal was as variable as the wood we were turning. Maxi's chisel was as hard as diamonds and its cut brittle and aggressive, while my choice of metal was hard and held its edge but had a cut that was smooth and silky. We shared the pleasure of exploring the different features of natural and man-made materials, and learning to use the various qualities to our advantage, as humans have done through their toolmaking career from the earliest times.

On one of our trio outings, Mr White spotted something that took his attention. Outside an ironmonger's that we were passing, a grimy cardboard box, which appeared to have been long forgotten in some back storeroom, lay open, offering round lengths of wood at a few pence per unit. Each piece was about ten inches long and an inch in diameter and was tapered at one end. Our knowledgeable companion picked up a piece and rubbed off the dust. 'They're boxwood,' he said, directing a controlled excitement our way. He wiped the faded label on the side of the box, and read, 'Lead-Working Mandrels.' 'They're what plumbers use,' he told us, and without saying more, he went into the shop and negotiated a price. For a few of the boss's shillings, we went away with the box and its contents.

Back at the workshop, the master handled a 'mandrel' lovingly as he enthused about the delights of boxwood. 'It's amazing to turn. The best wood is yellow. Carvers love it, they use it for making chess pieces. These'll make great handles for our tools.' We each put a piece in our lathe and quickly realized how unusual boxwood was to turn; it was hard and dense but so smooth and greasy that we could have imagined we were turning cheese. We were surprised by its bright colour and the curls of woodchips that fell and lay on the floor like golden locks of hair. We created our own design of handle and made ferrules from pieces of copper tubing, retrieved from a plumber's waste bin. Our tools took on a professional look, and were a joy to use. Their hardness saved us an immense amount of time, needing fewer stops to sharpen them, when we were proficient and counted the number of pepper mills we could make in an hour.

Some of our trio outings were less successful but still adventures in their own way. Our educational journey to work was lost temporarily when the cycling legs of our senior member began to tire and he decided to try some motorized assistance, appearing one morning riding an ancient autocycle. The first mile or two was exhilarating; with the old two-wheeler as our pacemaker, Max and I became racing cyclists in an attempt to keep up with the master. We could hear him talking loudly, probably proclaiming the joys of motorized travel but we were never quite within earshot to know. For our part, we worked hard to hold our place in the caravan of wheeled wonders. Hard work needed hard breathing, so we inhaled large quantities of the black oily smoke that the autocycle trailed behind it. Soon, pops and bangs heralded trouble; the smoke became blacker and the machine fell silent, quickly coming to a standstill by the side of the road. The weakness had been anticipated by the rider who, without hesitation, took from his pocket the appropriate spanner. While the sparkplug was removed and cleaned, Max and I took a moment to breathe clean air.

Once remedial work was complete, the rider remounted and pedalled energetically while Max and I pushed. After a hundred yards, as energy was fading, some popping and banging gave us extra strength, as this time, it indicated hope. The aged machine finally decided to run and our journey continued dubiously; sometimes faster than Max and I could pedal or, on up gradients, so slow as to require a hand on the boss's shoulder and a firm push while rider and helpers pedalled furiously. Regardless of the bursts of 'high speed', we arrived at our destination at the usual time. We were greeted by our colleagues, who were waiting to gain entry to the main house and begin their day's work. Our oily faces and dishevelled appearances caused amusement, and drew remarks that clearly needed an answer.

'Better than pedalling,' said Mr White, with a defiant grin, his comment bringing understanding agreement from some of the older employees.

'But we broke down,' said Max in truthful innocence, not really meaning to undermine the boss's defence.

'Like Aesop's fable of the hare and tortoise,' said the part-time packing and posting lady, who had once been a junior school teacher but was now retired and went out to work for the companionship.

The building was unlocked and we all went to our place of work.

The Trio

During the day, the boss came to the conclusion that the two-wheeled monster was not the solution to his present needs and said that once he had got 'the thing' home we would never see it again. However, his legs were still tired and, being a man not to give up easily, only a day or two went by before he came up with something he thought might be a better idea.

'Tomorrow, leave your bike at my house,' Mr White said to me. 'Leave your bike at home Robert, and meet us on the corner,' he said to Max. As instructed, I rode my bike to Mr White's house. When I arrived, he was sitting in the driving seat of an old car that had a great canvass top, which he was afraid to put down in case he could not put it up again, he said. The engine was running unevenly, in a way that was not reassuring. 'It's just warming up,' said Mr White, attempting to add the reassurance. 'Get in,' he said invitingly. I got in. We moved off uncertainly and continued in that way for half a mile or so until we reached the Nag's Head public house and the corner where Max was waiting for us.

'Get in, Robert,' Mr White proudly called to Max.

'What's this then?' said Max. 'That's nice, going to work in style today.'

Mr White smiled. He had probably not heard all that Max said but had detected pleasure in the words and accepted the cheery greeting. He sat back and drove on, with his arms straight out to reach the steering wheel. His chin was held high to aid his vision over the vast bonnet, which seemed excessively long unless it concealed a large high-powered engine.

After the gentle rise up Falling Lane, the engine warmed, ran more smoothly and was going well by the time we reached Merriman's Corner, a little further on. As we proceeded along Dawley Road in style, we tried to ignore the occasional 'cough' from under the bonnet, which caused the proud owner to comment, 'It's probably a sticky valve, nothing to worry about'. Half a mile or so short of where, on a previous morning, the autocycle had decided to go no further, we all heard clearly, coming from under the bonnet, cough cough cough. All that we heard after that was the whirring of wheels and tyres as they carried our enclosed comforts a few yards further before finally stopping by the side of the road.

Max and I got out, stretching ourselves in the sunlight and expending some of the energy saved by that day's means of travel. Mr White remained in the driver's seat, a little dejected but more puzzled than downcast. He examined the gauges in front of him, first with the ignition switched on and then with it switched off. He got out and lifted the bonnet, first the driver's side and then the passenger's side. From each approach, he stared and prodded and tugged on anything that might tell him something. Max and I knew very little about motorcars but we looked at the things Mr White looked at, in hope of showing our support in his moments of growing disappointment.

Our driver got back into his seat and checked the gauges on the dashboard once again. He decided to try pulling the starter, which briefly brought the engine to life, turning it over vigorously. Max unveiled a little knowledge of motorcars by shouting over the sound of the whirring engine and labouring starter motor, 'Make sure it's switched on when you pull the starter.' Making sure the ignition was switched on, Mr White pulled the starter again and a couple of times more. The engine now was turning over less briskly and our mentor, becoming as dejected as he was puzzled, said, 'I expect the battery's not much good either.'

Having returned to the passenger seat, Max had been observing the dashboard gauges. 'The petrol gauge doesn't move much when you turn the ignition on,' he said.

'It didn't when I put a gallon in this morning,' said Mr White.

'Only a gallon? Is a gallon enough?' said Max. 'My uncle puts in ten at a time.' After a respect-showing pause, which allowed Mr White time to recover from the enthusiasm of the enquiry, Max went on to ask, 'Will a gallon get us all the way to work?'

'It had better, otherwise it's going to be a dear job getting there,' said Mr White.

'The gauge says empty. Shall we try some more petrol?' said Max, convinced he had found the answer to the problem.

While Mr White was thinking about it, he got out of the car and

The Trio

opened the boot to see if he had put the petrol can in. By the time he found that he had, he had decided that to put some more petrol in was perhaps a good idea. ''Ere are, you two run back to the pumps that we passed next to those shops.' He gave Max the can. 'And you hang on to these four florins,' he said to me. 'That's eight bob, so I shall want some change,' he added. His reference to the amount revealed his distress at the cost of the morning's excursion.

It took a while before we returned with the petrol; the pumps were further away than our wishful thinking had calculated. The essential essence was poured into the car's petrol tank, which accepted it noisily; the liquid sounding as if it was hitting the bare metal of an empty vessel. The ignition was switched on and the starter pulled. The engine turned but did not fire. Hope could be heard fading in Mr White's words as he said, 'The battery's only got a couple more turns in it.'

Max revealed more of his mechanical knowledge. 'Perhaps it takes a few turns for the petrol to come through,' he said.

'That sounds right,' said Mr White. 'I'll give it one more try.' He pulled the starter, and the engine burst into life.

We arrived at work late. The car stood in the yard looking sorry all day. Mr White mumbled to himself from time to time about the price of petrol, and was beginning to sound as if he had come to the conclusion that the amount of the expensive liquid his pride and joy needed to get us to work made his grand plan non-viable. He finally decided he had better put in yet another gallon to make sure we all got home that evening. If he had borrowed the car, he gave it back. If he owned it, he sold it. We never knew the manner of the machine's going, but the once elegant car, with the high long bonnet that surely must have housed a powerful engine, was never seen again or even spoken of for a long time.

The old man's tired legs were pressed into further service as master and disciples resumed their cycle rides to work. Tranquillity was restored. Observations recommenced. All was enjoyed and appreciated even more than before. The pleasures became treasures with the space of years and, as memories tend to do, the sunny days and the happy days are the ones held most firmly in recollection.

Chapter 33

THE AUDITIONS

While I was working on the farm and, later, woodturning, I was, in any spare time I could find, teaching myself to play the clarinet. My early attempts to join my school friend Arthur and his group in playing the music of the old New Orleans jazzmen had been abandoned when I found that my ability to play 'by ear' was not good and I could not improvise a part that would blend with other players. Fortunately, I had been introduced to the romantic sounds of Tchaikovsky by 'Uncle' Bill, who had started in me a love of orchestral music. The idea of written music was not, therefore, alien to me, so perhaps I could explore the possibility of achieving my goal by learning to read and play the notes that others had decided for me.

I obtained a clarinet tutor book. It was under the name 'Otto Langey', and had been published many years before (when things were done thoroughly, it appeared). It had pages black with notes; scales, arpeggios and exercises in every key and mode. Without the discipline of a teacher to control my impatience, I turned the pages to find the easier and more playable passages. We are taught that if we cheat, the one most deceived is ourselves, and passing over the difficult exercises that full proficiency requires would prove this lesson to be true, and leave me with limitations in technique evermore.

One evening, when I was tightly enclosed in our scullery with my tutor book propped up on the white enamelled tabletop, the insurance man called, as he usually did on Fridays to collect premiums. The sound of my clarinet attracted his attention and he wanted to know more. A polite knock, and I beheld the uninvited visitor standing in the doorway with a broad grin on his enthusiastic face. 'That's a good noise you're making,' he said.

'Good' and 'noise' seemed to balance out, so I took it as a friendly

241

greeting, neither criticism nor compliment. He pointed to my Otto Langey, 'Oh, I know that one,' he said. At that moment, the book slipped on the smooth enamel of the tabletop as my improvised prop gave way. 'You need a music stand,' he said. Until that time, I had only seen jazz musicians who played without the need for music or stand, so the advice passed me by. 'That's an old clarinet,' he went on, adding quickly, 'nice,' so that this time 'old' and 'nice' balanced, with similar effect to his first remark. He asked if he could have a look. I hesitated. I knew that most people would immediately destroy the delicate reed by pressing the mouthpiece into their chest as they attempted to see where their fingers should be placed down the length of the instrument. I relinquished my hold reluctantly. He took my clarinet, and clearly knew how it should be handled. 'Could I have a blow?' he asked, by then his fingers correctly placed.

I was beginning to feel I could learn something, so I said yes. The insurance man blew but the instrument did not 'speak', as he put it. He pressed some pads and identified one or two that were leaking air. He worked on them, adjusted the reed and blew again. This time, rich low tones emerged then high melodic notes, which were so much better than I could make. I was delighted that my clarinet could 'sing' so beautifully, but, at the same time, was made aware that I had not yet learned to produce a true clarinet sound myself. Momentarily relieved of the pressure of his work, my self-appointed teacher of the evening relaxed and seemed younger. He blew a little more, and could see admiration radiating from my eyes. I saw the way ahead for myself, if only I persisted. He became talkative and spoke about his time as an army bandsman. The details I would forget, but the impression remained like a beckoning light. My practice sessions after that evening always brought the impromptu lesson to my thoughts. The rich sounds rang in my memory, I had been made aware that my instrument could do it, so it was up to me. I read and re-read what Mr Langey had written about the embouchure, correct breathing and filling the whole bore of the clarinet with vibrating air to create a full rich sound unique to the instrument. I practised and I blew until I rattled the cups on the dresser in the scullery corner.

One Clear Morn

One day at work, I was asked if I would be coming back to woodturning after I had finished my national service. I was told there would be a job for me, and I felt the same warmth and satisfaction as I had when I left the farm knowing I could return if I wished. I managed to answer gratefully but, in truth, was more concerned, at that moment, to ensure that I made good use of my compulsory two years of conscription. Disillusioned young men leaving the services, spoke of time wasted with endless 'square bashing' and having nothing to do in their spare time but hang around the NAAFI or go to the pictures. Many said they had learned nothing useful that would help them get back into 'Civvie Street'.

My thoughts went back to the insurance man who had spoken of the tuition he had received during his time as a military bandsman. He talked of Kneller Hall, it was the first time I had heard of the army's music college. But what was I thinking? I was not like him, when he played he sounded as I imagined a teacher would sound. I was just a beginner, I could not even think about trying to get into a band. At a more optimistic moment, I told myself that the ex-bandsman sounded as he did because he had been in the band, had received tuition and had played as a professional for some time. He was probably a beginner like me when he first went in. If he could do it, why could I not try? But how do I go about getting into a band? Where do I apply? Who do I ask?

One night, I was setting my alarm for an early start next morning when I thought of Mr Auditon, our first lodger, and his alarm clock with two bells on the top. Then, I remembered that he worked at the RAF camp at Uxbridge, and it occurred to me that they had a military band. I could hear myself saying, 'Why don't I go to see if I can get in?' Military bands had, until that moment, a positively khaki appearance in my imagination. Why had I not realized that the Royal Air Force Central Band was only a few miles away? What better way to find out about getting into a band than to go direct. I decided to make enquiries by telephone. My call bounced around the camp gently upward until I was speaking to someone of sufficient rank and musical interest to know that there was a band based there. He passed

The Auditions

me to the Band Office. Someone checked with someone else and I was told to report to a certain place at a certain time. I was delighted, I had an interview.

At the camp, I was challenged at several checkpoints, each time being directed onward in the general direction of the Band Room, where I was greeted by a warrant officer. For a few moments I felt like a VIP of the musical world. He was so polite as he showed me into a practice room and placed a piece of music on a stand, which had been set up in readiness. The warm welcome cooled a little as the brown leather case under my arm was spotted. It could be seen clearly that I was holding the lid in place, and its square tapered shape was obviously not the preferred fashion of the day. As the inside of the case was revealed, attention was drawn to the soft black lining, which I had accepted as normal until that day when I saw a newer example of the bright-red pile that would once have cosseted my instrument. Neither did my instrument seem to impress my interviewer, but he contained himself, making no comment other than to invite me to play a little to him. He opened the piece of music, passing over a page black with notes, depressingly similar to many in my omnibus tutor book, and pointed to a simple melody with which he considered I might begin.

Without giving myself time to look at the music, a common error made by beginners, so that the key and the time signature were taken into full account, I selected the places where my fingers should be positioned on my instrument to produce the first note I was to play. I recognized a minim and lunged in, stamping my foot for the two beats I knew it lasted. The next note was a dotted crotchet, which I was not so sure about, and I faltered. Within the one bar of music, the senior NCO had assessed that I was not built of the stern stuff needed to make an RAF bandsman. His interest now more openly fell upon my clarinet, making comments partly to me but mostly to himself. Many of his observations were outside my understanding at that time, they were clearly not compliments but neither were they totally offensive, showing a genuine curiosity for the most part and incomprehension for the remainder.

A lower ranking NCO popped his head round the door and the senior man called him in. My clarinet was passed back and forth like the oddity I was beginning to think it must be. The junior man was less restrained and his comments were obviously not compliments. Controlled chuckles were becoming more noticeable. It was a conversation that I was feeling less a part of as I stood-by, looking on. The junior man left and the warrant officer resumed his role as interviewer, and all the courtesies of my arrival returned. He thanked me profusely for coming and playing for him. He stood to attention and treated me as an equal, or even the VIP who had arrived a little earlier. I wanted to say 'Help!', 'What do I do to get in?', 'Where do I go from here?' Not a word of advice was forthcoming, and I remained silent, not knowing how or what to ask. He thanked me again and left. Had I been patted on the head and told to 'run along', the feeling would have been no less discouraging.

Full of youthful arrogance, complete recovery from the ordeal was achieved in a day or two, and rejection by the RAF had not the slightest affect upon my resolve. If they were unable to see my potential value to the clarinet-playing world, there must be something wrong with them, the fault could not possibly lie with me. I would try elsewhere. The question of 'where' rose again. There was still the army and the navy to go.

Mrs Rawlins, a neighbour who lived across the road from us and enjoyed chatting over cups of tea with Nan, had grown-up sons, now married and with homes of their own but still talked about with great pride, as if all their high achievements were only yesterday. One of her 'boys', who had been unruly and a great worry to her when he was young, had benefitted from his army training and the discipline that went with it. He looked immaculate turned-out in his dress uniform, Mrs Rawlins would tell on many occasions, and the fact was borne out by photographs displayed around her room. He had done 'so well' during his time with the Royal Artillery at Woolwich. 'They have a band, a good one,' said Mrs Rawlins to Nan, as they sipped their tea. It did not matter that my endeavours were the subject of teatime gossip, it had brought me information that could be useful and I

The Auditions

decided to act upon it. Woolwich was somewhere I could get to without great difficulty. I followed my previous tactics and an interview, or audition as they called it, was arranged. Assuming that I would again be asked to play a piece of music I had never seen, I had been concentrating on improving my 'sight-reading', and hoped to do better on my next try.

I presented myself at the place and time agreed. I managed to push my not-too-attractive case under my chair. My instrument was noticed, but observations were more sympathetic and more constructive. The army was much kinder than the air force, I thought, appearing to take an all-round view of the interviewee. My attempt to play a few bars was more satisfactory, but it was clear I was a beginner. Luckily, the interviewer was more interested in me as a person. He congratulated me on the progress I had made without help and praised my initiative in the way I had obtained an audition. He asked if I could afford to get myself a better clarinet. I had no idea how much I needed to 'afford', but I said that I could. 'Right,' he said. 'If you can, this man will take you on to teach you, and if you make good headway in the next few months he can recommend you for a further audition.' I was given the card of Henry Purcell, of Greenwich, who would help me on my way. Had I any knowledge of music, the name of 'Henry Purcell' for my teacher would have frightened me away. One of the great names in early English music meant nothing to me at that time in my life, so, again protected by ignorance, I clung carefully to the card of Mr Henry Purcell.

Whether I could afford a better instrument was in the balance; the subject had not arisen yet, but now I would have to discuss the matter with Nan. This time, I would not be asking her to finance one of my profit-making schemes that she seemed always to have faith in. This time I was 'in league' with the Government who were planning to take me away from her, as she had dramatically put it on more than one occasion, and I was asking her to help me desert her. I told her my story quietly and calmly, trying to appeal to her practical nature by saying that I had to go and that all I wanted was to make the time away useful rather than a waste. All that I said was listened to and considered in silence as she stared into her own unknown future, her face as grey as the mist into which she peered. She had dealt with many disappointments in her long life and she knew only positive ways to overcome them; no matter how bad the situation she confronted, the best had to be made of it. 'It's just common sense,' she would say. Common sense she had in abundance and it was her guiding light. The logic of my appeal had been fully understood and she would not destroy a chance I wanted to make for myself. She was aware, too, that I had a stake in the money under her wise control. I had never questioned handing over my earnings or needed to acknowledge that I was the main beneficiary of her spending – that was just the way it was. As always, the proposed expenditure was given serious consideration, and, on this occasion, in unemotional good grace, Nan raided her upstairs hiding places, found the money and told me to go and get my clarinet.

Chapter 34

SOHO

I had been given the name of a musical instrument manufacturer and retailer. They had, I was told, a small shop that specialized in woodwind instruments and it was there, I was advised, that I would find my clarinet. I wrote down details of the shop and the street in which it could be found. The names, unknown to me, raised no emotion, but when it was explained that I would have to negotiate my way around the streets of Soho, I was filled with an amount of trepidation equalled only by an inquisitiveness that would have to be satisfied. At that time, the Sunday newspapers appeared to have an obsessive interest – or perhaps a vested one – in filling their pages week by week with lurid stories of obscene goings-on in Soho. Salacious entertainments, films and magazines on offer in a sea of corruption, that appeared to be out of control to their sensation-seeking readers.

On the very first Saturday that I could arrange to be free, I set off to find my clarinet. I braced myself for adventure as I alighted the underground train at Piccadilly Circus. Out in the sunlight, I observed the great meeting of thoroughfares, known around the world for the statue of Eros that is its centrepiece. I crossed the grand avenues of Piccadilly and Regent Street and progressed onward to Shaftesbury Avenue, where, only a few yards along, I turned into the labyrinth of tiny streets of Soho.

Before going directly to my destination, I had my youthful curiosity to indulge, which led me to walk around looking at the street names. Many were known to me from the newspaper stories but the familiarity was not comforting, rather the knowledge added to my caution. I pushed my hand into my pocket to assure myself that my money was firmly enclosed. I was carrying more than I had ever done before and knew that I must take care in this place of such notoriety. I wandered along Denman Street, Frith Street, Wardour Street, Great

Windmill Street and into Archer Street, where musicians gathered, standing around in a hiring market waiting to be engaged by directors of music who wandered amongst them booking for a concert or a show.

On one unguardedly vulgar street, I saw an 'attraction' that, despite a large hoarding announcing it offered a striptease show, seemed less intimidating than many of its kind. Here, the style was of an ordinary cinema or theatre. I was drawn nervously to learn more. At that time of day there was only an empty facade to be seen, which emboldened my approach, as I could satisfy my lust for knowledge without being observed or harassed by a doorman, who I imagined must be on duty when the establishment was open for business.

The building had once contained an ordinary shop – butcher, baker, grocer perhaps – but was now open-fronted and built out like a tiny theatre foyer. A kiosk, where tickets could be purchased, was surrounded by photographs of scantily clad young women; revealing, but acceptable for a public place, being covered in flimsy garments or multitudes of ostrich feathers. Inside there was an unreal cloying decor. Sidewalls, which appeared to be made of an amount of papier mâché that would have made Hollywood proud, closed in towards an exit at the rear, covered by a well-fingered velvet curtain that was impossible to see past.

Before having the curtain pulled aside for him, a 'customer' would have to pass through a heavy-built turnstile, which would have been more suited to its earlier role at London Zoo or some other corporation assignment. In its present position it would be more than adequate to restrain an over-excited client. Its ferocity, softened only by a coat of pink paint, which although incongruous if examined in isolation, matched well with the general ambience of the decor as a whole. A single sign declared that a ticket to enter would cost seven shillings and sixpence.

A few doors along the same street was a similar enterprise, also offering delights of the flesh. It, too, had once been an ordinary shop but was now transformed into a foyer with photographs, ticket kiosk and decor all in shades of pinks and pastels. The turnstile was of a lighter construction and more fitting to its surroundings. All had been refurbished recently and the velvet curtain was less fingered. The sign at this establishment stated that a ticket to enter would cost ten shillings.

Further along was yet another foyer, more lavishly appointed in boudoir colours, ticket kiosk, photographs, papier mâché and all. Here the feeling was of much greater opulence; richly carpeted floor, drapes of pink satin, pristine velvet curtain at the rear exit door and, apparently, no need for a turnstile to restrain the kind of patron who would select this superior evening of visual pleasure. Here, a gentleman could wait his turn to pass, controlled only by a short rope of silk, sumptuously soft, in deepest pink. A large brass hook would be lifted to allow him through by an immaculately-dressed doorman, I imagined. Such extravagance was, of course, only available to those with a deeper pocket. The tariff displayed in the ticket kiosk showed that the price of entry here was twelve shillings and sixpence.

I walked on, wondering what could be the difference behind each velvet curtain. My thoughts raced but no substantial conclusions could be reached. My ruminations ceased abruptly when my attention was taken by a small crowd surrounding a man with a tray held in front of him. The tray was supported by a strap around his neck, like an ice-cream seller in the cinema. Excitable sounds drew me to join the group. The performer with the tray moved three upturned cups on a surface of green baize. Under one of the cups he placed an ivory dice, with dotted facets denoting numbers one to six. In his game, the symbols were disregarded and the only question was, where was the dice after the cups had been shuffled? For a wager of a half-crown, a crisp new one-pound note was on offer to anyone who could find the dice.

An onlooker, who had been drawn to the front of his fellows, passed a half-crown to the man and the dice was put in place. The cups were shuffled and the hopeful gambler made his choice. The dice was not under the cup selected. The player looked disappointed at his loss, but wagered another half-crown. He lost that, too.

'Third time lucky,' shouted the man with the tray, to rouse the crowd and encourage his 'customer' to risk another wager.

The betting man was persuaded, and handed over a third half-crown. This time he won, and was given a pound-note with great show, which pleased the crowd causing them to applaud as they joined in celebration of the winner's good luck. Now encouraged, the 'lucky' man handed over a fourth half-crown. He won again. The crowd became louder with excitement at the man's success. Others were now holding up half-crowns, keen to join the game and win one of the crisp new one-pound notes.

The first contestant was passed over for the next game, and the coin held high by another was accepted. The first man disappeared into the busy street with his winnings. The new player lost the first two games. Unlike his predecessor, he went on to lose two more before he gave up and vanished into the melee of the Soho street.

I was now directly in front of the performer and coming under the spell of the hysteria that was fuelling the mass around me. I found myself holding up a half-crown. My money was taken and I became a fully paid-up member of the possessed crowd. I selected an empty cup, and lost my money. I was foolish enough to place another bet, and then another, before coming to my senses. I put my hands firmly in my pockets and forced them to stay there. I walked away and on along the street. What had come over me? I was ashamed. Was I so arrogant as to think I could beat that man, obviously a trickster, at his own game? Was I trying to get something for nothing? That was not like me; there would have been no satisfaction even if I had won. And what was the result? I had lost seven shillings and sixpence, which had taken a lot of hard work to earn. I felt like Simple Simon going to the fair, or Jack who had taken a cow to market and was tricked out of it only to return home with a few beans. Losing the money hurt, and I promised myself I would never do it again. I walked on, grimly repeating my pledge.

As I turned a corner, there was a small gap between the properties, through which I could see the backs of the shops that contained the foyers of the striptease clubs I had examined a little earlier. Behind them, there seemed to be no extension to the buildings where the promised delights could take place. Instead, three rear exits opened onto a large area of muddy part-concreted yard. To the right of my view, on the opposite side of the yard to the row of shops, was a large black-painted structure of corrugated metal sheeting looking rather industrial at this time of the day. Above an ornate double door there was a full-width neon sign, which read 'Striptease this way'. No doubt the sign would be brightly lit when open for business and lead patrons to where the pleasures would take place whilst they indulged in an expensive drink or two from the bar.

The foyers were simply separate entrances to the same source of pleasure. One show, three entrances! First impressions, then, are not always what they seem. The man of modest means, the uncertain reveller and the bon viveur too, would rub shoulders after passing through the welcome of their choice into that muddy backyard. Perhaps only the regular visitor, who had surely selected the entrance of least cost, would be aware and enjoy his advantage as he crossed that starlit portal side by side with the well-healed gentleman who had paid so dearly in his desire for the best, his moment of superior luxury having passed so quickly as he now moved towards the brightly lit sign and, perhaps unknowingly still, was about to share his evening with all and sundry.

But I must get on to my important errand, I told myself. A few long strides took me past a coffee bar. What I saw inside halted my progress yet again. High stools were placed up to a narrow shelf across a large front window, so that two customers taking their coffee in the window were face to face with me as I passed. The two men were in animated conversation, laughing and seeming to be happy with their day. One was the man with the tray who had manipulated cups and dice. The other was the lucky customer who had lost two half-crowns but won two pounds gaining the applause of those around him as he convinced them to join the sport. He was the first to win, and the last, and now their secret was out.

Having satisfied my desire to know a little of Soho, I turned towards my destination. As I walked, I pondered on my findings of the day and reproached myself once more for my weakness in falling so easily under the spell of the clever practitioner of slight-of-hand. Finally, I arrived at the establishment that was my purpose for being in this part of London on that day. I entered the tiny shop. Woodwind instruments, clarinets, flutes, oboes and others I would hesitate to name, filled glass-fronted cabinets on one side of the shop from floor to ceiling. I stated clumsily that I wanted to buy a clarinet, aware that I had crossed the threshold into a world I knew little about. I stared into the assistant's eyes with such uncertainty as to be announcing my ignorance and pleading for his help. He stared back blankly, appearing to know that he had the advantage and was determined to enjoy the power I had just bestowed upon him. Giving him the benefit of the doubt, I judged that he would not intentionally be unhelpful. I decided I had better pull myself together, show confidence and give him more information about my needs. 'I want a Boehm system,' I said firmly, with all the assertiveness I could muster.

'They are all Boehm system,' he said coldly.

I had clearly not impressed him, and was beginning to think he might, after all, be deliberately unhelpful. I was suddenly self-conscious, hot, sticky and uncomfortable. The assistant lightly brushed the sleeve of his jacket with the backs of his fingers and my attention was drawn to his smart suit. I looked down at myself, I was wearing my best weekend clothes but they suddenly felt coarse and uncouth.

A curtain, which covered a doorway to a back room five or six steps above the shop floor, was moved aside and a stocky older man wearing a blue pinstriped suit peered down into the shop, he said nothing but his appearance had the affect of animating the assistant who then decided to show me a clarinet. Taking one from a high shelf in a cabinet, he said, 'This is the best model the company makes,' sounding as if he was recommending it to fit my needs. I was afraid to touch the beautiful item, feeling sure that my clumsy fingers would leave unsightly marks. I was told the price, and touching it became unnecessary. It was put back behind the glass doors.

Once again, the money in my pocket came to my mind. I had worried earlier in the day that I was carrying more than I had ever done before, but now I was confronted with the possibility that it would not be enough to obtain the instrument I needed to fulfil my ambition. Any remaining confidence I had, left me. What did I think I was doing trying to become something I was not and never could be? I should give up now before my foolishness went too far. How could I hope to compete, or even survive, with people like this? I could not even raise myself to the level of the shop assistant. I wanted to run from the shop, to run home, to return the money to its hiding place and take up my life where I belonged.

My agonizing was halted suddenly when the smart-suited young man laid an instrument on the counter in front of me, saying that he thought it might suit my needs and immediately stating the price, which was within my means. To my untrained eyes the clarinet was identical in appearance to the one so swiftly replaced in the cabinet. The assistant explained that this instrument was of the same high grade but contained some minor imperfection that labelled it a 'reject', a small blemish was the suggested reason. The blemish was, in fact, so small that our joint visual examination failed to find it. For a few moments, my doubts returned, had there been some obvious damage or lack of finish I would have been happier. Common sense was telling me that if the fault could not be seen it may well be in the basic construction and would affect the instrument's performance. The label of 'reject' was not reassuring either.

I was about to decide against the particular instrument when the previously unhelpful assistant moved around to my side of the shop counter and laid it in my hands, which were still nervously damp and becoming more so. The clarinet lay in them looking so out of place in my red work-damaged grasp; my nails manicured only by breakages on rough timber planks. My ability to apply the common sense thoughts of only moments before was lost in the discomfort of the situation. Slowly, I managed to steel myself and bring my concentration to bear on the clarinet alone. The magnificent instrument was already wearing evening dress in its ebony black and silver. I allowed myself to be dazzled. My dreams returned and I could hear myself filling a great hall with glorious sound. Momentarily, I saw myself in a year or two, at ease in the new life of my vision, and told myself that this clarinet could be my passport out of the dust of the factory. I could rise to its demands, I could learn, I could look smart like the shop assistant and to speak as he spoke. I could play my part in this better world that I wanted. Of course, it would not be easy and I would doubt myself many times, but I could not give up. Nan's words rang in my head, taunting, 'Don't start something yer can't finish' – 'If it was easy, it wouldn't be worth having'.

I looked deep into the shop assistant's eyes, and said, 'I'll have it,' and soon I was on my way home, forgetting any doubts that I had and peeping at my professional 'Boehm system' clarinet as it lay in the deep red fluffy pile of its new shiny black case.

Chapter 35

LEAVING HOME

In the coming days, I nervously attended my new clarinet. Its professional appearance was intimidating at first. I contented myself taking it out of its case to dust it, oil keys and springs, grease the corked joints and dust it once again before settling the magnificent piece back into the red deep-piled safety of its case.

Soon, I was putting the instrument together and carefully fitting a reed. With the fingering already under my control, I was able, after a little settling in, to play several simple scales. Time was then needed to familiarize my fingers with the many additional keys a Boehm system has to offer. More keys meant easier access to the full range of scales and arpeggios, but they would take time to learn. My already confessed lack of technique was no doubt furthered in my rush to pass through and beyond this valuable preparation.

To compensate for any lack of musical dexterity, I could, in time, boast a good full clarinet tone, which I acquired thanks to Uncle Fred's generosity (or perhaps a wish to save the hearing of his older sister). He allowed me to carry out my practice sessions in an old detached house that he had purchased and was planning to renovate at some future date. The empty rooms provided excellent acoustics where, without worry that anyone would be disturbed, I could project my sound through the whole house while dreaming of the concert hall that one day I would fill with my rich sounds.

It was not long before I was feeling confident enough to telephone Mr Henry Purcell, to arrange my first lesson with a professional player and teacher. I travelled to London each week and slowly became comfortable in his company. I welcomed eagerly the musical knowledge he could impart, and spent as much time as I could in the empty house putting into practise the ideas new to me.

As the months moved closer to the day of my 'call-up', Mr Purcell was as good as his word and recommended me for another audition with the Royal Artillery band. He gave me the date upon which I should present myself to Captain Brown at the band office of the Royal Artillery Mounted Band, Aldershot. It took a moment for this piece of news to register. Mounted! I was struggling to play a clarinet and I knew how difficult horses could be, the combination sounded more than I could manage. I was about to make some premature remark but was quickly dissuaded by laughter from my tutor. He had seen my reaction and hushed me, explaining that 'mounted' was in name only these days. He went on to tell me that, if accepted, I would be at Mons Officer Cadet School, where subalterns were turned out at a great rate. 'You'll love it,' he said. 'When the young second lieutenants perform for their proud parents on their passing-out parade, the band dresses up in all its finery: best blues, riding breeches, leather wellingtons, and spurs too. You'll have to learn not to trip over your spurs, but they do jingle so nicely when you all march on.' 'The ladies love it,' he added with an extra chuckle, and a look that appeared to contain some personal knowledge.

I left Henry Purcell for the last time that day, thanking him energetically for the help he had given me. My journey home was spent in a mix of excitement and apprehension, a condition that was becoming quite normal as I began to venture beyond my home territory. Until the date of my appointment with Captain Brown, the empty house was given great priority and my practise took on a meaningfulness more intense than before.

On the day of my audition, I decided to avoid plundering our limited funds further by anticipating my soldiering days and travelling in a way that was widely accepted for young servicemen at that time. A couple of rural stops between West Drayton and Staines on the single-carriaged 'pull and push' train and I was on the Great South West Road holding up my thumb and hoping for a lift. My wait was brief and I was loaded into the back of a large van. Some cardboard boxes, where I could sit, were indicated. I was asked where I was going, and assured that I would be dropped at the nearest point on the vehicle's journey. A low tailboard was swung up and fastened. As we moved off, the 'cargo' began to rattle. Apart from an empty space across the back of the vehicle where several travellers of my ilk could be accommodated, the van was full to the roof with empty milk bottles in metal crates. As we gathered speed, the rattle added a jingle, the combination increasing in volume, homogenizing like the milk that had been in the bottles, but here, into an inseparable ear-numbing noise that continued throughout the journey.

The van stopped. The driver appeared and let down the tailboard. Part hidden by his broad smiles, I could see his lips moving but could hear little over the ringing in my ears. He indicated the direction in which I was to walk, while shaking my hand vigorously and wishing me good luck, as if I was 'joining-up' to defend my country. I wondered if he had been a conscript in his time, or if his son was a currently serving soldier and he hoped someone was helping him as he was helping me. Without hearing my own words, I thanked him gratefully for the lift and his good wishes, and walked in the direction he continued to point for the next minute or two as he watched me go.

Long strides and deep breaths slowly brought back my hearing as I crossed a vast well-mown sports ground. I came to a broad avenue that I would later know to be Queen's Avenue, which ran from Aldershot town through the military heart of the region to the sprawling hamlet of Northcamp. A building unknown to me then, although the military prison's familiar name 'the glasshouse' was known around the world wherever British soldiers went, stood by the side of the avenue. I enquired but need not have done, as my van driver friend had dropped me, as he said he would, as near as he could to my destination. A short walk along Princess Avenue and I found myself at Mons Officer Cadet School.

As much as my journey had taken me into a different county, it had delivered me into another time. Mons Barracks had all the signs that it had been inhabited since the Victorian era and before. Single-story buildings, looking more tired now than they had once looked, surrounded a small parade ground. CO's Office, Adjutant's Office, Medical Room and various administrative quarters sat in a near-colonial style under tiled verandas. Quartermaster's Store and maintenance workshops were tucked away nearby, while in a more

Leaving Home

prominent position was the Guardroom, giving out all due signs of authority. Around the administrative buildings and parade ground there were accommodation blocks, which I would learn later were heated by coal fires and fitted with undoubtedly Victorian sanitary ware. One look inside, would prompt the question as to how many young men in the history of these buildings had made their temporary homes here before being sent to some hostile part of the world only to lose their lives, perhaps in the Boer Wars of South Africa's Transvaal, or in the war that would 'be over by Christmas', in France at Mons itself, or on the Somme, or at Ypres, where many succumbed to poison gas, or at Passchendaele, which sounds so sadly ill-named for a battlefield. Names of nearby barracks and surrounding roads would be a daily reminder, I thought, as I negotiated my way along Mafeking Road or Buller Road or Kitchener Road.

My instruction was to report to the Band Office. I was directed to a large red-tiled building, which I was told contained the office and practise room. The building had the appearance of a church hall in the style and time of its surroundings. It was set in a gravelled area at a considerate distance from any dwelling or place of work, presumably a kindness which allowed for the emitting sounds of a full-band practise. The office, I found, took up an insignificant part of the building. Its tiny space was filled by two desks and shelves overflowing with papers, folders and reference books of all kinds. A nervous little man, no more than five feet six inches in height, was hidden behind a large noisy typewriter, which I had heard even as I had knocked and been bid 'Come in'. He stretched up in his seat, to see over the machine, saying, 'Come in, come in. Captain Brown will be here in a minute.' Jock, as he invited me to call him only moments after I had stumbled into his domain, was the band clerk. I would learn that the smooth running of the band was mainly due to Jock's diligence; he dealt with every necessary detail and would only need to trouble Captain Brown on rare occasions, other than the daily routine of letter signing.

The conscientious clerk greeted me, and quickly suggested I might like to put my instrument together and warm up. Before waiting for my response, he propelled me gently through double doors into the large high-ceilinged band practise room. As the doors closed behind me I took a moment to glance around, hoping to allay the feeling that I had just been ushered into a dentist's waiting room. To my left, at the front of the room, was an upright piano. In one corner, at the back, were timpani and other percussion instruments. Across the back wall, were three wooden double-bass cases. Against remaining walls, were wooden chairs stacked in threes and fours, sufficient I imagined to accommodate all the players on a full-band practice day.

I took my clarinet from its case and put it together. I blew, and the sound echoed in the great void. I thought of the empty house and my desire to fill a large hall with sound. Here was my chance to try my wings, I knew that I could reach every corner of this special room. I might even impress my prospective director of music if he had arrived and was dealing with band matters in the little office next door. Momentarily, the thought that my uninvited offering might be overheard filled me with fear; it could be considered as showing-off if I played well or ridiculed if I played badly. To be judged, and perhaps laughed at, behind my back was unbearable. I was gripped with a nervous inertia. I decided to spend the waiting time readjusting my reed and checking my instrument, while asking myself, was this the life I really wanted and was my insecure nature up to it?

Before I had time to take flight or, alternatively, come to any positive conclusion, the door opened and Jock appeared, whispering feverishly as he shepherded me in to meet Captain Basil Brown, who greeted me pleasantly and listened to my audition piece, which I played without unreasonable nerves now that my judge was fully visible. The director of music pointed out that I had missed a beat, and told me that if I promised to work hard he would take me in. He left hastily, saying that his clerk would look after me. Jock said, 'Well done,' with a smile that faded quickly in his anxiety to complete the appropriate paperwork. 'You'll be in good company,' he said casually, as he hunted for more forms. 'We've auditioned several of you national service chaps lately.'

From the information Jock delivered piecemeal as he worked, I

Leaving Home

gathered that mostly band members arrived via boy service, where they had received a musical training under the guidance of Kneller Hall, the army's music college. National servicemen had made up the band's number for some years now, and two, who would be arriving at about the same time as me, might help me in my studies, Jock considered. They were older, having been allowed to defer their 'call-up' until finishing at university. In his desire to aid my progress (my performance of the morning no doubt telling him that I was going to need help), he spoke the newcomers' names clearly and with an emphasis that suggested I should remember them. Ian, he said, was at Cambridge, and Graham was an organ scholar at Oxford. 'They are both twenty-four and recently 'come down'.' I was ignorant of the last term and assumed they had 'come down on the train'. I was wise enough, however, to make a note of their names and remember them.

Jock then took on a stern approach, as he set about warning me that when I had finished my basic training I would have to insist that I had a place in the band and that is where I must be sent. 'You'll be the only one,' he said, 'the others will have postings to Germany, Gibraltar, Cyprus, Hong Kong and maybe other places around the world. If you don't keep telling them, you'll end up goodness knows where.'

As a relief from the serious message, and assuming that young men were interested in their appearance, Jock went on to say that, when I arrived back to take my place, I would be able to hand in my modern-day battledress at the quartermaster's store and draw my band uniforms. He confirmed what I had already been told about 'best blues', adding that on special occasions we would draw 'bearskins' as headgear. Most of the time, practise days and 'ordinary jobs', he went on, we wear khaki service dress. He was right, I liked the idea of being different from the 'ordinary' soldiers and thought the uniform of the First World War would be fitting to my surroundings. I was also delighted when told that my rank would be 'Musician', not 'Private' or 'Bandsman', the title seemed less military and fitted with youthful romantic notions. Jock saw my pleasure and was happy that he had done a good job promoting the band. He became bolder as he wished me good luck and sent me on my way.

My journey home was filled, as ever, with mixed feelings; elation that I had been accepted and an impatience to begin, while at the same time unease that I might become entangled in the military organisational mangle and find myself in some far-flung place. I had to content myself knowing that I could speak up if it became necessary. In the coming days, my clarinet practise took on an ever increasing seriousness as I waited for my call-up.

The anticipated government letter arrived in its own good time. My first instruction was to go to London for medical examination. A recall was necessary as the chest X-ray had failed me. Many young men would have been delighted to have been declined for a non-life-threatening problem. Foolish stories went around telling of ways to bring about rejection on medical grounds, such as drinking soapy water to produce a temporary uneven heartbeat, which would be sure to achieve refusal. By contrast, my consternation that I might be rejected and demand that 'I must be passed' because I was going to be a clarinet player in 'the band' caused the medical examiner and his staff great amusement. After a second examination, they teased me, saying I should not volunteer for any mountaineering but I was good enough for the band, adding that blowing a clarinet would do me good, and passing me A1.

Finally, the day of departure came. I made my way to West Drayton railway station where I presented my army travel warrant and boarded a steam train to Oswestry in Shropshire. The official letter in my pocket stated that I was to report to 67th Training Regiment Royal Artillery at Park Hall Camp, Rhyl, North Wales. I submitted willingly, even eagerly, to basic training, for, after all, it was an army band that I was joining so, quite understandably, I would first have to become a soldier. Being the Artillery, a thorough knowledge and competent use of guns was demanded, so, after being taught how to march on the parade ground and, later, drag half-hundredweight radio transmitters around the countryside or unroll several miles of telephone cable so that we could connect up a field telephone and ring back to base, only to be told to roll the wire up again, we went on to learn about guns. Training covered the full range of firearms: handguns, 303 rifles,

Leaving Home

tommy guns, Bren guns, Sten guns and 25-pound field cannons, with which we became quite adept at disturbing the denizens of the Welsh hillsides.

In my anxiety not to find myself shooting guns in some remote part of the world, I made sure to let it be known, as Jock had advised me, that the band in Aldershot was 'waiting impatiently' to count me amongst its number. I continued to broadcast that particular piece of information regardless of the amount of teasing, and sometimes stronger comments, it brought down upon me, teaching me quite early on that some very quaint notions were held about bandsmen. I received an extremely vigorous ribbing one day on the rifle range when, much to the amusement of my comrades, the sergeant in charge told me he considered that the world would be a safer place if I left guns alone and concentrated on my clarinet. His abrasive assessment followed an order to fire five rounds at the target in front of us. I had followed his orders meticulously, carrying out all the safety precautions we had been taught, and had achieved an average score. Unfortunately, the credits I had gained did not count towards my soldiering proficiency, as I had put my bullets into the target of the recruit next to me. He was also not pleased with me, as I had obliterated his excellent score!

As basic training was coming to an end, we spent time polishing boots, which we had already 'ironed' with a teaspoon heated over a candle to smooth them into black shiny mirrors, cleaning brass buttons and buckles, blancoing belts and gaiters, and pressing knife-edge creases in trousers and battledress blouses. On the last day, after a final inspection on the parade ground, travel orders were read out and small groups were marched away to find their allotted transport. I waited anxiously while my peers climbed into lorries that would take them to the railway station or other destinations. Numbers were reduced until Jock's words came true and I was the only one remaining. The order 'Dismiss' was shouted in my direction and, as the past weeks had trained me to do, I turned smartly and stamped my foot. I was given a railway warrant and told to return to my billet where I was to wait for my train.

One Clear Morn

I clutched at the railway warrant and read 'to Aldershot' several times to reassure myself. The train I was to catch left at ten o' clock next morning. All the equipment that I and my fellow trainees would not be taking with us had been handed in to the quartermaster's store, including mattresses and bedding. The training-camp staff, having done their job, were free of the responsibility of their charges and quickly dispersed in all directions homeward. I was left to my own devices. I decided that spending the night in an empty barrack room, on the wire base of a mattressless bed, in full kit and fully 'bulled' uniform, trying not to spoil the shine on my 'best boots', was a small price to pay for my first taste of being an individual once again, instead of the mere number I had been of late.

It was clear that the night was not going to be conducive to sleep, the hours would pass slowly and perhaps it would be a time for thought, creating a silent boundary between my old life and the one about to begin. I rolled my greatcoat to make a pillow, in hope of creating a little comfort on my wire crib. I lay back in modest ease, and unexpectedly submerged into sleep. Unfortunately, the tired mind plays tricks and, although I relinquished consciousness for only a few seconds, I found myself pulled into a cauldron of anxiety in which I was tormented with fears that I would be unable to hold my place amongst my new comrades in the band. Every one of them, I was certain, would be more clever than me. They would be talented, more socially adept and more confident. I saw myself as an outsider, ridiculed and scorned. I woke bathed in a cold sweat.

I decided I must remain awake and push such imaginings to the back of my mind. I endeavoured to list the strengths that I did have, and, although few seemed appropriate for the very different life I was about to enter, the exercise was uplifting and helped me to a better frame of mind. More easily conjured were excerpts of the rough and ready philosophy that had been quoted to me since my earliest childhood. The rawness of the words in my head filled me with a feeling of defiance and a determination not to be beaten. I gladly continued to recall the tried and tested parables of wisdom that were designed to exhort and encourage.

Leaving Home

As the demons of the night receded and a wakeful mind was once again in control, I told myself that this was no time for doubts, this was my chance to find that better life I wanted. This was the opportunity I had schemed and worked for, and now I must go forward with all the strength I could muster. I assured myself that if I lacked confidence, I would gain it as I mastered my instrument. If I was not as quick as my fellows, I would work harder and longer. If I lacked social skills, I would learn them. Whatever I needed to do, I would do.

As night moved towards day and the early light began to enter that empty barrack room with its many naked beds, I was already gathering my equipment together. There were hours to go before my train was due to leave, but I was determined not to miss it. As I packed my few belongings and carefully stowed my encased clarinet, I told myself once again, to help me on my way, that life owed me nothing; it was up to me to earn and claim what was mine. Once ready to depart, an educated man might have exclaimed 'Carpe diem!' I settled for 'OK, let's go!' So, with kitbag on my shoulder and clutching the small brown suitcase that I had arrived with, I began my second journey into the unknown. After leaving home on that fair morn just a few weeks earlier, nothing would ever be the same again; my education at the 'University of Life' would continue, but in ways I could never have known or even imagined.

THE END OF THE BEGINNING

Appendix

NAN'S GEMS OF WISDOM

Such a few words can be said in a moment and hold so much meaning, but it may take a lifetime to understand their wisdom.

Encouragements
Never say yer mother 'ad a jibber
There's no such word as 'can't'
A little help's worth all the pity
While you're sitting there having a rest, peel these spuds
Many hands make light work
Where there's a will, there's a way
Charity begins at home
God 'elps them that 'elps themselves

Warnings
Gotta live tomorrow, you know
If they put their fingers in the fire, would you?
Expect nothing and you'll never be disappointed
There's nothing as cold as charity
There's none so blind as them that won't see
Many a slip twixt cup and lip
Don't count your chickens before they're hatched
You make your own luck – good or bad
Be careful not to get out of the frying pan into the fire

Financial advice
Look after the pennies and the pounds will look after themselves
Money is a good servant but a bad master
Earn a pound, spend nineteen and six – that's happiness
Discount! They put it on before they take it off

Appendix

You've gotta speculate before you can accumulate
Nothing is cheap
The dearest is the cheapest in the long run

Disapproving comments
That's the pot calling the kettle black
Hansom is as hansom does
Self-praise is no praise
Actions speak louder than words

Self-defence
Don't start something you can't finish
If he hits you, give 'im the old one-two
The bigger they come, the 'arder they fall

General advice
Clean the corners and the middle will look after itself
Use plenty of elbow grease
Live and let live
Speak as you find
If you wish to live and thrive, let a spider run alive

Counselling of the day
If you can't get over it, get under it
Happiness is not getting what you want – it's wanting what you get
Life wasn't meant to be fair
Work it off
Make the best of it
Oh well, that's life

Printed in Great Britain
by Amazon